Nutrition

Second Edition

PEARSON

Boston   Columbus   Indianapolis   New York   San Francisco   Upper Saddle River

Amsterdam   Cape Town   Dubai   London   Madrid   Milan   Munich   Paris   Montréal   Toronto

Delhi   Mexico City   São Paulo   Sydney   Hong Kong   Seoul   Singapore   Taipei   Tokyo

Pearson

Editorial Director: Vernon R. Anthony
Executive Acquisitions Editor: Alli Gentile
NRA Product Development: Randall Towns and
  Todd Schlender
Senior Managing Editor: JoEllen Gohr
Associate Managing Editor: Alexandrina B. Wolf
Senior Operations Supervisor: Pat Tonneman
Senior Operations Specialist: Deidra Skahill
Cover photo: Amlet/Dreamstime.com

Cover design: Karen Steinberg, Element LLC
Director of Marketing: David Gesell
Marketing Manager: Derril Trakalo
Marketing Coordinator: Les Roberts
Full-Service Project Management: Barbara Hawk and
  Kevin J. Gray, Element LLC
Text and Cover Printer/Binder: LSC Communications
Text Font: Minion Pro, Myriad Pro Semicondensed

Photography Credits

Front matter: i Amlet/Dreamstime.com; vii (left) Suhendri Utet/Dreamstime; (right) Meryll/Dreamstime; viii (top) Mtr/Dreamstime; (bottom) Stratum/Dreamstime; ix (bottom left) Aprescindere/Dreamstime; xv (bottom left) Petar Neychev/Dreamstime; 15, 63, 145, 161, 258 Nikada/iStockPhoto

All other photographs owned or acquired by the National Restaurant Association Educational Foundation, NRAEF.

18 2023

ISBN-10:   0-13-218163-0
ISBN-13: 978-0-13-218163-1

ISBN-10:   0-13-272452-9
ISBN-13: 978-0-13-272452-4

Contents in Brief

Contents

About the National Restaurant Association and the National Restaurant Association Educational Foundation

Founded in 1919, the National Restaurant Association (NRA) is the leading business association for the restaurant and foodservice industry, which comprises 960,000 restaurant and foodservice outlets and a workforce of nearly 13 million employees. We represent the industry in Washington, DC, and advocate on its behalf. We operate the industry's largest trade show (NRA Show®, restaurant.org/show); leading food safety training and certification program (ServSafe®, servsafe.com); unique career-building high school program (the NRAEF's *ProStart®*, prostart.restaurant.org); as well as the *Kids LiveWell* program (restaurant.org/kidslivewell) promoting healthful kids' menu options. For more information, visit www.restaurant.org and find us on Twitter *@WeRRestaurants*, *Facebook*, and *YouTube*.

With the first job experience of one in four U.S. adults occurring in a restaurant or foodservice operation, the industry is uniquely attractive among American industries for entry-level jobs, personal development and growth, employee and manager career paths, and ownership and wealth creation. That is why the National Restaurant Association Educational Foundation (nraef.org), the philanthropic foundation of the NRA, furthers the education of tomorrow's restaurant and foodservice industry professionals and plays a key role in promoting job and career opportunities in the industry by allocating millions of dollars a year toward industry scholarships and educational programs. The NRA works to ensure the most qualified and passionate people enter the industry so that we can better meet the needs of our members and the patrons and clients they serve.

What Is the ManageFirst Program?

The ManageFirst Program® is a management training certificate program that exemplifies our commitment to developing materials by the industry, for the industry. The program's

most powerful strength is that it is based on a set of competencies defined by the restaurant and foodservice industry as critical for success. The program teaches the skills truly valued by industry professionals.

ManageFirst Program Components

The ManageFirst Program includes a set of books, exams, instructor resources, certificates, a new credential, and support activities and services. By participating in the program, you are demonstrating your commitment to becoming a highly qualified professional either preparing to begin or to advance your career in the restaurant, hospitality, and foodservice industry.

These books cover the range of topics listed in the chart above. You will find the essential content for the topic as defined by industry, as well as learning activities, assessments, case studies, suggested field projects, professional profiles, and testimonials. The exam can be administered either online or in a paper-and-pencil format (see inside front cover for a listing of ISBNs), and it will be proctored. Upon successfully passing the exam, you will be furnished with a customized certificate by the National Restaurant Association. The certificate is a lasting recognition of your accomplishment and a signal to the industry that you have mastered the competencies covered within the particular topic.

To earn this credential, you will be required to pass four core exams and one foundation exam (to be chosen from the remaining program topics) and to document your work experience in the restaurant and foodservice industry. Earning the ManageFirst credential is a significant accomplishment.

We applaud you as you either begin or advance your career in the restaurant, hospitality, and foodservice industry. Visit www.nraef.org to learn about additional career-building resources offered by the NRAEF, including scholarships for college students enrolled in relevant industry programs.

MANAGEFIRST PROGRAM ORDERING INFORMATION

Review copies or support materials

FACULTY FIELD SERVICES
Tel: 800.526.0485

Domestic orders and inquiries

PEARSON CUSTOMER SERVICE
Tel: 800.922.0579
http://www.pearsonhighered.com/

International orders and inquiries

U.S. EXPORT SALES OFFICE
Pearson Education International Customer Service Group
200 Old Tappan Road
Old Tappan, NJ 07675 USA
Tel: 201.767.5021
Fax: 201.767.5625

For corporate, government, and special sales (consultants, corporations, training centers, VARs, and corporate resellers) orders and inquiries

PEARSON CORPORATE SALES
Tel: 317.428.3411
Fax: 317.428.3343
Email: *managefirst@prenhall.com*

For additional information regarding other Pearson publications, instructor and student support materials, locating your sales representative, and much more, please visit *www.pearsonhighered.com/managefirst*.

Acknowledgements

The National Restaurant Association is grateful for the significant contributions made to this book by the following individuals.

Mike Amos
Perkins & Marie Callender's Inc.

Steve Belt
Monical's Pizza

Heather Kane Haberer
Carrols Restaurant Group

Erika Hoover
Monical's Pizza Corp.

Jared Kulka
Red Robin Gourmet Burgers

Tony C. Merritt
Carrols Restaurant Group

H. George Neil
Buffalo Wild Wings

Marci Noguiera
Sodexo—Education Division

Ryan Nowicki
Dave & Busters

Patricia A. Plavcan, MS, RD, LDN
Contributing Author

Penny Ann Lord Prichard
Wake Tech/NC Community College

Michael Santos
Micatrotto Restaurant Group

Heather Thitoff
Cameron Mitchell Restaurants

Features of the ManageFirst books

We have designed the ManageFirst books to enhance your ability to learn and retain important information that is critical to this restaurant and foodservice industry function. Here are the key features you will find within this book.

BEGINNING EACH BOOK

Real Manager

This is your opportunity to meet a professional who is currently working in the field associated with the book's topic. This person's story will help you gain insight into the responsibilities related to his or her position, as well as the training and educational history linked to it. You will also see the daily and cumulative impact this position has on an operation, and receive advice from a person who has successfully met the challenges of being a manager.

BEGINNING EACH CHAPTER

Inside This Chapter

Chapter content is organized under these major headings.

Learning Objectives

Learning objectives identify what you should be able to do after completing each chapter. These objectives are linked to the required tasks a manager must be able to perform in relation to the function discussed in the book.

Case Study

Each chapter begins with a brief story about the kind of situations that a manager may encounter in the course of his or her work. The story is followed by one or two questions to prompt student discussions about the topics contained within the chapter.

Key Terms

These terms are important for thorough understanding of the chapter's content. They are highlighted throughout the chapter, where they are explicitly defined or their meaning is made clear within the paragraphs in which they appear.

THROUGHOUT EACH CHAPTER

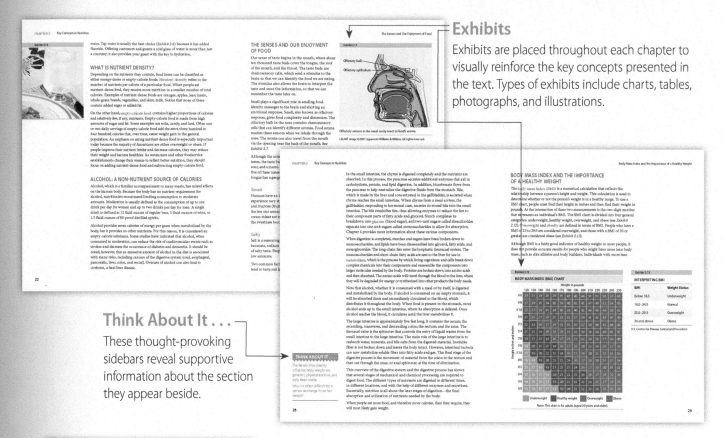

Exhibits

Exhibits are placed throughout each chapter to visually reinforce the key concepts presented in the text. Types of exhibits include charts, tables, photographs, and illustrations.

Think About It . . .

These thought-provoking sidebars reveal supportive information about the section they appear beside.

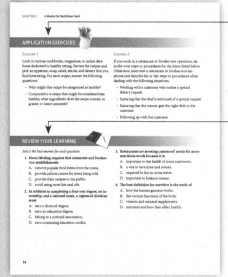

AT THE END OF EACH CHAPTER

Application Exercises and Review Your Learning

These multiple-choice or open- or close-ended questions or problems are designed to test your knowledge of the concepts presented in the chapter. These questions have been aligned with the objectives and should provide you with an opportunity to practice or apply the content that supports these objectives. If you have difficulty answering the Review Your Learning questions, you should review the content further.

AT THE END OF THE BOOK

Field Project

This real-world project gives you the valuable opportunity to apply many of the concepts you will learn in a competency guide. You will interact with industry practitioners, enhance your knowledge, and research, apply, analyze, evaluate, and report on your findings. It will provide you with an in-depth "reality check" of the policies and practices of this management function.

REAL MANAGER

Joyce Kerestes, MS, RD

Director

Department and Dietetic Internship
Patient Food and Nutrition Services
University of Michigan Health System

Philosophy: **Strive to bring a good attitude to work every day and to do your best by being responsible and adding value to your operation's vision and goals.**

MY BACKGROUND

I grew up on a small farm in central Minnesota, the oldest of four children. My mother was an elementary teacher and homemaker. She taught school for approximately 35 years—everyone in our small town knew my mom! My father was a purchasing agent and a farmer. He was also skilled at construction and built our family a new home when I was in high school. I attended Holdingford Public Schools all the way from Grades 1 to 12, and graduated valedictorian from my high school.

All in all, I recall a very happy childhood. We didn't have a lot of material things, but we never felt poor. We all worked hard on the farm. I kept busy picking up rocks, baling hay, and feeding animals. This was real farm-to-table before farm-to-table was popular! In fact, I think of myself as one of the original "foodies."

I had always loved science and math—and, of course, food. I also enjoyed helping people. So becoming a clinical dietician seemed like a natural progression. My major at the University of Minnesota was dietetics. To gain experience in the field and earn some money, I worked in nursing homes for a couple of summers. I learned nearly every position in the kitchen, from interacting with the geriatric residents to cleaning dining tables to cooking to opening the foodservice operation for the day. In retrospect, it really was a priceless experience.

MY CAREER PATH

After working in foodservice, my career goals focused on healthcare and clinical nutrition. After all, my interests included food, science, healthcare, and education. I graduated from the University of Minnesota with a BS in dietetics, completed a dietetic internship with an emphasis in clinical nutrition in Chicago, and earned a position at the University of Michigan Health System (UMHS) as a clinical RD (registered dietition).

I started volunteering for other projects, and soon I found that these projects earned me additional recognition. I found that I enjoyed organizing and managing. But I knew that I couldn't go any further in this area without additional studies.

So, after working in the field for several years, I decided to focus on graduate studies in the area of education. I received my MS in education from the University of Michigan. This laid the foundation for me to write the self-study for the reestablishment of the dietetic internship at UMHS.

Something I always think about: I am passionate about management and education, and I enjoy working with people. I'm so lucky to have found a position that enables me to incorporate all of these skills.

My first foodservice managerial position was as assistant director at a community hospital in southern Michigan. I was responsible for Patient Food and Nutrition Services. I learned so much! It was the first time I managed a union shop. A new replacement hospital was being constructed at the time, and I obtained invaluable experience in project management and kitchen design and layout, developing various processes and creating a departmental staffing plan.

Since 2000, I've been director of the Department and Dietetic Internship at a large academic medical center. I plan, organize, and direct the administrative and operational activities of the department and the dietetic internship. This includes ensuring compliance with regulatory agency requirements; and planning, organizing, and evaluating objectives, policies, procedures, and long-range programs consistent with institutional goals.

WHAT DOES THE FUTURE HOLD?

The future of nutrition and food science offers great opportunity. I think we'll be paying much more attention to the following:

- Food allergies and the creation of new food products in the marketplace to meet specific allergic needs

- Advanced nutrition research related to disease prevention and the management of obesity and oncologic and cardiac health

- New nutritional approaches to enhance the quality of life for the aging U.S. population

- Growth in the regulation and monitoring of food safety in the United States

- An increase in the areas of sustainability, local purchasing, and waste stream management

MY ADVICE TO YOU

I have learned many things from my mentors over the years. I'd like to pass those down to you. Remember to:

- Be fair and consistent.

- Adhere to your organization's policies and standard operating procedures.

- Document, document, document.

- Don't be afraid to spend money on yourself and your team to advance knowledge and career goals.

Remember: **Enjoy life and what you do. Life is not perfect; your attitude each and every day, as well as how you approach and deal with everything and everyone, will make a huge difference in your lifelong happiness and success.**

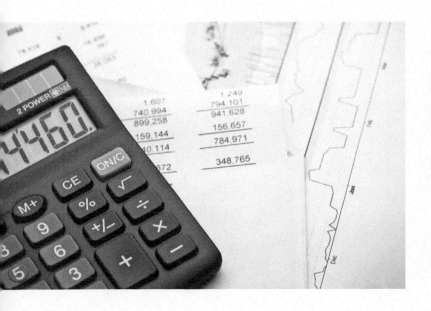

PART ONE
Understanding Nutrition Basics

CHAPTERS

1

A Market for Nutritious Food

INSIDE THIS CHAPTER

- A Growing Market for Healthy Menu Options
- Nutrition and Its Importance
- Opportunities for Foodservice Professionals
- Credible Sources of Nutrition Information

CHAPTER LEARNING OBJECTIVES

After completing this chapter, you should be able to:

- Recognize and explain the current market need for nutritious menu options.

- Define *nutrient* and *nutrition*.

- Identify health issues caused by poor nutrition.

- Explain opportunities for foodservice professionals with knowledge of nutrition.

- Identify industry trends in the area of nutrition.

- Identify credible sources of nutrition information.

KEY TERMS

CASE STUDY

Tyler is the owner of a busy family restaurant downtown. He was on his way home after a long but satisfying day of work. Tyler had reached the elevator to the parking garage when he overheard a conversation between two of his employees, a cook named Kenny and a member of his waitstaff, Jada.

"Did you see that special request for a gluten-free dish?" Jada asked Kenny. "How did you fill that order?"

Kenny responded, "I never worry about that kind of request. I just give them the regular menu item and pretend it is special. There's nothing to that stuff about gluten. I've never had anyone get sick from a meal I've served them. What's the difference, as long as they enjoy the food?"

Dismayed by the conversation, Tyler went home to think about how to address the situation.

1. What are the problems in Tyler's establishment?

2. What are the potential solutions to the problems?

3. How can Tyler determine that the problems have been solved?

Exhibit 1.1

People of all ages and ethnicities need balanced nutrition.

THINK ABOUT IT . . .

Why is it important for establishments to prepare meals in a manner that decreases calories, sodium, solid fat, and sugars?

A GROWING MARKET FOR HEALTHY MENU OPTIONS

This book is a guide for anyone involved in the restaurant and foodservice industry, including restaurant or foodservice managers, hospitality and culinary students, chefs, menu planners, and any other professionals engaged in the challenges and rewards of preparing and delivering food to the public. Restaurants and other foodservice establishments afford people the chance to experience new tastes and to savor favorite foods. They provide a place to celebrate, to socialize, and to conduct business. Customers travel with the confidence that they can dine safely when they arrive at their new destination. Whether by choice or by necessity, eating out at restaurants and other foodservice operations has become an enjoyable part of the American lifestyle.

Foods prepared outside of the home account for about one-third of the calories Americans consume and one-half of the money they spend on food each year. As the population continues to visit restaurants and foodservice operations on a regular basis, expectations for food and food products that meet customer needs have increased. Customers with specialized needs include those with celiac disease or gluten intolerance, those with allergies, and those who modify their entire diets due to diabetes or heart disease.

Beyond Foodhandling

Customers depend on restaurant and foodservice leaders to be knowledgeable about foodhandling and to meet food safety requirements. However, another set of issues and expectations is overshadowing these basic considerations. Healthcare providers are urging more and more Americans to decrease their dietary intake of calories, sodium, solid fats, and added sugar to curb or to avoid obesity, diabetes, and hypertension. Nutrition experts are encouraging the public to eat foods with higher levels of nutrients like fiber, vitamins, and minerals (*Exhibit 1.1*).

This trend affects local restaurant and foodservice operations because larger numbers of people are looking for dishes that fit their physicians' recommendations. The latest figures indicate that 72 percent of American men and 64 percent of American women are overweight, and about one-third of all adults are obese. In addition, 37 percent of the U.S. population has cardiovascular disease, 11 percent of the population over the age of 20 has diagnosed diabetes, and roughly 34 percent of the population has hypertension. The demand for more nutritious menu choices is extraordinarily high.[1]

[1] U.S. Department of Agriculture and U.S. Department of Health and Human Services, "Dietary Guidelines for Americans, 2010."

Menu-Labeling Legislation

A more recent change is menu labeling. To assist people who want to address their dietary requirements when eating out, recent Federal legislation, in addition to some state and local laws, mandates that restaurants and vendors with 20 or more locations must prominently label their menus with calorie counts for standard menu items. Establishments covered under this legislation must make additional nutritional data available to the public on-site. Details regarding the types of data will be covered later in this book. These changes require that foodservice operators be knowledgeable about nutrition and routine nutrition analysis, since they will be responsible for interpreting nutritional data and positioning it on their menus (see *Exhibit 1.2*).

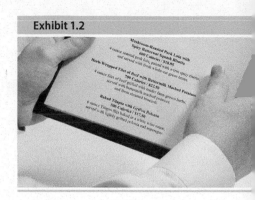

Exhibit 1.2

NUTRITION AND ITS IMPORTANCE

Before managers can assess recipes or revise menus to meet nutritional standards and guidelines, they will need to know why people should care about their dietary intake. Contained in the various foods we eat are varying amounts of chemical compounds called nutrients. Nutrients are essential to the body because they help it maintain, generate, and repair tissues. In order to maintain optimal health, we need to provide our bodies with most nutrients on a daily basis. Nutrition is the science of how the nutrients in food affect health. It includes the study of how the human body ingests, digests, absorbs, transports, and metabolizes food. Nutritionists also examine why people choose the foods they do.

Food provides the energy to build body structures and to power the many chemical reactions that enable the human body to function. Studies have shown that it is best for nutrients to come from the food people eat. This evidence reinforces the importance of every meal, whether it is eaten in or out of the home. Accessing nutritious food outside the home is a daily struggle for many people, and the stakes are high: insufficient or excess quantities of nutrients can result in impaired health. Many factors, some objective and some subjective, influence our food choices. Several of these factors are listed in *Exhibit 1.3* on the next page.

Good nutrition is important for all people at every age. When people do not have access to adequate amounts of nutritious food, they may experience negative health consequences such as weight loss, impaired immune systems, and anemia. Impaired immunity leaves people abnormally susceptible to infections and diseases such as colds and flu. A person who eats more than enough calories but has poor vitamin and mineral intake may become both obese and nutrient deficient.

Exhibit 1.3	

CHOOSING WHAT TO EAT

Factors That Influence Food Choices

Factor	Details
Personal preferences	Likes and dislikes gained from a variety of experiences
Traditions and habits	The results of never having been introduced to a food, or always having eaten a particular food
Philosophical and moral beliefs	Value judgments about consuming certain foods
Health concerns	A desire for health, longevity, and freedom from disease
Availability	What can be obtained or provided at the moment
Income level	Buying food within a particular budget or means
Convenience	The desired time and effort spent on obtaining and eating food
Parental influence	Parents' imposition of likes and dislikes on a child
Urban legends	Myths and rumors about eating or avoiding certain foods
Allergies	Avoidance of unpleasant or life-threatening allergic reactions
Emotions	Association of positive or negative feelings with certain foods
Social influences	Thoughts about what other people are eating or avoiding

People who consume too many calories, regardless of the food's nutritional content, may gain weight and increase their risk of developing diabetes and high blood pressure. Many people do not even realize that they are overeating. Overweight is often a result of gradual weight gain from consuming a few hundred unnecessary calories each day. Diabetes can result from a gain of just 25 to 40 extra pounds. What people choose to eat is ultimately up to them, but an informed choice is always a better one.

Long-term dietary choices may result in chronic disease due to the lack of a critical structural nutrient such as calcium. For example, repeated dietary shortages of calcium and vitamin D can eventually lead to osteoporosis. Inadequate levels of vitamin C cause a deficiency in one of the major antioxidant vitamins, leaving the cells unprotected from damage due to metabolic reactions. Consumption of more than the recommended daily amount of sodium can lead to high blood pressure.

OPPORTUNITIES FOR FOODSERVICE PROFESSIONALS

Some restaurants and foodservice operations have expanded their menus to include a wider variety of options that fit into healthy lifestyles. Others have begun marketing to people who find it difficult to eat out due to their need for special meals or products. Individuals who require gluten-free or allergy-free meals appreciate establishments that can meet their needs and carefully prepare their food.

When dining out, customers want good taste and value. They want food that is aromatic, colorful, and full of flavor (*Exhibit 1.4*). This is because people experience food through all five senses. And, contrary to popular belief, healthy, nutritious food can satisfy people's tastes—as long as the chef understands and applies nutrition principles when developing recipes.

THINK ABOUT IT . . .

Do you work in a restaurant or foodservice operation? What nutritional improvements can be made to your recipes and menu items? What populations do you serve, and how will they benefit from your changes?

Exhibit 1.4

Exhibit 1.5

The restaurant and foodservice industry is in dire need of professionals who are educated in nutrition and can provide nutritious food for all modern dining situations. When managers understand the dynamics of combining nutrition science and culinary art, they can meet their customers' need for nutrition and desire for sensory enjoyment. Foodservice professionals should understand how to prepare food that is both tasty and nutritious (*Exhibit 1.5*). This knowledge enables foodservice professionals to make a positive contribution to the expanding market for food outside the home. In return, restaurants and foodservice operations may find opportunities to grow larger and more successful. The following material describes specific markets that offer these types of opportunities. In addition, *Exhibit 1.6* lists some of the nutrition-related opportunities that exist within the current market.

Exhibit 1.6

NUTRITION-RELATED JOBS

College professor

Cook

Corporate chef

Culinologist

Diet Technician

Foodservice manager

Food scientist

Food technologist

Freelance instructor

Menu planner

Nutrition scientist

Private chef

Recipe developer

Research chef

Restaurant manager

Service staff

Adult Breakfast Skippers

Breakfast is still the meal that is most commonly eaten at home, especially among younger families. Yet, often it is only the children who eat breakfast; parents often skip this critical meal because they are caught up in the morning rush. This group of adults represents an important opportunity. The restaurant and foodservice industry currently targets breakfast sales for take-and-go items. This market has considerable potential for increased healthy options.

Home-Meal Replacements

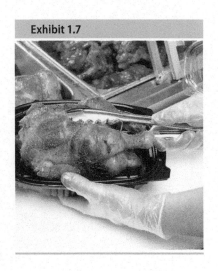

Exhibit 1.7

The market for home-meal replacements, which is food that has been prepared, cooked, chilled, and made ready for simple reheating, is a fast-growing segment of the restaurant and foodservice industry. People appear to be increasingly less willing to spend hours to prepare a meal.

The introduction of home-meal replacements added a new meaning to fast takeout food. Today, people can purchase home-replacement meals in a variety of ways. For example, expanded takeout areas at grocery stores provide complete meals (see *Exhibit 1.7*). Other operations deliver fully prepared meals, including those that comply with dietary restrictions. Some consumers assemble meals in the provider's kitchen facilities and take them home for later consumption. There are also special takeout services within conventional restaurants.

Changes in the Quick-Service Restaurant Segment

The quick-service restaurant industry is now providing more food alternatives. Many diners want both the convenience of eating quickly and the benefit of a healthy meal. The industry has responded well, as evidenced by the following offerings of food products:

- Baked, broiled, roasted, and flame-grilled meat and poultry
- More fresh fruit and vegetables
- Low-fat milk, milk shakes, smoothies, and ice cream
- Wraps with low-fat and whole-grain tortillas
- Salads with low-fat dressing and with or without grilled meat and fresh fruit
- Alternatives to fried side dishes, such as applesauce or fruit cups

Nutritious Cooking in Other Types of Dining Operations

Many foodservice dining operations have focused on healthier cooking for some time. These operations generally have a captive audience, meaning that many people visit and dine at the operation almost daily for one reason or another. Because the guests are often part of a captive audience, it is extremely important to ensure that nutrients are present in the meals and that the highest quality ingredients are used when possible.

Exhibit 1.8

1. **School and institutional foodservice:** These operations provide lunches to students in prekindergarten through 12th grade (*Exhibit 1.8*). Some schools also have breakfast programs. These operations are required to meet nutrient guidelines for government-funded breakfast and lunch programs.

2. **College and university foodservice:** These operations provide food for college students, faculty, staff, and campus visitors. Menus are varied and might be elaborate.

3. **Corporate dining:** Many office buildings and factories have cafeterias or vending services for their employees for breakfast and lunch. Some use catering services to achieve this.

4. **Healthcare foodservice:** These services provide meals to patients, employees, and visitors, many of whom have special dietary needs. Some hospitals also offer meals to go and cater special functions for doctors, staff, and members of the facility's board.

5. **Senior living centers:** These establishments provide varied dining services from typical restaurant fare to satisfying special dietary needs, depending on the residents' health status and ages.

6. **Correctional facilities:** Jail and prison cafeterias provide meals for inmates and employees, some of whom must follow special diets.

The Internet as a Food Market

The Internet has become a virtual food market. People use it for a variety of food-related functions that they used to fulfill through businesses, friends, or their own efforts. These functions are as follows:

- Ideas for meal planning
- Recipes
- Nutrition information
- Cooking demonstrations
- Cooking-equipment purchases
- Ordering food for delivery (from restaurants or grocery stores)

This area of the food industry offers opportunities for individuals with a restaurant or foodservice background and advanced knowledge of nutrition. It also may interest people who enjoy working with computers and using the latest technologies.

Private Chefs, Health Clubs, and Spas

Many people of means hire private chefs to cook healthy meals either for their entire families or for family members with special dietary needs. Entertainers, athletes, and other celebrities also hire private chefs because they know that nutritious eating will give them the stamina and energy to perform at their best.

Spas and health clubs often hire a professional with knowledge of nutritional cooking to satisfy the needs of guests through meal preparation or cooking classes. These chefs and cooks must be very creative in order to provide great-tasting, low-calorie foods. Since portions are usually small, spa and health-club chefs must understand how to incorporate flavor while using minimal ingredients.

The Food-Products Industry

The food-products industry is a multibillion-dollar business serving restaurant and foodservice operations as well as consumers. Food-product needs have changed in recent years. The industry is continually developing products that assist in reducing labor and food costs in restaurant and foodservice operations. It is also developing products that facilitate healthy eating. Food manufacturers use certain nutrients and processes for stabilization, binding, texture, and flavor enhancement. As nutrition researchers continue to discover how these nutrients and processes affect metabolic processes in the body, the food-products industry has to adjust.

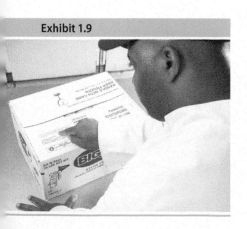
Exhibit 1.9

Skilled cooks must know how to use food products to produce actual dishes and menus in real-world settings. They also must be able to determine the value of these products by comparing food labels to analyze nutritional advantages (*Exhibit 1.9*) and then modify recipes and cooking methods to best utilize the products, all while keeping food and labor costs under control. Establishments need skilled managers to ensure that food sanitation and safety procedures are followed. Managers also must implement effective training to ensure that all staff members follow state and local regulations.

CREDIBLE SOURCES OF NUTRITION INFORMATION

Nutrition is a rapidly expanding field of knowledge, and it can be difficult to assimilate the changing and growing amounts of information. As consumer interest in nutrition grows, more restaurant and foodservice operations will need to be able to answer increasingly complex questions about the foods on their menus. Effectively evaluating the credibility of nutrition information is an important skill for any restaurant or foodservice manager.

To prepare employees to answer customers' questions, managers should lead training sessions to educate service staff about every menu item, and chefs should train cooks to understand the nutritional aspects of the food they are preparing. Now that menu labeling is mandated by law, more factual information will be, and must be, available.

Written Sources

The most knowledgeable restaurant and foodservice professionals use reliable and credible sources of information from trade associations like the National Restaurant Association and the Academy of Nutrition and Dietetics. Nonprofit associations for diseases like diabetes and cancer provide accurate information on their Web sites for professionals and the public alike. Other reliable sources include public reports of studies and surveys conducted by government agencies such as the Food and Drug Administration, the United States Department of Agriculture (USDA), and the United States Department of Health and Human Services (HHS).

Exhibit 1.10 provides a list of credible agencies and sources.

Exhibit 1.10

SELECTED CREDIBLE SOURCES OF NUTRITION INFORMATION

Government Resources

Centers for Disease Control and Prevention (CDC)
www.cdc.gov

Food and Drug Administration (FDA)
www.fda.gov

United States Department of Agriculture (USDA)
www.usda.gov

United States Department of Health and Human Services (HHS)
www.hhs.gov

USDA Center for Nutrition Policy and Promotion (CNPP)
www.cnpp.usda.gov

National Academy of Sciences (NAS)
www.nasonline.org

National Institutes of Health (NIH)
www.nih.gov

Professional Organizations

American Diabetes Association (ADA)
www.diabetes.org

Academy of Nutrition and Dietetics
www.eatright.org

American Heart Association (AHA)
www.heart.org

Institute of Food Technologists (IFT)
www.ift.org

National Restaurant Association (NRA)
www.restaurant.org

The Food Allergy and Anaphylaxis Network (FAAN)
www.foodallergy.org

International Food and Information Council (IFIC)
www.foodinsight.org

Manager's Memo

Although the Internet provides a rapid answer for most questions, when it comes to nutrition, managers must ensure that they are using reliable sources. While there are many credible resources available on the Internet, there is also a vast group of unreliable sites that provide questionable, confusing, or downright wrong information.

When planning nutrition programs for restaurants and foodservice operations, it is crucial to consult information that is agreed upon by experts in nutrition. The Dietary Guidelines for Americans, 2010, which is a comprehensive report required by law and produced by the United States Department of Agriculture (USDA) and the United States Department of Health and Human Services (HHS), meets this need. This report provides reliable, easy-to-understand information for the public. It can be found on the USDA Web site: MyPlate.gov.

Human Sources

To meet the demands for nutritional cuisine, many managers of restaurants, foodservice operations, and food companies hire specialists or contract with a third party for nutritional services such as developing and analyzing menus and recipes. A third-party consultant may be a **registered dietitian (RD)**, a **registered dietetic technician (DTR)**, or an American Culinary Federation **(ACF)-certified chef**. *Exhibit 1.11* provides further details about these three professions. RDs and DTRs are qualified to analyze recipes and menus and suggest modifications to address health concerns and special needs of customers and clients. ACF-certified chefs can select and prepare nutritional ingredients to make healthy menus of different cuisines.

Exhibit 1.11

THREE PROFESSIONS CONCERNED WITH NUTRITION

Profession	Education/Training
Registered dietitian (RD)	An RD must complete a four-year, Academy of Nutrition and Dietetics–approved undergraduate program, as well as advanced training through an internship or master's degree. After completing advanced training, the candidate must pass a national exam. To maintain RD status, RDs must meet continuing-education course requirements.
Registered dietetic technician (DTR)	A DTR must complete a two-year, Academy of Nutrition and Dietetics–approved undergraduate program and complete 450 hours of supervised practice. A national exam is available to further certify knowledge. To maintain DTR status, DTRs must meet continuing-education course requirements.
ACF-Certified Chef	An ACF-certified chef must satisfy ACF-established requirements that include a certain number of points earned from education, experience, and awards. In addition to culinary work, the candidate must complete 30 hours each of coursework in nutrition, food safety and sanitation, and culinary supervisory management. After meeting the point requirement, the candidate must pass a national certification exam and a proctored practical exam. To maintain certification status, continuing education must be completed.

SUMMARY

1. **Recognize and explain the current market need for nutritious menu options.**

   Recent statistics on the health of the nation indicate that most Americans are not healthy. Americans must change their lifestyle to improve their health, including eating more nutritious meals. Since many Americans dine out in restaurants and foodservice operations, there is a growing opportunity for the industry to meet their dietary needs.

2. **Define *nutrient* and *nutrition*.**

   Nutrients are chemical compounds contained in the food we eat. Carbohydrates, fiber, vitamins, and minerals are examples of nutrients. Nutrition is the science of how the nutrients in food affect health. It includes the study of how the human body ingests, digests, absorbs, transports, and metabolizes food. Nutritionists also examine why people choose the foods they do.

3. **Identify health issues caused by poor nutrition.**

   If people eat more calories than they need, they will become overweight and can develop obesity, diabetes, hypertension (high blood pressure), or cardiovascular disease. People with poor nutritional intakes can lose weight and develop nutrient deficiencies. They may also have impaired immunity. An example of a deficiency-related disease is osteoporosis, which is caused by a long-term lack of vitamin D and calcium.

4. **Explain opportunities for foodservice professionals with knowledge of nutrition.**

   In order to provide nutritious food for all modern dining situations, the restaurant and foodservice industry is in need of professionals who are educated about nutrition. There are opportunities in all facets of the restaurant industry, including family restaurants, quick-service restaurants, Internet markets, private establishments, colleges, correctional facilities, and schools.

5. **Identify industry trends in the area of nutrition.**

   The population of the United States is not healthy, and Americans are being advised to decrease their intakes of calories, sodium, solid fats, and added sugars to curb or to avoid obesity, diabetes, and hypertension. In addition, nutrition experts are encouraging the public to eat nutrient-dense foods with higher levels of fiber, vitamins, and minerals. The restaurant and foodservice industry is in need of professionals who are educated in nutrition and can provide nutritious food for all modern dining situations.

6. **Identify credible sources of nutrition information.**

   Credible sources of nutrition information include nutrition experts, government agencies, trade associations, and nonprofit organizations that represent major diseases and conditions such as diabetes.

APPLICATION EXERCISES

Exercise 1

Look at various cookbooks, magazines, or online databases dedicated to healthy eating. Review the recipes and pick an appetizer, soup, salad, entrée, and dessert that you find interesting. For each recipe, answer the following questions:

- Why might this recipe be categorized as healthy?

- Compared to a recipe that might be considered less healthy, what ingredients does the recipe contain in greater or lesser amounts?

Exercise 2

If you work in a restaurant or foodservice operation, describe your steps or procedures for the items listed below. Otherwise, interview a restaurant or foodservice employee and describe his or her steps or procedures when dealing with the following situations:

- Working with a customer who makes a special dietary request

- Ensuring that the chef is informed of a special request

- Ensuring that the runner gets the right dish to the customer

- Following up with the customer

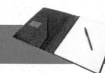

REVIEW YOUR LEARNING

Select the best answer for each question.

1. **Menu labeling requires that restaurant and foodservice establishments**
   A. remove popular food items from the menu.
   B. provide calorie counts for items being sold.
   C. provide their recipes to the public.
   D. avoid using most fats and oils.

2. **In addition to completing a four-year degree, an internship, and a national exam, a registered dietitian must**
   A. earn a doctoral degree.
   B. earn an education degree.
   C. belong to a national association.
   D. earn continuing education credits.

3. **Restaurants are meeting customers' needs for more nutritious meals because it is**
   A. important to the health of some customers.
   B. a way to save time and money.
   C. required by law in some states.
   D. important to balance menus.

4. **The best definition for *nutrition* is the study of**
   A. how the human genome works.
   B. the various functions of the body.
   C. vitamin and mineral supplements.
   D. nutrients and how they affect health.

5. About what percentage of Americans are obese?
   A. 11
   B. 15
   C. 33
   D. 65

6. A disease that can develop from a chronic deficiency of calcium and vitamin D is
   A. obesity.
   B. osteoporosis.
   C. iron-deficiency anemia.
   D. protein-energy malnutrition.

7. In addition to learning about sanitation, an ACF-certified chef must complete coursework in which area?
   A. Culinary supervisory management
   B. Recipe modification
   C. Menu planning
   D. Knife skills

8. What percentage of their daily calories do Americans consume from foods prepared outside the home?
   A. 13%
   B. 20%
   C. 27%
   D. 33%

9. The most reliable and credible source for nutrition information on the Internet would be
   A. an online vitamin store.
   B. a government agency.
   C. an advertisement.
   D. a blog.

10. The meal most commonly eaten at home is
    A. breakfast.
    B. brunch.
    C. lunch.
    D. dinner.

FIELD PROJECT

Visit at least three restaurants: a quick-service restaurant, an independent family restaurant, and a casual chain restaurant. Download a menu or obtain permission to take a menu or menu copy from each restaurant. If the menu is only a wall sign, copy it by hand. Review all three menus for the presence of healthy selections. For each establishment, answer the following questions:

- What are the healthy options on the menu?

- How, if at all, does the menu's presentation indicate that a menu item is healthy? For example, does the use of symbols, words, or proprietary names indicate a healthy menu selection?

- Does the establishment provide nutrient content on the menu or anywhere else?

2 Key Concepts in Nutrition

INSIDE THIS CHAPTER

- Food's Nutritional Value: The Six Basic Nutrients
- What Is Nutrient Density?
- Alcohol: A Non-Nutrient Source of Calories
- The Senses and Our Enjoyment of Food
- Digestion, Absorption, and Transport of Nutrients
- Body Mass Index and the Importance of a Healthy Weight

CHAPTER LEARNING OBJECTIVES

After completing this chapter, you should be able to:

- Define *calorie, nutrient density,* and *empty-calorie food* and explain why people should decrease consumption of empty-calorie food.

- Identify the six basic types of nutrients found in food and describe their characteristics.

- Describe the major functions of carbohydrates, proteins, lipids, vitamins, minerals, and water in the body.

- Explain the effect of alcohol consumption on the body.

- Explain how the senses affect a person's intake of food.

- Identify the structures of the digestive system and describe digestion, absorption, transport, and utilization of nutrients from food.

- Describe the body mass index and explain why it is important to achieve and maintain a healthy weight.

KEY TERMS

amino acid, p. 19

basal metabolism, p. 18

body mass index (BMI), p. 29

calorie, p. 18

carbohydrate, p. 18

digestion, p. 25

digestive tract, p. 26

empty-calorie food, p. 22

energy balance, p. 30

enzyme, p. 26

essential nutrient, p. 18

fatty acid, p. 20

fiber, p. 19

glucose, p. 28

high-density lipoprotein (HDL), p. 21

kilocalorie, p. 18

lipid, p. 20

low-density lipoprotein (LDL), p. 21

metabolism, p. 28

mineral, p. 21

nutrient density, p. 22

obesity, p. 29

overweight, p. 29

phytochemical, p. 21

protein, p. 19

vitamin, p. 21

CASE STUDY

John is a manager at a family restaurant in a busy suburban location. Recently he heard that the waitstaff was having trouble meeting the requests of some of the families who were steady customers. John wants to approach the owners about adding some healthier items to the menu, but he has decided to gather some data to support the need for this change before opening the discussion.

1. Why do you think John sees a need for healthier menu items in the market described above?

2. What can John do to obtain the data he needs to support these suggestions?

3. What obstacles do you think John might encounter as he works on his plan?

Exhibit 2.1

FOOD'S NUTRITIONAL VALUE: THE SIX BASIC NUTRIENTS

Chapter 1 explains why good nutrition is important for human health. Restaurant and foodservice managers should assist the public in maintaining good health by including menu items (*Exhibit 2.1*) that contribute to this goal.

As a review, nutrients are the chemical compounds found in the food we eat. They are essential to our existence because they enable the body to maintain, grow, and repair tissues. In the field of nutrition, the term essential nutrient indicates that a nutrient is required by the body and has to be obtained through the diet on a daily or near-daily basis. This chapter provides an overview of the main nutrients and their roles in maintaining body function and overall health. Later chapters will provide more details on each nutrient.

The amount of energy that a person derives from food is measured in units called kilocalories. A kilocalorie is the amount of energy needed to heat one kilogram of water (about 2.2 pounds) by approximately two degrees Fahrenheit (one degree Celsius). In the United States, when speaking about nutrition, nutrient composition, and dieting, the term *kilocalorie* is often shortened to calorie. Throughout this guide the term *calorie* will be used when discussing the amount of energy the body derives from food. Note that in scientific contexts, the word *calorie* technically refers to an energy unit one thousand times smaller than the kilocalorie.

Each day, a person requires enough food to meet his or her energy needs. This amount depends on factors such as age, gender, body size, and activity level. The body's biggest need for calories, 60 to 65 percent, is to support basal metabolism, which includes energy for functions such as respiration, muscle contraction, nervous system and hormonal functions, production of body heat, and circulation. The balance of a person's calorie needs is dedicated to physical activity, 25 to 35 percent, and thermic effect of food (TEF). TEF is the number of calories used to digest, absorb, and metabolize the food people eat. It usually accounts for 5 to 10 percent of daily calorie requirements.

There are six basic classes of essential nutrients in food: carbohydrates, proteins, lipids (which are fats and oils), vitamins, minerals, and water. People obtain these nutrients by ingesting, digesting, and absorbing food. Because carbohydrates, proteins, and lipids provide energy, they are often referred to as the energy-yielding nutrients.

Carbohydrates

The first group of energy-yielding nutrients is the carbohydrates, which contain the elements carbon, hydrogen, and oxygen. This basic class of nutrients includes starch, sugar, and dietary fiber. Carbohydrates provide the body with four calories of energy per gram of food eaten. Food that contains large amounts of carbohydrates is referred to as carbohydrate food.

Carbohydrates are divided into two categories: simple and complex. The simple carbohydrates are sugars from sources such as table sugar, honey, maple syrup, milk, fruit, soft drinks, and energy drinks. On the other hand, foods like pasta, bread, rice, tortillas, cereal, and potatoes contain complex carbohydrates (see *Exhibit 2.2*). Due to their more complicated chemical structure and fiber content, complex carbohydrates take more time to digest than simple carbohydrates do. Fiber is a complex carbohydrate that cannot be digested by the human body but goes through the digestive tract and provides bulk for regularity.

In recent years, carbohydrates have become nutrients of contention because many people think that eating any amount of carbohydrates will make them particularly likely to gain weight. This is not true. The primary role of carbohydrates in the diet is to supply energy. If a person expends all the calories that he or she has eaten, it is unlikely that the person will gain weight regardless of the food's carbohydrate content. Most people need not fear carbohydrates as a food category because the actual culprits in weight gain are lack of exercise and excess calories from *all* nutrient sources.

It is necessary to keep all nutrients, in the right proportions, in the diet. Consuming carbohydrates helps people utilize dietary protein for more specialized purposes by sparing it from being used as an energy source. The U.S. government recommends that 45 to 65 percent of a person's daily caloric intake come from carbohydrates. Chapter 4 will cover carbohydrates in greater detail.

Proteins

A protein is a large, complex molecule whose primary role is to provide amino acids, which are chemical compounds that have special functions in the body. Amino acids build and repair muscles; supply nitrogen for tissue growth and maintenance; maintain fluids; keep the body from getting too acidic or basic; and act as transporters of lipids, vitamins, minerals, and oxygen as part of the blood. The body also uses protein to form enzymes, hormones, and antibodies.

Twenty amino acids can be found in food. However, only nine of them must be obtained from food each day, since the body can produce the other acids on its own. The nine amino acids that we must get from food each day are considered the essential amino acids. The acids that the body can produce are referred to as the nonessential amino acids.

It is preferable for the body to use carbohydrates and lipids for fuel before using protein as an energy source. When needed, however, protein can provide four calories per gram of food eaten. People who follow low-carbohydrate diets depend on higher amounts of protein to provide energy.

Exhibit 2.2

Exhibit 2.3

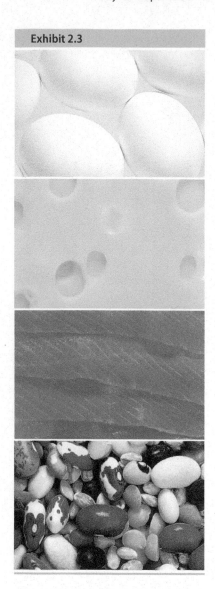

Protein can be found in abundance in meat, eggs, cheese, beans, nuts, seeds, legumes, and milk (*Exhibit 2.3*). Vegetables and grains also contain protein. Restaurant and foodservice professionals should note that vegetarian customers maintain diets that draw proteins mostly (or, in the case of vegans, solely) from vegetables and grains. The government recommends that protein account for 10 to 35 percent of a person's daily caloric intake. More details about protein are provided in chapter 4.

Lipids

The last type of energy-yielding nutrient is a lipid. The three categories of lipids are triglycerides, cholesterol, and phospholipids. About 95 percent of the lipids we eat are triglycerides. Triglycerides are the fats and oils that people get from food or produce within their bodies. Fat is usually defined as a lipid that is solid at room temperature, and oil is a lipid that is liquid at room temperature. Triglycerides are composed of an alcohol molecule and three fatty acids. A fatty acid is an organic molecule found in animal and vegetable fats. It consists of a carbon and hydrogen chain with an acid at one end. Food items that are high in lipids include butter, lard, vegetable oil, nuts, sour cream, and cream cheese (see *Exhibit 2.4*). Lipids provide abundant energy because each gram contains nine calories, which is more than twice the amount yielded by carbohydrates or protein. The government recommends that lipids account for 20 to 35 percent of daily caloric intake.

Exhibit 2.4

Much of the public has a skewed perception of the amount of lipids that should be in their diet. Some people believe their diets should be entirely lipid-free. This is incorrect and harmful, since the absence of essential lipids can cause fatty acid deficiency. A deficiency of essential fatty acids causes flaky skin, diarrhea, delayed wound healing, and infection. Fatty acid deficiency is not common in the population because two to three tablespoons of plant oils eaten each day will provide enough essential fatty acids to avoid a deficiency. Diets that are low in lipids appear to decrease the body's production of high-density lipoprotein (HDL), or good cholesterol, which is believed to protect the cardiovascular system. HDL, which has high amounts of protein and smaller amounts of cholesterol and triglyceride, is believed to help reduce low-density lipoprotein (LDL), or bad cholesterol. See chapter 4 for more information about lipoproteins.

Saturated fats are considered to be unhealthy because they raise the level of LDL in the body. Thus, the U.S. government has recommended that people decrease their dietary intake of saturated fat. Despite the warnings of doctors nationwide, heart disease remains the number one cause of death in the United States.

Knowing how the intake of lipids affects the body will help restaurant and foodservice professionals alter recipes and menus to meet the needs of their customers. Chapter 4 will cover lipids and heart disease in greater detail.

Vitamins and Minerals

Vitamins are organic compounds, while minerals are inorganic elements. These nutrients are considered non–energy yielding nutrients. Non–energy yielding nutrients are essential nutrients that provide no calories but are needed for regulatory activities of the body. The body needs both vitamins and minerals in relatively small amounts in order to regulate metabolic processes involved in growth, reproduction, and the operation and maintenance of the body. In addition, minerals such as calcium, phosphorus, and magnesium serve as structural components of the body. Though they do not provide calories, vitamins and minerals are found in small quantities in many different types of food. It is generally considered that food is a better source of vitamins and minerals than pills and other supplements. See *Exhibit 2.5.*

Vitamins are divided into two general types: fat soluble and water soluble. Fat-soluble vitamins are stored by the body, while water-soluble vitamins are not. Phytochemicals, also known as phytonutrients, are plant chemicals that may assist the body in preventing or fighting diseases. Beta-carotene, which is found in carrots and other orange vegetables, is one example of a phytochemical that aids the body as an antioxidant.

Water: The Most Important Nutrient

Water is the most important of the six basic nutrients. It is essential to all forms of life. By weight, about 50 to 70 percent of the human body is water. It is a perfect medium for the body's metabolic processes. Water either participates in or is a by-product of most metabolic reactions. In addition, water aids in temperature regulation, waste removal, and hydration. Without water, life would not exist.

Most people get 80 percent of their water from beverages and 20 percent from food. Drinks such as coffee, iced tea, soda, and juices consist primarily of

Exhibit 2.5

Food should be people's primary source of vitamins and minerals in most circumstances.

Exhibit 2.6

water. Tap water is usually the best choice (*Exhibit 2.6*) because it has added fluoride. Offering customers and guests a cold glass of water is more than just a courtesy; it also provides your guest with the key to hydration.

WHAT IS NUTRIENT DENSITY?

Depending on the nutrients they contain, food items can be classified as either energy-dense or empty-calorie foods. Nutrient density refers to the number of nutrients per calorie of a particular food. When people eat nutrient-dense food, they receive more nutrition in a smaller number of total calories. Examples of nutrient-dense foods are oranges, apples, lean meats, whole-grain breads, vegetables, and skim milk. Notice that none of these contain added sugar or added fat.

On the other hand, empty-calorie food contains higher proportions of calories and relatively few, if any, nutrients. Empty-calorie food is made from high amounts of sugar and fat. Some examples are soda, candy, and lard. Often one or two daily servings of empty-calorie food add the extra three hundred to four hundred calories that, over time, cause weight gain in the general population. An emphasis on eating nutrient-dense food is especially important today because the majority of Americans are either overweight or obese. If people improve their nutrient intake and decrease calories, they may reduce their weight and become healthier. As restaurants and other foodservice establishments change their menus to reflect better nutrition, they should focus on adding nutrient-dense food and subtracting empty-calorie food.

ALCOHOL: A NON-NUTRIENT SOURCE OF CALORIES

Alcohol, which is a familiar accompaniment to many meals, has mixed effects on the human body. Because the body has no nutrient requirement for alcohol, nutritionists recommend limiting consumption to moderate amounts. Moderation is usually defined as the consumption of up to one drink per day for women and up to two drinks per day for men. A single drink is defined as 12 fluid ounces of regular beer, 5 fluid ounces of wine, or 1.5 fluid ounces of 80-proof distilled spirits.

Alcohol provides seven calories of energy per gram when metabolized by the body, but it provides no other nutrients. For this reason, it is considered an empty-calorie substance. Some studies have indicated that alcohol, when consumed in moderation, can reduce the risk of cardiovascular events such as strokes and decrease the occurrence of diabetes and dementia. It should be noted, however, that an excessive amount of alcohol in the diet is associated with many risks, including cancers of the digestive system (oral, esophageal, pancreatic, liver, colon, and rectal). Overuse of alcohol can also lead to cirrhosis, a fatal liver disease.

THE SENSES AND OUR ENJOYMENT OF FOOD

Our sense of taste begins in the mouth, where about ten thousand taste buds cover the tongue, the roof of the mouth, and the throat. The taste buds are chemosensory cells, which send a stimulus to the brain so that we can identify the food we are eating. The stimulus also allows the brain to interpret the taste and store the information, so that we can remember the taste later on.

Smell plays a significant role in sending food-identity messages to the brain and eliciting an emotional response. Smell, also known as olfactory response, gives food complexity and dimension. The olfactory bulb in the nose contains chemosensory cells that can identify different aromas. Food aroma reaches these sensors when we inhale through the nose. The aroma can also travel from the mouth via the opening near the back of the mouth. See *Exhibit 2.7.*

Exhibit 2.7

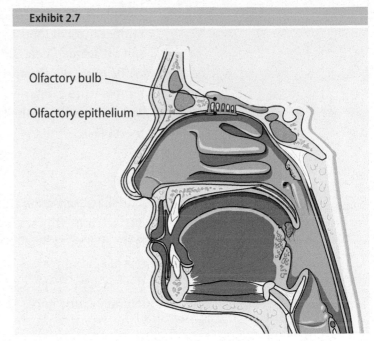

Olfactory bulb

Olfactory epithelium

Olfactory sensors in the nasal cavity react to food's aroma.

Although the combination of taste and aroma produces thousands of distinct tastes, the taste buds translate only five primary tastes: sweet, salty, bitter, sour, and umami. Research suggests that all parts of the tongue can detect all five of these tastes. Thus, contrary to popular myth, it is unlikely that the tongue has a geographic region for each taste.

THINK ABOUT IT . . .

Why is your ability to taste food impaired when you have a stuffy nose from a head cold?

Sweet

Humans have an inherent preference for the sweet taste. We tend to experience very strongly the types of sugars that come from cane, beet, honey, and fructose (fruit sugar) (*Exhibit 2.8*). However, the lower the temperature, the less our senses perceive the sweet taste. One example is ice cream. Ice-cream mixes are extremely sweet when first mixed, but when they are frozen, the sweetness becomes much less noticeable.

Salty

Salt is a seasoning that enhances the flavor of food. Sodium chloride, sodium benzoate, sodium fluoride, and other sodium compounds give the impression of salty taste. People can condition their preference for salt to either high or low amounts.

Two common factors affect the perceived saltiness of food. First, smokers tend to taste salt less vividly and, therefore, tend to salt food more heavily.

Exhibit 2.8

Cooks who smoke should be wary of over salting food. Second, the temperature of food affects how salty it tastes; the hotter the food, the less salty it seems. A classic example is over salting of soup. If the soup is salted while hot, the salty taste becomes more predominant as it cools. The best temperature range at which to taste food that is served hot is between 70 and 105 degrees Fahrenheit (21 and 41 degrees Celsius); this yields the food's truest taste.

Sour

The sharp sensation that we call a sour (acid) taste is found in foods such as citrus fruits, wines, vinegar, and oxalic acid from spinach, rhubarb, and other leafy greens. Skilled chefs use sour tastes to balance and enhance flavor. The use of acid in recipes can trick the tongue into thinking that there is more salt than is actually present. So before reaching for the salt shaker, try a squeeze of lemon or lime juice.

Bitter

Nature has provided humans with a sensory system that prevents us from ingesting food poisons and bitter tastes. Poisonous alkaloid food is most associated with bitterness. Food items and components such as Brussels sprouts, spinach, chocolate, caffeine, saccharin, and quinine contain alkaloid compounds that give a bitter and astringent taste.

Umami

Umami is recognized as the fifth taste sensation and is associated with the amino acid glutamate. The word *umami* is derived from the Japanese language, and many Japanese dishes contain this flavor. Examples of umami flavor include monosodium glutamate (MSG), mushrooms, seaweed, soy products such as soy sauce and miso, meat, corn, peas, fish, tomatoes, and cheese. Umami is a subtle taste sensation and can round out the flavor of other types of food. By using umami, cooks can create many savory and delicious food items with little or no salt.

Spice: Not Quite a Taste

The taste of spicy or hot food is not a taste, exactly, but rather a response to an acid-like chemical irritation to the tongue. The trigeminal nerve, centered in the tongue, picks up this response and sends it to the brain as pain. People can condition this response over time by increasing the spiciness of the food they eat. On the other hand, overuse of this type of food can "burn" the palate and desensitize the ability to taste milder food. Sources of spicy or piquant food include chilies, peppercorns, horseradish, and mustard.

Building a Palate

The brain collects the sensory stimuli associated with eating food and tells us whether the overall sensation is pleasurable or painful. Later, when the same taste and aroma combination is received, the brain recognizes this food as something liked or disliked. Over a period of time, a person builds a palate, or a memory stamp of food flavor profiles. The same response can occur when a person chews food. As food is chewed and swallowed, the nose receives the gases by way of the opening at the back of the throat, and this triggers the same response to the recognition of the food. Thus, the nose is the primary source of taste perception. That is why a person with a cold cannot taste food well.

As people age, their senses of smell and taste diminish. Starting at around 40 years of age, people experience an incremental loss of taste perception each decade, until there is a total loss of up to 70 percent by age 70. This loss can have a significant impact on health because older adults have an increasing tendency to choose food that is heavily salted, fried, high in fat, or high in sugar in an attempt to maintain the sensation of taste. These types of food contribute little to a healthy diet. The complete loss of smell is called anosmia, which can be extremely dangerous for older adults living alone. With this condition, the appetite usually diminishes, possibly resulting in malnutrition.

We perceive flavor through all our senses. When we see a very attractively presented dish, we anticipate its taste. Smell and taste sensations work together to provide most of the flavor. People describe the consistency or feel of food in the mouth as important as well; for example, a high-fat ice cream is often described as creamy. When entering an establishment, guests can often hear the sizzling of steaks or the accompanying sound of a flaming dish as it is served. These sounds can add to the excitement and pleasure of eating.

DIGESTION, ABSORPTION, AND TRANSPORT OF NUTRIENTS

The adage "You are what you eat" reminds us that everything we eat is important to our health. Every morsel we eat is broken down through digestion and absorbed into our bodies. Our food choices, along with our genetics, daily habits, and environment, determine our overall health.

Digestion is the process of breaking food down to its simplest or most elemental parts, which the body can then absorb and use. Digestion is much more than just the physical and chemical breakdown of food; it also includes the senses. Seasoned restaurant and foodservice professionals know the importance of creating an appetizing ambience for their diners. This helps to engage the customer in the enjoyment of food, and the anticipation of food actually begins the digestive process.

REAL MANAGER

FOOD MATTERS

Early in my career as a registered clinical dietician at a hospital, I ran into a situation that has stayed with me to this day. We admitted a very badly injured female teenager in need of serious care.

Of course all patients need sufficient calories and protein, and the hospital food was good and nutritious, but sometimes she had to feel like a teenager! So, to break the monotony, I would sometimes stop at a local fast-food restaurant and buy her a meal.

Well, she was hospitalized for over a year, but she did recover. Flavor and presentation can be as important as nutrition, and I became even more convinced that nutrition needs to feed the body *and* the soul.

Exhibit 2.9

THE DIGESTIVE SYSTEM

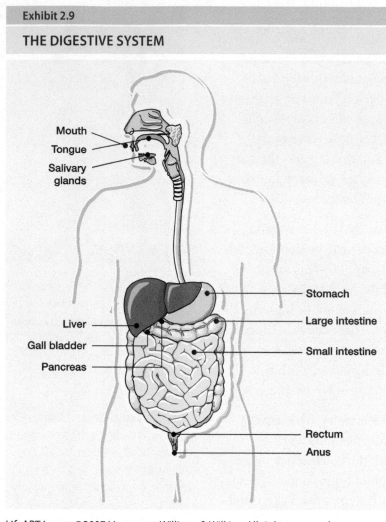

Mouth
Tongue
Salivary glands

Stomach
Large intestine
Small intestine

Liver
Gall bladder
Pancreas

Rectum
Anus

The digestive system is the body's food-breakdown machine. The process occurs in the digestive tract, a hollow, muscular tube that extends from the mouth to the anus. The **digestive tract** is composed of the oral cavity, the pharynx, the esophagus, the stomach, the small intestine, the large intestine, the rectum, and the anus. The liver, pancreas, and gall bladder also participate in digestion by secreting fluids into the tract (see *Exhibit 2.9*).

The digestive process consists of both the physical movement of food through the digestive tract and the chemical breakdown that happens along the way. The physical process reduces the size of the food by grinding (via the teeth) and churning (via the stomach) it as it moves along the tract. The chemical process consists of the secretion of enzymes and other fluids that the body produces. These fluids chemically separate the components of food into their simplest form, thus preparing the food material for absorption by the body. **Enzymes** are protein substances that speed up metabolic reactions. Various digestive enzymes are usually very efficient at breaking down food materials.

The digestive tract has many layers: an inside lining called the mucosa, a mucous membrane that protects the lining of the tract and provides secretions from underlying tissue; the submucosa, which has connective tissue and blood vessels; a layer of muscle; and the serosa, which lines the abdominal cavity and provides a passage for blood vessels, nerves, and the lymphatic system. Throughout the process of digestion, an involuntary wave of contraction called peristalsis propels food down the tract. In the small intestine, food is further broken down until the fragments are completely mixed with the intestinal secretions. All of these digestive processes are under hormonal and enzymatic control.

Exhibit 2.10

The mouth accepts the food and starts both mechanical and chemical digestion (*Exhibit 2.10*). The teeth masticate (chew) the food. This step consists of grinding the food into smaller pieces and mixing it with saliva. There are three sets of salivary glands in the mouth. They produce approximately 1 to 1.5 liters of fluid each day to keep both food and the tissue inside the mouth moist. As food touches the tongue, its tastes are revealed and the taste buds transmit an impulse to the brain. The parotid salivary gland is responsible for secreting an enzyme called salivary amylase, which starts the digestion of starch. The tongue then positions the masticated food to be swallowed.

The masticated food passes through the pharynx to the esophagus on its way to the stomach. Once food leaves the mouth and journeys toward the stomach as a wet, soft ball, it is called a bolus. Peristalsis propels the bolus through the esophagus to the stomach, where the lower esophageal sphincter opens to allow entry. Normally, the sphincters, which are powerful muscles, only allow a one-way trip; they close once partially-digested food has been passed on to the next phase of digestion.

The functions of the stomach are to store food temporarily, to mix it mechanically, and to continue chemical digestion. The stomach produces hydrochloric acid, pepsin (which is an enzyme that digests protein), and intrinsic factor. The body will later use intrinsic factor to enable the absorption of vitamin B12. All of this mixing, along with the addition of acid and enzymes, produces a thin fluid called chyme.

The watery chyme passes through the pyloric sphincter as it moves from the stomach to the small intestine. The small intestine is approximately 20 feet long. It has fingerlike projections called villi (the singular is villus) that increase the surface area and, thus, the absorptive capacity of the small intestine. On each villus are epithelial cells that have microvilli. Inside the villi are capillaries—tiny blood vessels that carry the digested nutrients through the blood to the liver. The lymphatic vessels, part of the immune system, absorb the dietary fats, which will then travel by the blood to the heart, as shown in *Exhibit 2.11.*

Exhibit 2.11

VILLI

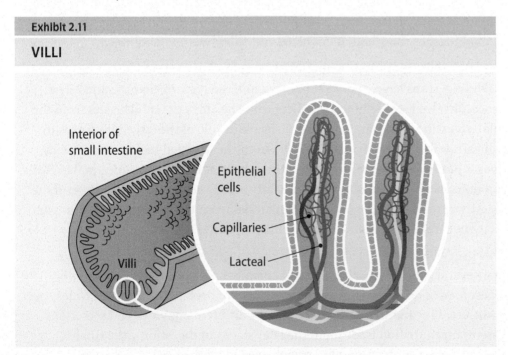

Interior of small intestine

Epithelial cells

Capillaries

Lacteal

Villi

The villi are tiny fingerlike projections that absorb nutrients and pass them into the bloodstream.

In the small intestine, the chyme is digested completely and the nutrients are absorbed. In this process, the pancreas secretes additional enzymes that aid in carbohydrate, protein, and lipid digestion. In addition, bicarbonate flows from the pancreas to help neutralize the digestive fluids from the stomach. Bile, which is made by the liver and concentrated in the gallbladder, is secreted when chyme reaches the small intestine. When chyme from a meal arrives, the gallbladder, responding to hormonal cues, secretes its stored bile into the small intestine. The bile emulsifies fats, thus allowing enzymes to reduce the fats to their component parts of fatty acids and glycerol. Starch completes its breakdown into **glucose** (blood sugar), and two-unit sugars called disaccharides separate into one-unit sugars called monosaccharides to allow for absorption. Chapter 4 provides more information about these various components.

When digestion is completed, starches and sugars have been broken down to monosaccharides, and lipids have been disassembled into glycerol, fatty acids, and monoglycerides. The long-chain fats enter the lymphatic (immune) system. The monosaccharides and short-chain fatty acids are sent to the liver for use in **metabolism**, which is the process by which living organisms and cells break down complex chemicals into their components and reassemble the components into larger molecules needed by the body. Proteins are broken down into amino acids and then absorbed. The amino acids will travel through the blood to the liver, where they will be degraded for energy or synthesized into other products the body needs.

Note that alcohol, whether it is consumed with a meal or by itself, is digested and metabolized by the body. If alcohol is consumed on an empty stomach, it will be absorbed there and immediately circulated to the blood, which distributes it throughout the body. When food is present in the stomach, more alcohol ends up in the small intestine, where its absorption is delayed. Once alcohol reaches the blood, it circulates until the liver metabolizes it.

The large intestine is approximately five feet long. It contains the cecum; the ascending, transverse, and descending colon; the rectum; and the anus. The ileocecal valve is the sphincter that controls the entry of liquid wastes from the small intestine to the large intestine. The main role of the large intestine is to reabsorb water, minerals, and bile salts from the digested material. Insoluble fiber is not broken down and leaves the body intact. However, intestinal bacteria can now metabolize soluble fiber into fatty acids and gas. The final stage of the digestive process is the movement of material from the colon to the rectum and then out through the anus, or anal sphincter, at the time of elimination.

This overview of the digestive system and the digestive process has shown that several stages of mechanical and chemical processing are required to digest food. The different types of nutrients are digested at different times, in different locations, and with the help of different enzymes and secretions. Essentially, nutrition is all about the later stages of digestion—the final absorption and utilization of nutrients needed by the body.

When people eat more food, and therefore more calories, than they require, they will most likely gain weight.

THINK ABOUT IT . . .

The factors that directly influence body weight are genetics, physical exercise, and daily food intake.

Why is it often difficult for a person to change his or her weight?

BODY MASS INDEX AND THE IMPORTANCE OF A HEALTHY WEIGHT

The body mass index (BMI) is a numerical calculation that reflects the relationship between a person's height and weight. This calculation is used to determine whether or not the person's weight is in a healthy range. To use a BMI chart, people must find their height in inches and then find their weight in pounds. At the intersection of these two measurements is the two-digit number that represents an individual's BMI. The BMI chart is divided into four general categories: underweight, healthy weight, overweight, and obese (see *Exhibit 2.12*). Overweight and obesity are defined in terms of BMI. People who have a BMI of 25 to 29.9 are considered overweight, and those with a BMI of 30 or greater are considered obese (see *Exhibit 2.13*).

Although BMI is a fairly good indicator of healthy weight in most people, it does not provide accurate results for people who might have more lean body mass, such as elite athletes and body builders. Individuals with more lean

---

Exhibit 2.12

BODY MASS INDEX (BMI) CHART

Weight in pounds

Height	120	130	140	150	160	170	180	190	200	210	220	230	240	250
4'6	29	31	34	36	39	41	43	46	48	51	53	56	58	60
4'8	27	29	31	34	36	38	40	43	45	47	49	52	54	56
4'10	25	27	29	31	34	36	38	40	42	44	46	48	50	52
5'0	23	25	27	29	31	33	35	37	39	41	43	45	47	49
5'2	22	24	26	27	29	31	33	35	37	38	40	42	44	46
5'4	21	22	24	26	28	29	31	33	34	36	38	40	41	43
5'6	19	21	23	24	26	27	29	31	32	34	36	37	39	40
5'8	18	20	21	23	24	26	27	29	30	32	34	35	37	38
5'10	17	19	20	22	23	24	26	27	29	30	32	33	35	36
6'0	16	18	19	20	22	23	24	26	27	28	30	31	33	34
6'2	15	17	18	19	21	22	23	24	26	27	28	30	31	32
6'4	15	16	17	18	20	21	22	23	24	26	27	28	29	30
6'6	14	15	16	17	19	20	21	22	23	24	25	27	28	29
6'8	13	14	15	17	18	19	20	21	22	23	24	25	26	28

Height in feet and inches

▢ Underweight   ▢ Healthy weight   ▢ Overweight   ▢ Obese

Note: This chart is for adults (aged 20 years and older).

Exhibit 2.13

INTERPRETING BMI

BMI	Weight Status
Below 18.5	Underweight
18.5–24.9	Normal
25.0–29.9	Overweight
30 and above	Obese

U.S. Centers for Disease Control and Prevention

THINK ABOUT IT . . .

To calculate your BMI, use this equation:

$$\left(\frac{\text{Weight in pounds}}{} \div \frac{\text{Height in inches}^2}{} \right)$$
$$\times \ 703 \ = \ \text{BMI}$$

For example, one person is 5 feet 8 inches tall and weighs 185 pounds:

$$(185 \div 68^2) \times 703 = 28.1$$

This BMI indicates an overweight individual.

body mass weigh more because lean body mass is heavier than fat mass. This difference in proportion can yield an inaccurate measurement.

Healthy weight adults store most of their fat below the skin, or subcutaneously. However, if they store fat more around the waist, it can increase their risk of health problems. Women with waist sizes larger than 36 inches and men with waist sizes greater than 40 inches are storing fat in their midsections. This can lead to increased risk of cardiovascular disease and type 2 diabetes.

According to the U.S. government's Dietary Guidelines for Americans, 72 percent of men and 64 percent of women in the United States are overweight, and about one-third of these adults are obese. In addition, and this may be the worst news, 18 percent of American children aged 12 to 19 are obese. Today, the major causes of morbidity (disease rate) and mortality (death rate) in the United States involve poor diet and a sedentary lifestyle. Worrisome diseases and conditions include cardiovascular disease, hypertension, type 2 diabetes, obesity, osteoporosis, iron-deficiency anemia, oral disease, malnutrition, and some cancers. One particularly alarming trend is that children are being diagnosed with diseases like type 2 diabetes because they are obese. This requires a call to action from all members of the community to help children reduce their weight and improve their health. Restaurant and foodservice operations can help counteract these trends by providing nutritious food that is low in solid fat, added sugar, and sodium. There is a large population of adults and children who need to reduce their weight due to obesity or type 2 diabetes. This population represents a significant market for the restaurant and foodservice industry.

Weight Adjustments

In general, three factors determine an individual's body weight: genetics, daily physical activity, and daily food intake. For individuals who are at an ideal or healthy weight, the goal is to maintain energy balance by eating the same number of calories that they are utilizing or expending daily, assuming that their level of physical activity remains consistent.

When someone is overweight or obese, the idea is to decrease caloric intake to create a deficit, or negative calorie balance, in order to lose weight. Exercise is also necessary to maintain a healthy body. It is particularly important to exercise regularly when trying to lose weight. On the flip side, if an individual is underweight, the goal is to increase food intake to create a positive energy balance in order to achieve weight gain.

Although overall weight-loss strategies sound simple, many people find it difficult to lose weight and then to keep it off. When people become overweight or obese, metabolic changes throughout the body can cause resistance to weight loss. In addition, when people have gained weight, they often do not have the same capacity to exercise that they once had, and it takes a concerted effort for them to get back to engaging in strenuous activity on a daily basis. People who are trying to lose weight have to create a deficit of 3,500 calories in order to lose one pound of body weight. This means eliminating at least five hundred calories per day to lose a pound of weight per week if exercise remains consistent. This task is often more challenging than it sounds.

Children and Weight

Both increased caloric intake and lack of physical activity contribute to obesity in children. According to the report of the 2010 Dietary Guidelines for Americans, in 2007, the prevalence of obesity in children was 10 percent for children aged 2 to 5, 20 percent for children aged 6 to 11, and 18 percent for adolescents aged 12 to 19. Considering the numbers of overweight and obese children, there is an increased need for parents to supervise the meals that their children eat. Parents have the greatest potential to be change agents in decreasing this obesity epidemic. They must teach their children how to eat healthfully, yet they should focus on the quality of the diet rather than on the quantity of calories. Schools and other institutions responsible for the diets of children and teens should do the same. These institutions should make an effort to offer healthful, appealing choices that assist children with their decisions. As they grow, children and teens need monitoring in order to ensure that their weight remains healthy into adulthood.

SUMMARY

1. Define *calorie*, *nutrient density*, and *empty-calorie food* and explain why people should decrease consumption of empty-calorie food.

   The amount of energy that a person derives from food is measured in units called calories. A calorie is the amount of energy needed to heat one kilogram of water (about 2.2 pounds) by approximately two degrees Fahrenheit (one degree Celsius). Nutrient density refers to the number of nutrients per calorie of a food. For the most part, if you eat nutrient-dense food, you receive more nutrition in a smaller number of total calories. An empty-calorie food is one that contains higher proportions of calories but few if any nutrients. Empty-calorie food usually contains high amounts of sugar and fat. Often one or two servings of empty-calorie food per day can add the extra three hundred to four hundred calories that cause weight gain in the general population. Therefore, it would be wise for most people to decrease consumption of these foods.

2. **Identify the six basic types of nutrients found in food and describe their characteristics.**

    The six essential nutrients are carbohydrates, proteins, lipids, vitamins, minerals, and water. Carbohydrates include starch, sugar, and dietary fiber. Carbohydrates provide the body with four calories of energy per gram. Proteins are large, complex molecules that contain long chains of amino acids. Lipids can be triglycerides, cholesterol, or phospholipids. Lipids provide abundant energy, as each gram contains nine calories. Vitamins are organic compounds, while minerals are inorganic elements. Both are needed in relatively small amounts by the body for regulation of metabolic processes. Water is the most important nutrient. It is a universal solvent and a critical component of metabolic processes.

3. **Describe the major functions of carbohydrates, proteins, lipids, vitamins, minerals, and water in the body.**

    The primary role of carbohydrates in the diet is to supply energy. The primary function of protein is to provide amino acids, which the body uses to build and repair muscles and other tissues. In addition, the body uses protein to form enzymes, hormones, and antibodies. Lipids provide energy at a rate of nine calories per gram of food eaten.

    Vitamins and minerals are needed in relatively small amounts by the body for regulation of metabolic processes. Water is essential to all forms of life. It is a perfect medium for the metabolic processes of the body. In addition, water aids in temperature regulation, waste removal, and hydration.

4. **Explain the effect of alcohol consumption on the body.**

    Alcohol has mixed effects on the body. Some studies have indicated that alcohol, when consumed in moderation, can reduce the risk of cardiovascular events and decrease the occurrence of diabetes and dementia. However, an excessive amount of alcohol in the diet is associated with cancers of the digestive system as well as cirrhosis, a fatal liver disease.

5. **Explain how the senses affect a person's intake of food.**

    There are five recognized primary tastes: sweet, salty, bitter, sour, and umami. In addition, when we see a very attractively presented dish, we anticipate its taste. Smell and taste sensations work together to provide most of the flavor. People also describe the consistency or feel of food in the mouth as important. The sizzling of steaks or the accompanying sound of a flaming dish as it is served can also add to the excitement and pleasure of eating.

6. **Identify the structures of the digestive system and describe digestion, absorption, transport, and utilization of nutrients from food.**

    The structures of the digestive system include the oral cavity, the pharynx, the esophagus, the stomach, the small intestine, the large intestine, the rectum, the anus, the liver, the gallbladder, and the pancreas.

    The digestive process includes both the physical movement of food down the digestive tract and the secretion of enzymes and fluids. The teeth chew the food, the salivary glands secrete saliva, and the stomach holds and mixes the food. The small intestine is responsible for most digestive and absorptive roles. The major role of the large intestine is to reabsorb water, minerals, and bile salts. The rectum stores the waste, and the anus allows for elimination. The liver produces bile, the gallbladder stores it, and the pancreas adds bicarbonate and enzymes to the chyme in the small intestine for the final phase of digestion.

When digestion is completed, starches and sugars have been broken down into monosaccharides, and lipids have been disassembled into glycerol, fatty acids, and monoglycerides. The long-chain fats enter the lymphatic system. The monosaccharide and short-chain fatty acids are sent to the liver for use in metabolism. Proteins are broken down into amino acids and then absorbed, and the amino acids travel through the blood to the liver to be used by the body.

7. **Describe the body mass index and explain why it is important to achieve and maintain a healthy weight.**

The body mass index (BMI) is a numerical calculation that reflects the relationship between a person's height and weight. This calculation can indicate if the person's weight is in a healthy range. Statistically, individuals who have high BMI values are at increased risk of what are generally referred to as the chronic diseases. These diseases include obesity, type 2 diabetes, arthritis, cardiovascular disease (including high blood pressure, or hypertension), stroke, and coronary heart disease.

APPLICATION EXERCISES

Exercise 1

Match the organ on the left with its function on the right.

Component(s) of the Digestive System	Function
_____ Mouth, teeth, tongue, and salivary glands	A. Mixes chyme with bile and pancreatic juices to ensure complete digestion; products of digestion are absorbed here.
_____ Pharynx	B. Muscular sphincter that releases waste
_____ Esophagus	C. Performs metabolic regulation and produces bile
_____ Stomach	D. Stores and concentrates bile
_____ Small intestine	E. Secretes enzymes and bicarbonate to digest starches, proteins, and fats
_____ Large intestine	F. Common passage for swallowing food
_____ Rectum	G. Reabsorbs water and bile; compacts waste
_____ Anus	H. Receives the bolus and mixes it into a liquid; adds acids and enzymes to digest proteins
_____ Liver	I. Stores wastes until they can be eliminated
_____ Gallbladder	J. Grinds food into smaller pieces and mixes it with saliva
_____ Pancreas	K. Transports the bolus to the stomach

Exercise 2

Food items can be classified generally by the energy-yielding nutrients they contain. Some food items have empty calories, while others are nutrient dense. See how well you can distinguish them. Indicate with a check mark the major nutrient contributions of each of these food items. Also indicate whether each is high or low in nutrient density. (All the food items listed in the table contain vitamins and minerals in varying levels.)

Food	Carbohydrate	Protein	Lipid	High or low nutrient density
Bacon				
Baked beans				
Cookies				
Corn				
Cream cheese				
Eggs				
Grapefruit juice				
Grapes				
Green beans				
Ham				
Jelly beans				
Nonfat milk				
Pasta				
Rice cereal				
Salmon				
Sirloin steak				
Sour cream				
Tofu				
Waffles				

REVIEW YOUR LEARNING

Select the best answer for each question.

1. **Oils and fats are part of a class of nutrients called**
   A. amino acids.
   B. proteins.
   C. starches.
   D. lipids.

2. **Carbohydrate and protein food items yield how many calories per gram?**
   A. 2
   B. 4
   C. 6
   D. 8

3. **Proteins are complex compounds formed by long chains of**
   A. starch.
   B. cholesterol.
   C. amino acids.
   D. phospholipids.

4. **Studies have suggested that moderate consumption of alcohol has**
   A. some beneficial effects on health.
   B. some detrimental effects on health.
   C. no known effects on health.
   D. mixed effects on health.

5. **The three energy-yielding nutrients are**
   A. proteins, vitamins, and lipids.
   B. proteins, carbohydrates, and minerals.
   C. carbohydrates, lipids, and vitamins.
   D. carbohydrates, proteins, and lipids.

6. **What is the most important nutrient to the body?**
   A. Carbohydrates
   B. Proteins
   C. Lipids
   D. Water

7. **Which carbohydrate found in food is NOT digested by the human body?**
   A. Fiber
   B. Sugar
   C. Starch
   D. Maltose

8. **Cookies, candies, and sweetened beverages are considered what type of food?**
   A. Nutrient-dense
   B. Empty-calorie
   C. Healthy
   D. Fast

9. **Sugars are absorbed in the**
   A. small intestine.
   B. large intestine.
   C. stomach.
   D. liver.

10. **Bile is produced in the liver and stored in the**
    A. pancreas.
    B. gallbladder.
    C. large intestine.
    D. small intestine.

3 Understanding Nutritional Standards and Guidelines

INSIDE THIS CHAPTER

- A Healthy Diet
- Dietary Reference Intakes
- Dietary Guidelines for Americans 2010
- USDA's MyPlate
- Food Labeling

CHAPTER LEARNING OBJECTIVES

After completing this chapter, you should be able to:

- Define *Recommended Dietary Allowance, Adequate Intake, Tolerable Upper Intake Level*, and *Estimated Energy Requirement.*

- Determine the amounts of carbohydrate, protein, and fat recommended for healthy diets.

- Identify recommended estimates of calorie needs and daily fluid intakes.

- List the current recommendations for daily intake of sodium.

- State the importance of achieving calorie balance to maintain weight.

- Locate the nutrition facts label and the ingredient list on food packages, and describe how the daily values, nutrition facts label, and ingredient list are used in restaurants and foodservice operations.

- Identify major allergens on an ingredient list.

KEY TERMS

Acceptable Macronutrient Distribution Range (AMDR), p. 39

Adequate Intake (AI), p. 39

allergen, p. 55

Daily Value (DV), p. 52

Dietary Guidelines for Americans 2010, p. 42

Dietary Reference Intakes (DRIs), p. 38

Daily Reference Value (DRV), p. 52

Estimated Average Requirement (EAR), p. 39

Estimated Energy Requirement (EER), p. 39

food label, p. 51

healthy diet, p. 38

nutrition facts label, p. 52

Recommended Dietary Allowance (RDA), p. 39

Reference Daily Intake (RDI), p. 52

Tolerable Upper Intake Level (UL), p. 39

USDA Organic, p. 57

CASE STUDY

Luisa is a foodservice manager for a large company that operates facilities serving lunches to employees in corporate settings. It is her job to travel to various sites and monitor the facilities. There were several customer complaints from one site, so she visited the site to help solve the problems. Here are a few of the comments from customers:

- The food is often very salty.

- I have high blood pressure, and the cook is not helping.

- The portion sizes are too large for lunchtime fare.

- Can you tell the cook not to add so much salt to the food?

- I have allergies and am unsure what I can eat for lunch.

    1. What are the problems at this site?

    2. What can be done to correct the problems?

    3. What nutrition standards or guides can Luisa use to educate staff about changes that will satisfy customers?

    4. How can Luisa best communicate these changes to the operators of the facility?

A HEALTHY DIET

A healthy diet is one that contains nutrient-dense food choices from the five food groups. It contains all essential vitamins and minerals, as well as enough fiber, fluid, and phytochemicals to maintain good health. In addition, a healthy diet is balanced in calories, ensuring that people neither exceed nor dip below their ideal weight. Last but not least, diners should *enjoy* food that comprises a healthy diet! Combining all these elements every day is a tall order for most people with busy lifestyles. Most people have very little education in nutrition and therefore rely on food professionals to provide basic information on how to eat well.

Nutrition professionals use standards and guidelines to teach consumers how to achieve a healthy diet. This chapter will introduce these standards and guidelines in a way that helps restaurant and foodservice professionals plan menus for their customers. Chapters 1 and 2 established that the market for nutritious food is gaining strength as people address their need to maintain or improve their personal health or that of their families. Customers and clients are looking to restaurants and foodservice operations to provide meals that are both appetizing and in line with dietary recommendations.

Much of the information presented in this book is meant to help restaurant and foodservice professionals as they develop nutritional programs designed to fulfill their customers' expectations for both good taste and healthy choices.

THINK ABOUT IT . . .

How can restaurant and foodservice operators increase their understanding of nutrition and offer healthier menu items? How can they help guests make more informed decisions?

DIETARY REFERENCE INTAKES

The Dietary Reference Intakes (DRIs) are recommended daily nutrient and energy intake amounts for healthy people of a particular age range and gender, based on current scientific evidence. They are issued by the Food and Nutrition Board of the Institute of Medicine, National Academy of Sciences. The DRIs are updated as new research indicates that a particular nutrient needs to be adjusted for optimal health. Although most people initially used the DRIs to respond to nutritional deficiencies, the current focus is to help the public make the connection between nutrition and good health. The DRIs can be used to plan diets for both individuals and groups. For example, the Estimated Average Requirement (EAR) discussed below is the basis for determining the Recommended Dietary Allowance (RDA) (also discussed below) as well as planning national nutrition programs and setting government policy.

The DRIs are presented in tables. This arrangement allows the user to locate values for each nutrient easily. The macronutrients are presented in gram quantities, and the micronutrients are presented in either milligram or microgram quantities. When analyzing recipes for sodium content, the DRI value will be used as the standard for comparison.

The DRIs provide the following types of nutrient intake values:

- **Estimated Average Requirement (EAR):** The estimated average daily dietary intake level that meets the nutritional requirements of half the healthy people of a particular age range and gender.

- **Recommended Dietary Allowance (RDA):** The average daily dietary nutrient intake sufficient to meet the nutrient requirement of nearly all (97 to 98 percent) healthy individuals of a particular age and gender group.

- **Adequate Intake (AI):** The daily dietary intake level assumed to be adequate for good health when there is insufficient evidence to set an RDA.

- **Tolerable Upper Intake Level (UL):** The highest level of daily nutrient intake that poses no risk of adverse health effects to almost all individuals of a certain age range.

In addition to the values for nutrients, the DRIs include two values for energy:

- **Estimated Energy Requirement (EER):** The dietary energy intake believed to maintain energy balance in a healthy adult of a certain age, gender, weight, height, and level of activity.

- **Acceptable Macronutrient Distribution Range (AMDR):** The range of intakes for a particular energy source, such as carbohydrates (45 to 65 percent), lipids (20 to 35 percent), and protein (10 to 35 percent), that reduces risk of disease while providing enough essential nutrients. The AMDR shown in *Exhibit 3.1* is for adults. It is expressed as a percentage of total energy intake because it does not depend on other energy sources or an individual's caloric needs. More information about the DRIs can be found at the Food and Nutrition Information Center of the USDA Web site *fnic.nal.usda.gov/dietary-guidance/dietary-reference-intakes.*

Exhibit 3.1

ACCEPTABLE MACRONUTRIENT DISTRIBUTION RANGE (AMDR)

Nutrient	Percent
Carbohydrates	45 to 65 percent
Proteins	10 to 35 percent
Lipids	20 to 35 percent

Adapted from *Dietary Reference Intakes for Energy, Carbohydrate, Fiber, Fat, Fatty Acids, Cholesterol, Protein, and Amino Acids (Macronutrients).* ©2005 by the National Academy of Sciences.

A Focus on Water

The DRIs address the human body's dietary need for the most important essential nutrient: water. The body is almost two-thirds water by weight. Water is critical for survival and good health because it provides a medium in which the chemical reactions of the body take place. Because water is also needed to cool the body, the amount of water that each person requires will vary with external temperature, amount of physical exercise, and number of calories eaten. Men usually need about 3.7 liters of water per day, and women need about 2.7 liters.

Thirst is generally the best sign of water needs. People meet most of their daily water needs by consuming either pure water or other beverages (*Exhibit 3.2*). A small part of our water intake is derived from the food we eat.

Exhibit 3.2

Reading the DRIs

As shown in *Exhibit 3.3*, the DRI tables are organized according to gender and age. The tables in this guide contain values for the RDA, AI, and UL. In addition, each nutrient has separate recommended values for pregnant and lactating women. The EAR is not included because it is used primarily for research and for planning federal nutrition programs.

Exhibit 3.3

DIETARY REFERENCE INTAKES FOR MAJOR MINERALS

	Male 9–18 yrs	Male 19–70 yrs	Male >70 yrs	Female 9–18 yrs	Female 19–70 yrs	Female >70 yrs	Male and female 19–70 yrs
	RDA/AI	RDA/AI	RDA/AI	RDA/AI	RDA/AI	RDA/AI	UL
Major Minerals							
Calcium (mg)	1,300	1,000	1,200	1,300	1,000–1,200	1,200	2,000–2,500
Chloride (mg)	2,300	2,000–2,300	1,800	2,300	2,000–2,300	1,800	3,600
Magnesium (mg)	240–410	400–420	420	240–360	310–320	320	350
Phosphorus (mg)	1,250	700	700	1,250	700	700	4,000
Potassium (mg)	4,500–4,700	4,700	4,700	4,500–4,700	4,700	4,700	-------
Sodium (mg)	1,500	1,300–1,500	1,200	1,500	1,300–1,500	1,200	2,300

Additional DRI tables can be found in chapter 5.
Adapted from Dietary Reference Intakes (DRIs), Recommended Dietary Allowances (RDA), and Adequate Intakes (AI)—Food and Nutrition Board, Institute of Medicine, National Academy of Sciences.

The Role of DRIs in Menu Planning

Dietary planning, whether for an individual or for a group, involves developing a diet that is nutritionally adequate without being excessive. A foodservice operation can help its customers achieve adequate nutrient intakes by using the DRIs as a reference.

As stated earlier in this chapter, DRIs consist of several different types of reference values. The RDA and AI are recommendations for adequate nutrient intakes for the majority of healthy individuals. By referring to the AI for calcium, for example, a menu planner can determine that the recommended amount of calcium for adults aged 19 to 50 is one thousand milligrams per day. This might encourage the planner to add menu items that are good sources of calcium. In addition, it might confirm that existing menu items provide appropriate amounts of this nutrient.

The UL provides the maximum intake limits for each nutrient. For most nutrients this amount is difficult to reach just by eating food; it can be reached only when people consume vitamin and mineral supplements. One exception to this generalization is sodium. Some people think that vitamins and minerals should be taken in large doses in order to avoid deficiency diseases. The UL is helpful when trying to demonstrate to individuals that they are taking too many nutrients, or too much of a particular nutrient, for the good of their health. The public is often surprised to hear that taking too much of certain vitamins and minerals through supplements can have a negative impact, such as increasing the risk of developing certain types of cancer.

It is easy to exceed recommended amounts of sodium because it does not take much salt (sodium chloride) to reach the DRI level of fifteen hundred milligrams of sodium, and some meals may even reach the UL of twenty-three hundred milligrams. Restaurants and other foodservice operations should seek to increase food's flavor through other ingredients and to use salt moderately. This strategy of increasing flavor while reducing sodium takes culinary skill, and it is aided by the use of standardized recipes to ensure that sodium levels remain the same with each preparation, regardless of the preparer.

Meal planning for institutional settings requires that managers know the nutritional needs of the group they serve. The RDAs and AIs are essential for planning meals that target those groups. Some menu planning is dependent on established standards, such as those for the National School Lunch and School Breakfast programs. New standards effective 2012, mandate that meals include more fruits, vegetables, and whole grains, while scaling back calories. Low-fat milk must be served and the amount of sodium in meals decreased. These changes align with recommendations of the Dietary Guidelines for Americans. Meal planners in institutional settings, such as the school shown in *Exhibit 3.4*, must ensure that the nutrient requirements of the program are met each day.

Finally, DRIs are useful in another way. Restaurant managers, foodservice operators, and chefs can refer to these guidelines when helping staff to understand nutritional information.

THINK ABOUT IT . . .

Why might a restaurant or foodservice operation perform a nutritional analysis of its menu items? What are the advantages of gathering this information? Are there any potential disadvantages?

Exhibit 3.4

DIETARY GUIDELINES FOR AMERICANS 2010

Dietary Guidelines for Americans 2010 is a document that provides information and advice on food choices, healthy weight, and disease prevention for people aged two years and above. This report is mandated by legislation and is produced jointly every five years by the United States Department of Agriculture (USDA) and the United States Department of Health and Human Services (HHS). The advice is gathered from a thorough review of current scientific research. The report both provides dietary recommendations and indicates the strength of the evidence that supports those recommendations. One of the principles of the Dietary Guidelines is that nutrients should be obtained through food. In some cases, however, fortified food and dietary supplements may be helpful in meeting nutrient needs.

Normally the Dietary Guidelines report is released to a healthy population. However, the 2010 report was released at a time of crisis. Today, the majority of the U.S. population is overweight, and people have an increased risk of chronic diseases like diabetes, hypertension, and heart disease. The 2010 report acknowledges that Americans make their own food and physical-activity choices. It also states, however, that people cannot change their diets unless they have the opportunity to purchase nutritious food. Because of the strength of evidence that obesity is harmful to human health, government officials are making concerted efforts to encourage healthy eating in all areas of the country and in all types of markets.

Major changes are necessary to curb the incidence of overconsumption by the populace. Many restaurants and foodservice operations have already begun initiatives to provide more nutritious choices and to offer consumers the opportunity to purchase reduced portion sizes. For example, some restaurants participate in the Healthy Dining program, which helps customers locate restaurants that have adapted their menus to include more nutritious food. In addition, the Kids LiveWell[SM] program focuses on providing nutrient-rich menu options, including fruit, vegetables, lean protein, whole grains, and low-fat dairy products, while limiting unhealthy fats, sugars, and sodium.

The 2010 Dietary Guidelines contain two main concepts that the public should embrace. These are followed by 23 key recommendations for all Americans and 6 recommendations for specific population groups. Restaurant and foodservice professionals should be familiar with the two main concepts as well as some of the key recommendations presented below.

Concepts

Concept one: Maintain calorie balance over time to achieve and sustain a healthy weight: This guideline encourages the public to eat smaller portions and to exercise daily in order to decrease weight. It is all about balancing the number of calories eaten with the amount of calories expended through physical activity. When the number of calories ingested is equal to the number expended, people maintain their weight. As mentioned previously, a person's estimated energy requirement (EER) depends on body size, gender, physical activity, and age.

Concept two: Focus on consuming nutrient-dense foods and beverages: To increase their chances of losing weight and improving their health, Americans should focus on eating foods that are nutrient dense. This involves consuming fewer sugar-sweetened beverages, solid fats, and refined grains.

Key Recommendations
BALANCING CALORIES TO MANAGE WEIGHT

- Prevent and/or reduce overweight and obesity through improved eating and physical activity behaviors.

- Control total calorie intake to manage body weight. For people who are overweight or obese, this will mean consuming fewer calories from foods and beverages.

- Increase physical activity and reduce time spent in sedentary behaviors.

- Maintain appropriate calorie balance during each stage of life: childhood, adolescence, adulthood, pregnancy and breastfeeding, and older age.

FOODS AND FOOD COMPONENTS TO REDUCE

- Reduce daily sodium intake to less than 2,300 milligrams (mg), and further reduce intake to 1,500 mg among persons who are 51 and older and those of any age who are African American or have hypertension, diabetes, or chronic kidney disease. The 1,500 mg recommendation applies to about half of the U.S. population, including children, and the majority of adults.

- Consume less than 10 percent of calories from saturated fatty acids by replacing them with monounsaturated and polyunsaturated fatty acids.

- Consume less than 300 mg per day of dietary cholesterol.

- Keep trans-fatty acid consumption as low as possible by limiting foods that contain synthetic sources of trans fats, such as partially hydrogenated oils, and by limiting other solid fats.

- Reduce the intake of calories from solid fats and added sugars.

- Limit the consumption of foods that contain refined grains, especially refined-grain foods that contain solid fats, added sugars, and sodium.

- If alcohol is consumed, it should be consumed in moderation, up to one drink per day for women and two drinks per day for men, and only by adults of legal drinking age.

FOODS AND NUTRIENTS TO INCREASE

Individuals should meet the following recommendations as part of a healthy eating pattern while staying within their calorie needs:

- Increase vegetable and fruit intake.

- Eat a variety of vegetables, especially dark-green vegetables, red and orange vegetables, and beans and peas (*Exhibit 3.5*).

- Consume at least half of all grains as whole grains. Increase whole-grain intake by replacing refined grains with whole grains.

- Increase intake of fat-free or low-fat milk and milk products, such as milk, yogurt, cheese, or fortified soy beverages.

- Choose a variety of protein foods, which include seafood, lean meat and poultry, eggs, beans and peas, soy products, and unsalted nuts and seeds.

- Increase the amount and variety of seafood consumed by choosing seafood in place of some meat and poultry.

- Replace protein foods that are higher in solid fats with proteins that are lower in solid fats and calories and/or are sources of oils.

- Use oils to replace solid fats where possible.

Choose foods that provide more potassium, dietary fiber, calcium, and vitamin D, nutrients that are typically low in American diets. These foods include vegetables, fruits, whole grains, milk, and milk products.

Exhibit 3.5

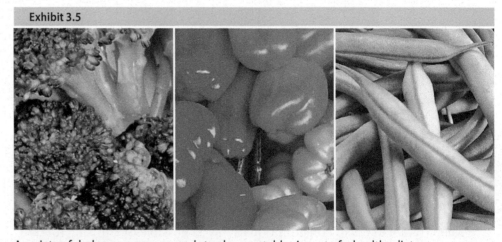

A variety of dark green, orange, and starchy vegetables is part of a healthy diet.

BUILD HEALTHY EATING PATTERNS

- Select an eating pattern that meets nutrient needs over time at an appropriate calorie level.

- Account for all foods and beverages consumed and assess how they fit within a total healthy eating pattern.

- Follow food safety recommendations when preparing and eating foods to reduce the risk of foodborne illnesses.

Women capable of becoming pregnant:

- Choose foods that supply heme iron, which is more readily absorbed by the body, additional iron sources, and enhancers of iron absorption such as vitamin C–rich foods.

- Consume 400 micrograms (mcg) per day of synthetic folic acid from fortified foods and/or supplements, in addition to food forms of folate from a varied diet.

Women who are pregnant or breastfeeding:

- Consume 8 to 12 ounces of seafood per week from a variety of seafood types.

- Due to high methyl mercury content, limit white (albacore) tuna to 6 ounces per week and do not eat the following four types of fish: tilefish, shark, swordfish, and king mackerel.

- If pregnant, take an iron supplement, as recommended by an obstetrician or other health care provider.

Individuals ages 50 years and older:

- Consume foods fortified with vitamin B12, such as fortified cereals, or dietary supplements.

Selected Messages for Consumers from the Dietary Guidelines for Americans

The federal government selected the following messages to encourage the public to make changes in their dietary intake. These changes will hopefully improve Americans' overall health. Managers and other foodservice operators may want to utilize these simple, easily remembered messages in materials they develop for their operation or for their staff.

BALANCING CALORIES

- Enjoy your food, but eat less.
- Avoid oversized portions.

FOODS TO INCREASE

- Make half your plate fruits and vegetables.
- Switch to fat-free or low-fat (1%) milk.

FOODS TO REDUCE

- Compare sodium in foods like soup, bread, and frozen meals—and choose the foods with lower numbers.

- Drink water instead of sugary drinks.

From the U.S. Department of Health and Human Services and U.S. Department of Agriculture, *Dietary Guidelines for Americans 2010.*

Exhibit 3.6

It is critical that restaurant and foodservice managers and staff understand these messages so that when a menu is developed or when a customer makes a special request based on dietary needs, the staff can respond appropriately. Managers should train their staff to communicate with customers about ingredients, preparation, and potential options so that orders can be taken efficiently (*Exhibit 3.6*).

Most Americans do not realize how many calories they need. Neither do they realize that they often exceed their recommended calorie intake. According to the Dietary Guidelines, adult women need an estimated sixteen hundred to twenty-four hundred calories per day, and men need two thousand to three thousand calories per day. (See *Exhibit 3.7* for recommended calorie levels for children and adults at different activity levels.)

Exhibit 3.7

ESTIMATED CALORIE NEEDS PER DAY BY AGE, GENDER, AND PHYSICAL ACTIVITY LEVEL

| Gender | Age (years) | Physical Activity Levels | | |
		Sedentary	Moderately Active	Active
Child (female and male)	2–3	1,000–1,200	1,000–1,400	1,000–1,400
Female	4–8	1,200–1,400	1,400–1,600	1,400–1,800
Female	9–13	1,400–1,600	1,600–2,000	1,800–2,200
Female	14–18	1,800	2,000	2,400
Female	19–30	1,800–2,000	2,000–2,200	2,400
Female	31–50	1,800	2,000	2,200
Female	51+	1,600	1,800	2,000–2,200
Male	4–8	1,200–1,400	1,400–1,600	1,600–2,000
Male	9–13	1,600–2,000	1,800–2,200	2,000–2,600
Male	14–18	2,000–2,400	2,400–2,800	2,800–3,200
Male	19–30	2,400–2,600	2,600–2,800	3,000
Male	31–50	2,200–2,400	2,400–2,600	2,800–3,000
Male	51+	2,000–2,200	2,200–2,400	2,400–2,800

Amounts are rounded to the nearest two hundred calories. An individual's calorie needs may be higher or lower than these average estimates.

Adapted from page 14 of the *Dietary Guidelines for Americans 2010*.

USDA'S MYPLATE

In 2011, the USDA introduced a new food guide icon called MyPlate. It was designed to assist consumers in making better food choices. Food guides are important because they translate the DRIs and Dietary Guidelines into actual food groups. The new MyPlate icon will be used as a communication tool for the public, and all messages will be based on the content of the Dietary Guidelines for Americans. The MyPlate image does not demonstrate specific amounts of food to eat. People can find out the number of calories they need each day by using the daily food plan on the MyPlate Web site. This plan provides the appropriate number of calories and the amounts of food recommended from each food group.

MyPlate Food Group 1: Grains

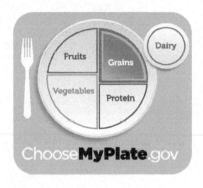

Food that contains grains is important to eat because it furnishes many nutrients, including fiber, thiamin, niacin, riboflavin, folate (folic acid), iron, magnesium, and selenium. Grains are carbohydrates, and they provide a large percentage of our daily energy needs. Examples of this food group are breads, pasta, rice, tortillas, grits, oatmeal, and cornmeal. The recommendation for adults is to get half of their grains, a minimum of three ounces daily, from whole grain food items. Most refined grains are enriched. Enrichment restores a portion of the thiamin, riboflavin, niacin, folic acid, and iron that have been removed during refining. Fiber is not replaced as part of the enrichment program.

Whole grains include all parts of the grain: the bran, the germ, and the endosperm. Whole grains have been found to be heart healthy, and they may lower the risk of obesity and type 2 diabetes. Some whole grains add significant amounts of fiber to the diet.

A one-ounce equivalent of grain is one slice of bread, ½ cup of oatmeal, one cup of ready-to-eat cereal, ½ cup of rice, or one 6-inch-diameter flour or corn tortilla.

MyPlate Food Group 2: Protein

Proteins are important because they supply amino acids. Amino acids contain the nitrogen that allows the body to grow, maintain, and repair tissues. The protein food group consists of meat, poultry, fish, eggs, beans, peas, seeds, and nuts. For people who eat meat regularly, beans and peas are counted as vegetables. Meat, poultry, fish, and eggs are excellent sources of animal protein and contain other nutrients like B vitamins (including B_6 and B_{12}), iron, and zinc. Animal sources of protein also contain cholesterol and saturated fat, however; so leaner cuts are advised. Vegetarian options in the protein food group include beans, peas, and soy—which contain both soluble and insoluble fiber and have important nutrients like iron and zinc—plus nuts and seeds. The recommended amount of protein varies from person to person. Most Americans get adequate amounts of protein.

One equivalent of protein is one ounce of meat, poultry, or fish; ¼ cup of cooked beans; one egg; one tablespoon of peanut butter; or ½ ounce of nuts or seeds. The number of equivalents a person needs to consume will depend on individual calorie needs.

MyPlate Food Group 3: Vegetables

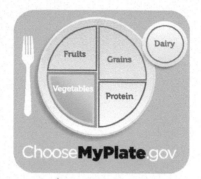

Note that in MyPlate, vegetables and fruit together should take up half of a person's plate. All vegetables, as well as 100 percent vegetable juices, belong in this food group. Raw, cooked, frozen, canned, or dried/dehydrated vegetables are acceptable choices for meeting the recommendations, but you must cook vegetables in a way that conserves vitamins and minerals.

The vegetables are classified into subgroups: dark-green vegetables like spinach and broccoli, starchy vegetables, red and orange vegetables, beans and peas, and other vegetables. An equivalent of vegetables is equal to one cup of raw or cooked vegetables, one cup of vegetable juice, or two cups of raw, leafy greens.

MyPlate Food Group 4: Fruits

This food group contains all types of fruit and 100 percent fruit juice. Fruit may be fresh, canned, frozen, or dried, and it may be whole, cut up, pureed, or juiced. Unlike vegetable juice, which has fewer calories per portion than solid vegetables do, fruit juice is a concentrated form of calories. It is important to watch the portion size and number of portions available to children to make sure that fruit juice fits into their daily calorie needs. Fruit and fruit juice are sources of dietary fiber, vitamin C, folate, and potassium.

A cup equivalent of fruit is equal to one cup of fresh strawberries, one cup of fresh orange juice, ½ cup of raisins, one cup of canned peaches, or one large banana.

MyPlate Food Group 5: Dairy

This food group contains all fluid milk and many products made from milk. Some dairy products are not included in this group because they do not provide enough calcium and have more solid fat. Examples are cream cheese, sour cream, and butter. The dairy group provides the body with calcium, potassium, vitamin D, and protein. Choose low-fat or fat-free products when selecting from this group. Dairy food contributes to bone health, lower blood pressure, and lower risk of cardiovascular disease. A one-cup equivalent of dairy is equal to one cup of milk, one cup of yogurt, or one cup of calcium-fortified soy milk; 1.5 ounces of natural cheese, two ounces of processed cheese, ½ cup of ricotta cheese, or two cups of cottage cheese. The following equivalents are also included, although they are higher in solid fats and added sugars: one cup of pudding made with milk, one cup of frozen yogurt, and 1.5 cups of ice cream (a scoop of ice cream is equivalent to 1/3 cup of milk).

Crafting a Healthy Plate

Ultimately, the information included in MyPlate is meant to help Americans create a healthy plate of food at every meal. This process starts with the table shown earlier in *Exhibit 3.7*, which provides calorie levels that reflect healthy intakes for all ages. Individuals have different eating patterns. The factors that affect food choices include age, habits, environment, and economic factors. *Exhibit 3.8* shows how a healthy plate containing all five food groups could look at levels of two thousand and twenty-four hundred calories. Oils are not included as a food group, but they do contain essential fatty acids. People must get these from foods like nuts or seeds, or from small amounts of various oils used in cooking.

Exhibit 3.8

MYPLATE FOOD CATEGORIES

Grains	Vegetables	Fruits	Dairy	Protein
Examples of Food				
Bread Cereal Rice Pasta	Dark green vegetables Orange vegetables Starchy vegetables Dry beans and peas Other vegetables	Apricots Apples Bananas Grapes Raisins	Milk Cheese Yogurt Ice cream Cottage cheese	Meat Fish Fowl Eggs Dry beans and peas Nuts and seeds
Daily recommendations for females (F) and males (M), ages 19 to 30*				
F 6 ounces **M** 8 ounces At least one-half of the servings should be whole grain.	**F** 2½ cups **M** 3 cups Eat more dark green and orange vegetables and dry beans and peas.	**F** 2 cups **M** 2 cups Eat a variety. Choose fresh, frozen, canned, or dried fruit. Limit daily intake of fruit juices.	**F** 3 cups **M** 3 cups Choose low-fat or fat-free milk products.	**F** 5½ ounces **M** 6½ ounces Select lean or low-fat meat and poultry. Select fish high in omega-3 fatty acids more often.
Serving Equivalents				
One ounce equivalent: 1 slice bread 1 cup cereal ½ cup cooked rice or pasta	**One cup equivalent:** 1 cup cooked or raw vegetables 2 cups leafy greens	**One cup equivalent:** 1 cup fruit ½ cup dried fruit	**One cup equivalent:** 1 cup milk or yogurt 1½ ounces natural cheese 2 ounces processed cheese	**One ounce equivalent:** 1 ounce meat, fish, or poultry ½ cup cooked dry beans or peas 1 egg 1 tablespoon peanut butter ½ ounce nuts or seeds

*These recommendations are based on 2,000 and 2,400 calorie diets. Adapted from the U.S. Department of Agriculture My Pyramid.

The equivalents for the various food groups are often smaller than most people realize. The daily recommendation of five to eight equivalents of grain might seem large until consumers realize that an ounce of grain is a very small amount. For example, according to MyPlate, one equivalent of pasta is equal to one-half cup. However, many people eat a cup or more of pasta in a meal and thus consume two or more equivalents of grain.

Meals at restaurants and foodservice establishments sometimes provide customers with half or more of their daily calorie allotments. In general, restaurant portion sizes have been larger, often much larger, than the equivalents used in food guides such as MyPlate. The same is true of the total volume of most packaged food.

Research indicates that people generally eat more food than they need if it is served to them. Restaurants and foodservice operations can help their customers stay within their daily calorie allotments by implementing the following tactics:

- Provide several portion sizes of a given menu item.
- Provide an easy way for a customer to eat a portion of food and take the rest home.
- Provide an easy way for customers to split an entrée with others in their dining party.

Menu Planning with MyPlate

Many of this chapter's suggestions for applying the Dietary Guidelines for Americans to menu planning also apply to using MyPlate. Here are two suggestions:

- MyPlate provides a visual model of how to portion a plate. Over half the plate should consist of vegetables and fruit, and the other half should be divided between the protein group and the grain group.
- To provide a more balanced menu, foodservice and restaurant professionals should use MyPlate as a quick guide to what constitutes a healthful diet. Then they can plan menus that help customers get the most nutrients for the calories when eating at these establishments.

Exhibit 3.9

Since restaurant meals are probably not the only meals customers will eat during the day, establishments might consider gearing their portions to a percentage of the recommended amounts suggested for each food group. For example, MyPlate recommends a daily intake of 5 to 6.5 one-ounce equivalents of meat. If an establishment currently offers eight-ounce steaks, its managers might consider changing the portion size to four or five ounces (*Exhibit 3.9*). Alternatively, they may want to add a four-ounce steak as a menu item for customers who prefer a smaller portion.

Restaurant and foodservice professionals should work to offer a variety of food items to cover all food groups. They should also select lean meat and reduce the amount of fats and oils used in cooking. By doing this, an operation can offer a wide variety of healthful meals that its customers can enjoy without exceeding nutritional recommendations.

MyPlate can be found at the Web site of the Center for Food and Nutrition Information of the USDA at *www.choosemyplate.gov*.

FOOD LABELING

Restaurant and foodservice operators need to understand food labeling in order to determine the contents of food they will order, prepare, or serve to customers. The Nutrition Labeling and Education Act of 1990 (NLEA) was an amendment to the Food, Drug and Cosmetic Act that provided the framework for the food label that is now nearly universal on packaged food. This label lists the nutrients included in the product, along with their amounts. It is another tool that helps consumers in implementing the DRIs and Dietary Guidelines. The food label takes the guesswork out of buying packaged or canned food. It allows consumers to compare these types of food by their nutritional value.

The Food Label

The NLEA provides the Food and Drug Administration (FDA) with specific authority to require nutrition labeling of most food products regulated by the agency. The legislation specifies which food products require labels, details what must be included on a food label, and describes the companies and food products that are exempt from providing complete nutrition information. In addition, the NLEA requires that all health claims and nutrient-content claims, such as "high fiber" and "low fat," be consistent with agency regulations.

Under NLEA, some food items are exempt from nutrition labeling:

- Food shipped in bulk, as long as it is not for sale in that form
- Medical food, such as that used to meet special patient needs
- Plain coffee and tea, some spices, and other food items that contain no significant amounts of any nutrients

The NLEA allows nutritional information about game meat, such as deer, bison, and quail, to be provided on counter cards or other point-of-purchase materials rather than on individual packages. Finally, nutrition labels are voluntary for many raw food items, such as fruit and vegetables.

Manager's Memo

Managers should educate their staff about nutrition principles to improve both employee wellness and the profit of the operation. Employees who have a basic understanding about food may start to change their own dietary habits and improve their health. This can lead to less down time for employees whose health issues will often be a reflection of those in the populace. In addition, employees who understand the importance of nutrition to health can appreciate customers whose health conditions mandate that they follow special diets. The Web site *choosemyplate.gov* provides an abundant amount of information on nutrition that can be presented in training programs. Employers could also invite a registered dietitian to speak about various conditions and the dietary restrictions that might be requested. The importance of listening carefully to guest requests and responding appropriately to situations involving gluten intolerance or allergen information cannot be overemphasized.

Labeling of Meat

The United States Food Safety and Inspection Service (FSIS) adopted a rule called "Nutrition Labeling of Single-Ingredient Products and Ground or Chopped Meat and Poultry Products" that went into effect on January 1, 2012. Retailers are now required to provide nutrition information for the "major" cuts of meat and poultry. They can place this information on a label or at the point-of-purchase (POP). The "nonmajor" cuts of single-ingredient, raw meat and poultry products are not required to have nutrition labeling; but if plants or retailers voluntarily provide nutrition information, it has to comply with the requirements for the major cuts. Nutrition information is also required for ground meat and poultry products. Unlike whole muscle cuts, ground products will be required to bear nutrition labeling on their packages, unless they are exempted. Failure to provide nutrition information in accord with this rule renders a product misbranded.

Exhibit 3.10

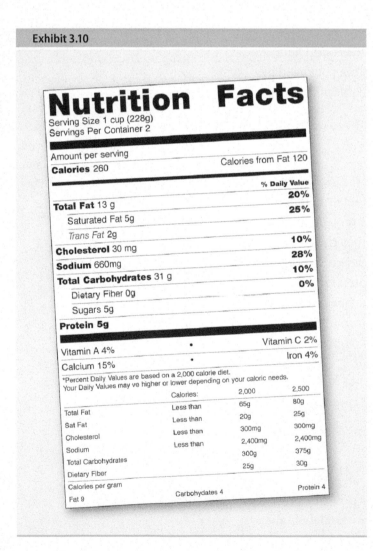

The Nutrition Facts Label

The nutrition facts label is the part of the food label that contains the nutrition information required by the FDA (see *Exhibit 3.10*). It is usually located on the back or side of the package. The nutrition facts label can be a useful tool in designing a balanced, varied, and healthful diet and in selecting food items for a diet that will meet the dietary guidelines. In addition, learning how to read and use nutrition information can help people avoid food allergens, plan special diets, and cut back on calories, total fat, cholesterol, and sodium.

DAILY VALUES (DVs)

Each nutrient on the nutrition facts label is reported as a percentage of the Daily Values (DVs). These are food-label reference values determined from the FDA's Reference Daily Intakes (RDIs) and Daily Reference Values (DRVs). The Reference Daily Intake (RDI) is a nutrient value for vitamins and minerals set by the FDA to formulate the Daily Value. The Daily Reference Value (DRV) is the nutrient-intake value for protein, carbohydrate, fat, and other components, such as cholesterol, set by the FDA to formulate the Daily Value. Providing DVs on the nutrition facts label helps people see how different types of food contribute to their overall daily diet. Although all food has nutrient value, it is important to provide the percentages of daily values so people can compare food products.

The DVs are provided in percentages based on a two-thousand-calorie diet, to which a single serving of a food item contributes. For example, a food that has 13 grams of total fat would show a percent Daily Value (% DV) of 20, which means that a serving of that food contributes 20 percent of the total daily fat grams that an individual should consume if he or she is following a two-thousand-calorie diet. Since calorie needs vary from one person to the next, the % DVs can be tailored to meet individual needs. They can also be used as a guide to the relative amount of certain nutrients in a serving of a given food. See *Exhibit 3.11* for selected daily values given in the amount on which the label percentages are based.

Exhibit 3.11

SELECTED DAILY VALUES (DVs)

Nutrient	Unit of measure	DV
Total fat	grams (g)	65
Saturated fatty acids	grams (g)	20
Cholesterol	milligrams (mg)	300
Sodium	milligrams (mg)	2,400
Total carbohydrate	grams (g)	300
Fiber	grams (g)	25
Protein	grams (g)	50
Vitamin A	international unit (IU)	5,000
Vitamin C	milligrams (mg)	60
Calcium	milligrams (mg)	1,000
Iron	milligrams (mg)	18

MANDATORY COMPONENTS OF A NUTRITION FACTS LABEL

The FDA requires that a nutrition facts label have certain nutrient components because these nutrients address current health concerns. The order in which the nutrients must appear reflects the current priority of dietary recommendations. The mandatory components are as follows:

- **Serving size and servings per container:** The standard serving size is the basis for reporting each food's nutrient content. It is defined as the amount of food customarily eaten at one time for each food category. To report the serving size, the FDA allows the use of common household measures or units, such as cup, tablespoon, teaspoon, piece, slice, or part (such as "1/8 pizza"), and common household containers used to package food products, such as a jar. Ounces may be used, but only if a common household unit does not apply. The standard serving size is followed by the metric amount, such as the number of grams. The servings per container reflects how many servings are contained within the package. The size of the serving on the food package influences the number of calories, as well as all the nutrient amounts listed on the top part of the label.

- **Total calories and calories from fat:** The label must list the caloric content of one serving of the food, as well as the number of calories from fat contained in a single serving.

Exhibit 3.12

ORDER FOR LISTING OPTIONAL VITAMINS AND MINERALS

Vitamin D

Vitamin E

Thiamin

Riboflavin

Niacin

Vitamin B$_6$

Folate

Vitamin B$_{12}$

Biotin

Pantothenic acid

Phosphorus

Iodine

Magnesium

Zinc

Copper

Note: These vitamins and minerals must be listed when added to a food as a nutrient supplement or when used as the basis of a health claim.

- **Total fat and saturated fat:** The label must list the total grams of fat in one serving and the number of grams of saturated fat in one serving, which are included in grams of total fat per serving.

- **Trans fat:** All labels must list grams of trans-fatty acid, also called trans fat, which has been shown to have a harmful effect on cholesterol levels and heart health. As with the other fats, the amount of trans fat is listed as the number of grams in one serving.

- **Cholesterol:** Cholesterol is listed in milligrams and the percentage of DV. It is based not on calories but on a daily recommendation of three hundred milligrams or less.

- **Sodium:** The DV is set at twenty-four hundred milligrams for sodium, and this will be reflected in the values and percentages on the food label.

- **Total carbohydrate, dietary fiber, and sugars:** Both dietary fiber and the total amount of sugar are included in a food's total carbohydrate content. Sugar can be naturally occurring in a food or it can be added. Currently, added sugar is included as part of the total sugar on the label as it is not required to be listed separately. Dietary fiber has been associated with decreasing cholesterol and aiding in food transportation through the digestive tract.

- **Protein:** This reflects the total number of grams of protein in one serving.

- **Vitamin A, vitamin C, calcium, and iron:** The FDA requires that the label list vitamins A and C and the minerals calcium and iron because of their connection to health conditions like osteoporosis and anemia. *Exhibit 3.12* shows the allowable optional vitamins and minerals that can be listed.

NUTRITION FACTS AND CHILDREN

There are some variations in the format of the nutrition facts label. For example, labels of food items for children under two years of age must not list information about saturated fat, polyunsaturated fat, monounsaturated fat, cholesterol, calories from fat, or calories from saturated fat. This is to prevent parents from incorrectly assuming that infants and young children must restrict fat intake. During these two years, fat is crucial to ensure adequate growth and development.

Ingredient Labeling

Ingredients must be declared on all food items with more than one ingredient. Ingredients must be listed in order by the weight contained in the product; the ingredient of greatest weight is listed first.

FOOD ADDITIVES

Because some people are allergic to certain additives, the ingredient list must include the following:

- FDA-certified color additives, such as FD&C Blue No. 1, by name
- Sources of protein hydrolysates, which are used in food as flavors and flavor enhancers such as MSG
- Caseinate as a milk derivative for food that claims to be nondairy, such as coffee whiteners

JUICES

The NLEA requires a declaration of the total percentage of juice in beverages that are claimed to contain juice. In addition, the FDA has established criteria for naming juice beverages. The label of a multi-juice beverage whose predominant juice is present in small amounts must state that the product is flavored with that juice or state the amount of the juice in a 5 percent range. For example, a product with a small amount of cranberry juice must use the phrases *cranberry-flavored juice blend* or *juice blend with 2 to 7 percent cranberry juice*.

ALLERGENS

Food allergens are substances that can cause an allergic reaction for some people. The Food Allergen Labeling and Consumer Protection Act (FALCPA), effective January 1, 2006, requires food labels to disclose whether a food contains one or more of the eight major allergens: milk, eggs, peanuts, tree nuts, fish, shellfish, soy, and wheat. These are shown in *Exhibit 3.13*.

Exhibit 3.13

MAJOR ALLERGENS

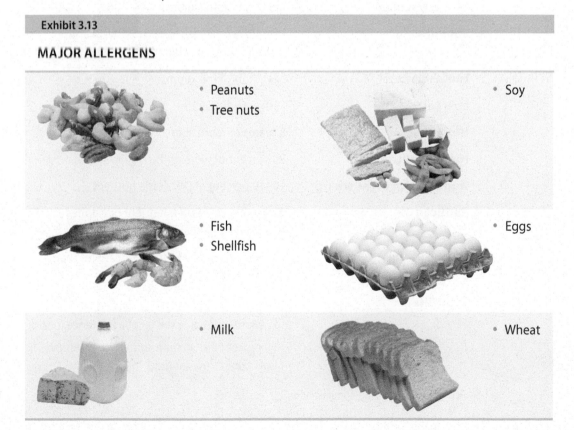

- Peanuts
- Tree nuts

- Soy

- Fish
- Shellfish

- Eggs

- Milk

- Wheat

Exhibit 3.14

INGREDIENTS: BROCCOLI SPEARS IN SAUCE CONTAINING WATER, ENZYME MODIFIED BUTTER, SUGAR, SALT, MODIFIED CORN STARCH, XANTHAN GUM, SODIUM STEAROYL LACTYLATE, ARTIFICIAL COLOR.
CONTAINS MILK INGREDIENTS.

DISTRIBUTED BY **Ouska Sales, Inc.**
GENERAL OFFICES **NEWTON IA 50208 USA**

PRODUCT OF USA

The ingredient list for this food product points out that it contains milk, a major food allergen.

This information is required on both domestically manufactured and imported packaged food items that are subject to regulations. FALCPA regulations extend to retail and foodservice establishments such as bakeries, food kiosks at malls, and carryout operations. (See *Exhibit 3.14*.)

Labeling Terms

Prior to the NLEA, food manufacturers had no restrictions on using terms such as *light* or *low-calorie*. The term *light*, or *lite*, could refer to anything from the amount of calories or fat to the color of the food. To protect consumers from misleading advertising, regulators defined the descriptors to be used to indicate the level of a nutrient in a food. *Exhibit 3.15* lists some of the key terms and their definitions.

Exhibit 3.15

NUTRIENT CONTENT LABELING TERMS

Term	Definition (amount per serving)
Calorie-free	Less than 5 calories
Sugar-free, fat-free	Less than 0.5 grams
Low fat	3 grams or less total fat
Low saturated fat	1 gram or less
Low sodium	Less than 140 milligrams
Very low sodium	Less than 35 milligrams
Cholesterol-free	Less than 2 milligrams of cholesterol and 2 grams or less of saturated fat
Low cholesterol	Less than 20 milligrams
Low calorie	Less than 40 calories
High fiber	5 grams or more fiber
High in (nutrient)	20 percent or more of the DV for the nutrient
Good source of (nutrient)	10–19 percent of DV for the nutrient
Reduced	25 percent or less of a nutrient or calories than the regular product
Less	25 percent less of a nutrient or calories than a reference food
Light/lite	Either: • ½ less calories or ½ the fat of a reference food • 50 percent less sodium content in an already low-calorie, low-fat food

Source: U.S. Food and Drug Administration

Labeling Food as Healthy

According to the FDA, a food item must meet all the following requirements to be labeled "healthy":

- Low in fat and saturated fat
- Limited amounts of cholesterol and sodium
- Single-item food must provide at least 10 percent of one or more of the following:
    - Vitamin A
    - Vitamin C
    - Iron
    - Calcium
    - Protein
    - Fiber
- Meal-type products, such as frozen entrées, must provide 10 percent of two or three of the nutrients named above, in addition to meeting the other criteria. The sodium content cannot exceed 360 milligrams per serving for individual food items and 480 milligrams per serving for meal-type products.

Certain food, such as some raw, canned, and frozen fruit and vegetables and certain cereal-grain products, is exempt from this rule and can be labeled "healthy" as long as it does not contain ingredients that change the nutritional profile.

Labeling Organic Food

Food labeled with the USDA Organic seal must be at least 95 percent organic and must meet USDA organic standards. These standards include the use of renewable resources and the conservation of soil and water in growing food. In addition, organic food is grown without the use of conventional pesticides, fertilizers made with synthetic ingredients or sewage sludge, bioengineering, or ionizing radiation. Animals are given no antibiotics or growth hormones.

The word *organic* may appear on packages of meat, milk, eggs, cheese, and other single-ingredient food items. Truthful claims, such as *free-range*, *hormone-free*, and *natural*, may also appear on food labels; however, these terms are not interchangeable with the term *organic*.

THINK ABOUT IT . . .

What are the advantages and disadvantages of allowing companies to make nutrient-content claims and health claims about their products?

Exhibit 3.16

This food product claims to be heart healthy. Note the use of symbols and descriptions.

Health Claims

Claims for relationships between a food or nutrient and the risk of a health-related condition are allowed. They can be made in several ways (see *Exhibit 3.16*), including the following:

- Third-party references, such as the National Cancer Institute
- Symbols, such as a heart
- Descriptions

The claim cannot state the degree of risk reduction and can use only the words *may* or *might* in discussing the nutrient or food–disease relationship. Claims also must state that other factors play a role in the particular disease, and they must be phrased so that the relationship between the nutrient and the disease is understood.

Examples of health-claim rules include the following:

- **Calcium and osteoporosis:** To carry a claim relating calcium and osteoporosis, a food must contain 20 percent or more of the DV for calcium (two hundred milligrams) per serving, have a calcium content that equals or exceeds the food's content of phosphorus, and contain a form of calcium that can be readily absorbed in the body. The claim must name the target group most in need of adequate calcium and note the need for exercise and a healthy diet. A product that contains 40 percent or more of the DV for calcium must state that a total dietary intake greater than 200 percent of the DV for calcium (two thousand milligrams or more) has no additional known benefit.

- **Fat and cancer:** To carry a claim relating fat and cancer, a food must meet the nutrient-content claim requirements for the term *low fat*.

- **Saturated fat and cholesterol and coronary heart disease:** A claim relating saturated fat and cholesterol to coronary heart disease may be used if the food meets the definitions for the nutrient-content claims "low saturated fat," "low cholesterol," and "low fat," or, if the food is fish or game meat, "extra lean."

- **Fiber-containing grain products, fruit, and vegetables and cancer:** To carry a claim relating fiber and cancer, a food must be or contain a grain product, fruit, or vegetable and meet the nutrient-content claim requirements for the term *low fat*, and, without fortification, it must be a "good source" of dietary fiber.

- **Fruit, vegetables, and grain products that contain fiber and risk of coronary heart disease:** To carry a claim relating fiber and coronary heart disease, a food must be or contain fruit, vegetables, or grain products; meet the nutrient claim requirements for "low saturated fat," "low cholesterol," and "low fat"; and contain, without fortification, at least 0.6 grams of soluble fiber per serving.

- **Sodium and hypertension (high blood pressure):** To carry a claim relating sodium and hypertension, a food must meet the nutrient-content claim requirements for "low sodium."

- **Fruit and vegetables and cancer:** A claim regarding cancer may be made for fruit and vegetables that meet the nutrient-content claim requirements for "low fat" and, without fortification, for a "good source" of one or more of these nutrients: dietary fiber, vitamin A, or vitamin C.

- **Folic acid and neural tube defects:** A claim relating folic acid and neural tube defects is allowed on dietary supplements that contain sufficient folate and on conventional food items that are naturally good sources of folate, as long as they do not provide more than 100 percent of the DV for vitamin A as retinol or preformed vitamin A or vitamin D. For example, the claim can read, "Healthful diets with adequate folate may reduce a woman's risk of having a child with a spinal cord defect."

- **Dietary sugar alcohols and dental caries (cavities):** A claim relating dietary sugar alcohols and dental caries applies to food products, such as candy or gum, containing sugar alcohols (xylitol, sorbitol, mannitol, maltitol, isomalt, or lactitol), hydrogenated starch hydrolysates, or hydrogenated glucose syrups, alone or in combination.

- **Soluble fiber from certain types of food, such as whole oats and psyllium seed husk, and heart disease:** To carry a claim relating soluble fiber and heart disease, the label must state that fiber must be part of a diet low in saturated fat and cholesterol, and the food must provide soluble fiber. The amount of soluble fiber in a serving of the food must be listed on the nutrition facts label.

Using the Food Label in a Restaurant or Foodservice Setting

Since food labels are primarily applied to packaged food, a restaurant or foodservice operation's opportunity to use the food label will depend on the amount of packaged food used by the operation. For operations that use packaged food, menu planners and chefs can use the food label in the following ways:

- **To determine the serving size and number of servings in a container:** This information can help in specifying the number of containers of the packaged food that are needed in a standardized recipe.

- **To refer to the nutrient listing and DVs:** This is done to compare food and to select food low (5 percent or less) in fat, sodium, and sugar, and high (20 percent or more) in vitamin A, vitamin C, and calcium.

- **To scan the ingredient list for allergens:** This information can be included on the menu and can be provided to servers.

- **To review deliveries to ensure that food products match food ordered:** This is especially important if a specific type of product, such as a salt-free, organic, or whole-grain product, was ordered.

SUMMARY

1. **Define *Recommended Dietary Allowance, Adequate Intake, Tolerable Upper Intake Level*, and *Estimated Energy Requirement*.**

   The Recommended Dietary Allowance (RDA) is an average daily dietary nutrient intake sufficient to meet the nutrient requirement of nearly all (97 to 98 percent) healthy individuals of a particular age and gender group. The Adequate Intake (AI) is the assumed daily dietary intake level of healthy people when there is insufficient evidence to set an RDA. The Tolerable Upper Intake Level (UL) provides the upper intake limits for each nutrient. The Estimated Energy Requirement (EER) is the calorie intake that maintains energy balance in a healthy adult of a certain age, gender, weight, height, and level of activity.

2. **Determine the amounts of carbohydrate, protein, and fat recommended for healthy diets.**

   According to the Acceptable Macronutrient Distribution Ranges, in a healthy diet carbohydrate should provide about 45 to 65 percent of the calories, protein should provide about 10 to 35 percent of the calories, and lipids or fats should provide about 20 to 35 percent of the calories.

3. **Identify recommended estimates of calorie needs and daily fluid intakes.**

   People have different calorie needs depending on their gender, age, body size, and activity level. According to the Dietary Guidelines for Americans 2010, adult women need about sixteen hundred to twenty-four hundred calories per day, and men need two thousand to three thousand calories per day.

   Water needs are variable, depending on the environment, temperatures, and the amount of calories expended. Adult females should consume approximately 2.7 liters of water per day, and adult males should consume about 3.7 liters per day.

4. **List the current recommendations for daily intake of sodium.**

   The Dietary Reference Intake (DRI) value for sodium is fifteen hundred milligrams per day. The Tolerable Upper Intake Level (UL) is twenty-three hundred milligrams per day. Most adults should try to consume less than twenty-three hundred milligrams of sodium per day to prevent hypertension. People 51 years of age and older, or those who are African-American or have diabetes, hypertension, or chronic kidney failure, should consume less than fifteen hundred milligrams of sodium per day.

5. **State the importance of achieving calorie balance to maintain weight.**

   Individuals who maintain their calorie balance over time usually achieve and sustain a healthy weight. An individual should match the number of calories eaten with the number of calories expended each day to maintain his or her weight.

6. **Locate the nutrition facts label and the ingredient list on food packages, and describe how the daily values, nutrition facts label, and ingredient list are used in restaurants and foodservice operations.**

The nutrition facts label is the part of the food label that contains the nutrition information required by the FDA, such as allergens, total fat, sodium, cholesterol, and calories. The ingredient list is in a separate place on the label. It lists the ingredients in descending order by weight.

In a restaurant or foodservice operation, the food label can be used to determine the serving size, the number of servings in a container, the ingredients list, and the daily values. It can be used to check for allergens. Staff responsible for receiving deliveries can review the label to ensure that the food product received matches the food ordered. This is especially important if a specific type of product, such as a salt-free, organic, or whole-grain product, was ordered. The daily value can be used to increase or decrease specific nutrients when menu planning or to determine whether a product has too much sodium for a special recipe.

7. **Identify major allergens on an ingredient list.**

As of 2006, food labels must disclose whether a food contains one or more of the eight major food allergens: milk, eggs, peanuts, tree nuts, fish, shellfish, soy, and wheat.

APPLICATION EXERCISES

Exercise 1

Find the Dietary Guidelines for Americans 2010 on the USDA Web site, *www.choosemyplate.gov*.

Read the Executive Summary for the Dietary Guidelines and select two of the key recommendations. Then summarize the selected recommendations and write a paragraph or two about how a restaurant or foodservice operation might apply them in their business.

Finally, answer the following question: How might these guidelines affect the businesses from these perspectives?

a. financial performance

b. customer satisfaction

c. health of the customers

Exercise 2

If you are employed at a restaurant or foodservice establishment, use the storeroom or product information sheets, which may contain labeling information, to complete this assignment. Gather four labels from the operation. If you are not currently employed at a restaurant or foodservice establishment, find four labels in your kitchen at home. Read the labels, and then answer the following questions for each label:

- How is the product used in the operation or at home? Is this product eaten as is, or is it part of a recipe?

- Does the product have any of the big eight allergens mentioned in the chapter?

- Does the product make either a nutrient-content claim or a health claim?

Exercise 3

Contact a local food-products company and request a short interview with a quality-assurance specialist. In the interview, focus on the nutrition facts label for one of the company's products, and ask the quality-assurance specialist to describe the process by which the label component "calories per serving" was determined. Write a few paragraphs explaining what you learned about the process. What surprised you? Did the process seem rigorous? Explain.

REVIEW YOUR LEARNING

Select the best answer for each question.

1. What is the Dietary Reference Intake (DRI) value that is defined as sufficient to meet the nutrient requirement needs of nearly all healthy individuals of a particular age and gender?

   A. EAR

   B. RDA

   C. AI

   D. EER

2. What is the Tolerable Upper Intake Level (UL) for sodium for a healthy 45-year-old man?

   A. 1,200 milligrams

   B. 1,500 milligrams

   C. 1,800 milligrams

   D. 2,300 milligrams

3. What percentage of MyPlate should be covered by fruit and vegetables?

   A. 25

   B. 30

   C. 45

   D. 50

4. What amount of cooked oatmeal or rice equals a one-ounce equivalent of grain according to MyPlate?

   A. ½ cup

   B. ¾ cup

   C. 1½ cups

   D. 1¾ cups

5. According to the Dietary Guidelines for Americans 2010, what percentage of a person's daily caloric intake should come from saturated fat?

   A. <10

   B. <20

   C. <30

   D. <40

6. What reference value is used to determine nutrient percentages on the food label?

   A. Estimated Average Requirement

   B. Dietary Reference Intake

   C. Adequate Intake

   D. Daily Value

7. In what order do items appear on the ingredient list of a food label?

   A. Ascending by measure

   B. Alphabetical by ingredient name

   C. Descending by weight

   D. Descending by order in which ingredients are added

8. What are the two main concepts that were presented in the Dietary Guidelines for Americans 2010 to assist individuals in improving their health?

   A. Calorie balance and eating more dark-green vegetables

   B. Weight control and eating more fruit daily

   C. Weight loss and eating more whole grains

   D. Calorie balance and eating more nutrient-dense food

9. **Approximately what percentage of a person's daily dietary intake of grains should come from whole grains?**

   A. 10
   B. 25
   C. 50
   D. 75

10. **What are the four micronutrients that are required to appear on a food label?**

    A. Calcium, potassium, vitamins A and D
    B. Iron, potassium, vitamins A and D
    C. Calcium, iron, vitamins C and D
    D. Iron, calcium, vitamins A and C

FIELD PROJECT

For this project, you will use the Key Concepts and the Recommendations or the Selected Messages from the Dietary Guidelines for Americans.

1. Review the menu of a restaurant in your area. Plan either an advertisement for the operation, or signage and table-tents, which connect foods on the menu with the recommendations from the Guidelines. These could be used in promotions for healthier menu items or as informative pieces on signage. Develop a presentation for your items that could be presented to your teacher, fellow students, or the manager of the operation.

2. Design a training session based on the Dietary Guidelines for Americans for staff at your operation or for other students in your class. Develop innovative ways to present the messages knowing that staff may have limited knowledge of nutrition.

4

The Energy Nutrients: Carbohydrate, Protein, and Lipid

INSIDE THIS CHAPTER

- Carbohydrate Basics
- Carbohydrates and Their Effect on Health
- Protein Basics
- Protein and Food Allergies
- Lipid Basics
- Metabolic Effects of Alcohol

CHAPTER LEARNING OBJECTIVES

After completing this chapter, you should be able to:

- Identify the Acceptable Macronutrient Distribution Range (AMDR) and the Recommended Dietary Allowance (RDA) for carbohydrate, protein, and lipid.

- Identify the types of carbohydrates, their food sources, and their importance in the diet.

- Identify the types of dietary fiber, their food sources, and their importance to health.

- Explain diabetes and its causes and effects.

- Identify the dietary sources and functions of protein, and explain what essential amino acids and incomplete, complete, and complementary proteins are.

- Identify the big eight allergens and their relationships to protein.

- Describe the types and characteristics of lipids and their importance in health.

KEY TERMS

adipose tissue, p. 73

alpha-linolenic acid, p. 86

cholesterol, p. 83

complete protein, p. 79

complex carbohydrate, p. 69

diabetes mellitus, p. 74

dietary fiber, p. 69

essential amino acid, p. 79

essential fatty acid, p. 86

glucagon, p. 72

glycogen, p. 72

hydrogenated, p. 85

hyperglycemia, p. 74

incomplete protein, p. 79

insulin, p. 72

ketosis, p. 73

lecithin, p. 86

linoleic acid, p. 86

lipoprotein, p. 89

monounsaturated, p. 84

nitrogen balance, p. 78

omega-3 fatty acid, p. 91

omega-6 fatty acid, p. 91

phospholipid, p. 83

plaque, p. 83

polysaccharide, p. 69

polyunsaturated, p. 84

saturated fatty acid, p. 84

simple carbohydrate, p. 67

sterol, p. 83

sucrose, p. 68

trans fat, p. 85

triglyceride, p. 84

unsaturated fatty acid, p. 84

CASE STUDY

Ricardo is a restaurant manager in a prominent city hotel. His day-to-day responsibilities include ensuring that special luncheon and dinner buffets are set up on time and that food is replenished as necessary. During a recent conference for health professionals held in the hotel, Ricardo observed that the buffet line had stopped and people were standing with their plates and waiting for food. He approached the buffet table and observed that there was a plate full of white bread remaining, but there was no whole-grain bread left. When the waitstaff returned, Ricardo learned that the operation was out of whole-grain products. He apologized to the people waiting in line. Although the patrons indicated their disappointment, they made alternative food selections and the line moved again.

1. What is the problem in this situation?

2. What do you think the customers expected?

3. What can Ricardo do to prevent this type of situation in the future?

CARBOHYDRATE BASICS

Carbohydrate, protein, and lipid are known as the energy nutrients because they fuel the body and its processes. Knowing the characteristics, functions, and nutritional significance of these substances is critical to achieving balanced, healthy meals and menus at any restaurant or foodservice operation. It is also crucial for restaurant and foodservice professionals to understand how these nutrients relate to disease conditions and food allergies.

Carbohydrates are essential nutrients, and they are the body's preferred source of fuel, providing four calories of energy per gram. They are important in menu planning because sources of carbohydrate are found in all five food groups.

Structure and Sources of Carbohydrates

A carbohydrate is an organic chemical that consists of only carbon, hydrogen, and oxygen atoms in various numbers and arrangements. An organic chemical is one consisting of chains or rings of carbon atoms along with other atoms. Since a carbon atom is designated by the letter *C*, a hydrogen atom by an *H*, and an oxygen atom by an *O*, carbohydrates can be designated as CHO.

The Food and Nutrition Board of the National Academy of Sciences set the Acceptable Macronutrient Distribution Range (AMDR) for carbohydrate for adults at 45 to 65 percent of daily calories. This means that diets planned with this carbohydrate range in mind will meet the needs of most individuals. (See *Exhibit 4.1*.)

Carbohydrate intakes for each individual fluctuate daily depending on the food chosen. Although some people decide to follow a low-carbohydrate diet as a lifestyle choice, the Recommended Dietary Allowance (RDA) for carbohydrate is set at a minimum of 130 grams per day for adults and children over one year of age (see *Exhibit 4.2*). Carbohydrate is an important source of glucose, which is the body's blood sugar. Consuming the right amount of carbohydrate to meet an individual's needs for glucose without causing weight gain is one main goal of a healthy diet. Individuals should be cautious that they do not take in too many carbohydrates.

According to nutrition surveys in the United States, for people over the age of two, the largest sources of sugar by percentage of calories are soft drinks, energy drinks, sport drinks, grain-based desserts, sugar-sweetened fruit drinks, dairy-based desserts, and candy. *Exhibit 4.3* details the carbohydrates found in some common foods.

In some cases, individuals may require particularly high levels of carbohydrate in their diet. For example, endurance athletes may need

Exhibit 4.1

Nutritious and tasty meals should be 45 to 65 percent carbohydrate.

Exhibit 4.2

DIETARY REFERENCE INTAKES FOR CARBOHYDRATE

Age	Recommended daily carbohydrate intake (grams)
0–6 months	60
7–12 months	95
1 year or more	130

Exhibit 4.3

CARBOHYDRATE CONTENT IN COMMON FOOD ITEMS

Food	Amount	Carbohydrate content (grams)
Romaine lettuce	1 c shredded	1.8
Summer squash	1 c	3.8
Apple	1 raw with skin	19.1
Pasta with meatballs	1 c	28.0
Glazed donut	1 medium	30.4
Vanilla ice cream	1 c	31.2
Carbonated cola	12 oz	35.4
Applesauce, canned, sweetened	1 c	44.0
Egg bagel	4-in. diameter	47.2

Adapted from U.S. Department of Agriculture, Agricultural Research Service. 2011. USDA National Nutrient Database for Standard Reference, Release 24.

to raise their overall carbohydrate percentage to 60 or 65 during training and competition. When planning training tables or competition meals for athletes, the amount of carbohydrate may seem out of proportion with other meal components, such as protein and fat. However, this amount of carbohydrate provides the energy required for athletes to compete successfully in their events.

Simple Sugars

Carbohydrates are classified as either simple or complex. The names of the sugars are derived from the term *saccharide*, which means "sugar." The simple carbohydrates are sugars that consist of monosaccharides and disaccharides. A monosaccharide, as the name suggests, is a single-unit sugar, while disaccharides are two monosaccharides bonded together to form two-unit sugars. The monosaccharides are glucose, fructose, and galactose. The disaccharides are sucrose, lactose, and maltose. All carbohydrates must be digested to one of the monosaccharides to be absorbed by villi in the small intestine.

MONOSACCHARIDE

Sugars in food consist of both naturally occurring and refined sugars. For example, honey (*Exhibit 4.4*) is simply collected from honeycombs and filtered, making it minimally processed. Table sugar, however, is a refined sugar because it has been extracted from the juice of either sugarcane or sugar beets.

THINK ABOUT IT . . .

How much added sugar do you consume each day? What foods in your diet provide the most sugar? What foods in a typical restaurant or foodservice establishment are sources of added sugars?

Exhibit 4.4

Exhibit 4.5

MONOSACCHARIDES

Name	Food sources
Glucose	Honey, corn syrup
Fructose	Honey, tree fruit, berries, melons, some root vegetables (beets, sweet potatoes, parsnips, onions)
Galactose	Not present in significant quantities in food; it is part of the disaccharide lactose

Source: U.S. Department of Agriculture

Restaurant managers and foodservice professionals must be able to identify the sugars in recipes, in menus, and on processed-food labels. For example, glucose is not used alone in cooking, but it may be found in processed food or food products. The natural form of glucose is known as dextrose.

Fructose is referred to as fruit sugar. The sweetest of the sugars, it is found in fruit and honey. Fructose can be found in many beverages as high-fructose corn syrup because of its capacity to sweeten. Both honey and corn syrup, which are used routinely in cooking, contain glucose in a mixture with other sugars (see *Exhibit 4.5*).

The third monosaccharide, galactose, is considered a nutritive sweetener because it has food energy, but it is less sweet than glucose and not very water soluble.

DISACCHARIDES

The disaccharide sucrose is referred to as table sugar. Found in kitchens in many forms, it is also known as plain sugar, brown sugar, and confectioner's sugar. Sucrose is ideal for cooking and baking. The second-sweetest sugar next to fructose, sucrose's solubility and viscosity make it versatile in the kitchen. However, sucrose is a big contributor to dental caries (tooth decay) because the bacteria that live in the mouth can rapidly consume sucrose and use it for energy. These bacteria produce acids that destroy the enamel of the tooth.

Lactose, the combination of galactose and glucose, is called milk sugar. Lactose is widely known for the problems people encounter when they have lactose intolerance and cannot break down this sugar during digestion.

Exhibit 4.6

DISACCHARIDES

Name	Food source(s)
Sucrose (table sugar)	Extracted from the juice of sugarcane, sugar beet, sorghum or the sap of maple trees
Lactose (milk sugar)	Milk
Maltose (malt sugar)	Grains; also produced by the breakdown of starch

Source: U.S. Department of Agriculture

However, many lactose-intolerant people can digest the amount of lactose in a glass of milk if they drink it with a meal or in small amounts over the course of a day. People with lactose intolerance also may tolerate yogurt and aged cheese. Lactose intolerance is quite variable; some people are more intolerant of this sugar than others.

Maltose (malt sugar) is the disaccharide consisting of a glucose bonded to another glucose molecule. It is found in grains as a by-product of the digestion of starches. Consuming large amounts of refined grains can lead to increased blood-glucose levels because of the eventual release of glucose as maltose is broken down. This contributes to high blood-sugar levels, which will be discussed in detail later in this chapter. *Exhibit 4.6* details each of these disaccharides.

SUGARS IN COOKING

The sugars discussed in the previous section are generally available in the following products:

Exhibit 4.7

- Caramel (*Exhibit 4.7*)
- Confectioner's sugar (powdered sugar)
- Corn syrup
- Dextrose
- Fructose
- Fruit juices and fruit reductions
- Glucose
- High-fructose corn syrup
- Honey
- Invert sugar
- Maltose
- Malt syrup
- Maple syrup
- Molasses
- Sucrose (table sugar)
- Turbinado sugar

Complex Carbohydrates: Polysaccharides

Complex carbohydrates contain numerous combinations of saccharides, including the oligosaccharides and the polysaccharides. Oligosaccharides are relatively small complex carbohydrates composed of three to ten sugar molecules. **Polysaccharides** (*poly-* means "many") are composed of long chains of glucose molecules and therefore take much longer to digest than sugar. Examples of polysaccharides are starch and fiber. In addition to their value as fuel, these carbohydrates provide an abundance of other nutrients, such as vitamins, minerals, and fiber. Good food sources of complex carbohydrates are pasta, rice, breads, beans, legumes, and vegetables.

OLIGOSACCHARIDES: SMALL CHAINS OF STARCH

Two oligosaccharides of note are raffinose and stachyose. Because the enzymes in the small intestine cannot break down these molecules, raffinose and stachyose pass into the large intestine, where intestinal bacteria can metabolize them. This process produces gas. Some extremely nutritious food items, including lima beans, dried peas, and soybeans, contain raffinose and stachyose. Beans contain both soluble and insoluble fibers that, in addition to their protein content, make them a very desirable food in the diet.

DIETARY FIBER

Dietary fiber is another type of carbohydrate that contains long strands of bonded glucose molecules. But it is different from starch in that human digestive enzymes cannot break it down. In the stomach, fiber provides a feeling of fullness or satiety, and since it is slow to leave the stomach, the consumer feels full for a significant period of time. Because of this effect, fiber

THINK ABOUT IT . . .

What fibrous foods do you eat? What sources of fiber are on the menu at your favorite restaurant? Have you ever requested whole-grain products? Why or why not?

helps with weight control. It passes through the small intestine intact, or undigested. In the large intestine, bacterial enzymes can break down some types of fiber, and this process produces fatty acids and gas.

One of the health benefits of fiber is that it resists digestion and maintains its bulk. Diets that contain adequate fiber support regularity. Having adequate fiber in the diet may decrease the incidence of hemorrhoids, diverticular disease of the colon, and cardiovascular disease. Although experts disagree about whether increasing fiber helps to prevent colon cancer, studies show that populations with high fiber intakes have lower rates of colon cancer. This result may stem from the phytochemicals contained in high-fiber foods.

Dietary fiber is classified as soluble or insoluble. Insoluble fiber does not dissolve in water; it simply passes through the digestive tract. Soluble fiber dissolves in water to form a soft gel that connects to bile salts and reduces cholesterol in the blood. It may also inhibit glucose absorption and thus prevent excessive swings of blood sugar.

Fiber is best obtained by eating high-fiber food because the bulk and nutrients of these types of food contribute to a healthy diet. Good sources of soluble and insoluble fiber are provided in *Exhibit 4.8*, while *Exhibit 4.9* shows recommended daily amounts of fiber intake.

Exhibit 4.8

SOURCES OF DIETARY FIBER

Soluble	Insoluble
• Legumes (peas, soybeans, and other beans) • Oats • Some fruit (especially apples, bananas, and berries) • Some nonroot vegetables (especially broccoli and carrots) • Most root vegetables (especially potatoes and yams, but the skins are insoluble fiber)	• Whole-grain food • Bran • Nuts and seeds • Vegetables such as green beans, cauliflower, zucchini, celery • Skins of some fruit, including tomatoes • Skins of potatoes and yams

Exhibit 4.9

ADEQUATE INTAKE OF FIBER

Age (years)	Males	Females
	(grams per day)	
1–3	19	19
4–8	25	25
9–13	31	26
14–18	38	26
19–30	38	25
31–50	38	25
51–70	30	21
70+	30	21

Adapted from *Dietary Reference Intakes for Energy, Carbohydrate, Fiber, Fat, Fatty Acids, Cholesterol, Protein, and Amino Acids (Macronutrients)*. ©2005 by the National Academy of Sciences.

Whole Grains: An Opportunity to Meet Customer Needs

Whole grains, or food made from them, contain all the nutritionally essential parts of the grain: the bran, the endosperm, and the germ (see *Exhibit 4.10*). The bran is the outer layer, which contains the highest percentage of fiber and nutrients. It is the same part of the grain found in bran cereal. The endosperm is the starchy layer, which is the largest part of the grain and provides flour for white bread and pastries. The germ is a small, nutrient-rich inner layer. Wheat germ, for instance, is sold separately for cooking and baking.

The official definition of a whole grain includes the following: when grain is processed by crushing, cracking, pearling, or some other process (including cooking), the whole-grain product should have about the same ratio of nutrients found in the original grain or seed. Some examples of common whole grains are brown rice, oats, wheat, barley, and quinoa.

WHY WHOLE GRAINS?

Whole-grain food has many health benefits. Health studies have linked the consumption of whole grains to a decrease in the incidence of cardiovascular disease, improved function of the large intestine, and improved blood-glucose control among people with diabetes. Whole grains contain high levels of antioxidants and high amounts of minerals, including magnesium. The benefits of whole grains are just now being fully appreciated.

The Food and Drug Administration (FDA) allows companies to make the following health claim for whole-grain products that contain 51 percent or more of whole grain by weight: "Diets rich in whole-grain food and other plant food, and low in total fat, saturated fat and cholesterol, may reduce the risk of heart disease and certain cancers."[1] Whole grains should be part of a healthy diet, either as grains or ground into flour (*Exhibit 4.11*).

Currently, nutrition professionals are making a concerted effort to teach the public about whole grains, including what types of food to eat when dining out. Customers who want to eat for health are now making it known that they want whole-grain foods. Customers who do not find these options may not always voice their disappointment; instead, they will simply go to a different establishment next time. Restaurants and foodservice professionals should take advantage of this opportunity to increase their business by attracting customers who prefer nutrient-dense food choices such as whole grains. Including whole-grain items on menus and in recipes should not be overly difficult because whole grains are versatile and can be used in main dishes, side dishes, salads, soups, bakery items, and desserts.

[1]*Notification for a Health Claim Based on an Authoritative Statement: Whole Grain Foods and Heart Disease, Food and Drug Administration, 11/25/03.*

Exhibit 4.10

WHOLE-GRAIN COMPONENTS

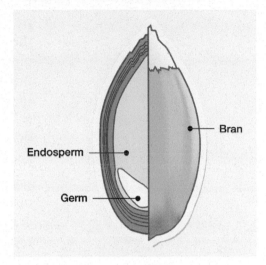

Bran

Endosperm

Germ

Food made from whole grains contains all the essential parts of the grain: bran, endosperm, and germ.

THINK ABOUT IT . . .

Have you ever eaten a whole-grain food alternative such as whole-grain bread or pasta? How did it differ in taste from the non–whole-grain item?

Exhibit 4.11

Since 1942, flour has been enriched with thiamine, riboflavin, niacin, and iron as part of the U.S. government's grain-enrichment program. This program was created in response to the devastation caused by pellagra during the Great Depression. Pellagra is a disease caused by a lack of niacin and protein in the diet. In 1996, the grain-enrichment program was amended to include folic acid, a form of the vitamin folate, in an effort to decrease the incidence of spina bifida, which is a birth defect connected with insufficient levels of this water-soluble B vitamin. Enriching a food such as flour restores the above-named nutrients, which are removed during the processing of a whole grain into a refined product. Although the enrichment program mandated that manufacturers return specific nutrients to processed grains, not all nutrients get restored to the level at which they appear in the original grain. In particular, fiber and trace elements like magnesium and zinc are not restored. As a result, enrichment falls short of mimicking the whole grain.

The color of bread is not an indication of whether it is made with whole grains; in fact, its color may be due to food coloring. The label should state that the bread contains whole grains or whole wheat, and *whole grain* or *whole wheat* should be the first ingredient listed. Words like *stone-ground* do not necessarily indicate that the product is whole grain. Since customers in a restaurant or foodservice operation cannot see the nutrition labels on the components of the food they order, managers should make this information available in some other way. Menu descriptions are one way to indicate that whole grains are being used.

Metabolism of Carbohydrates

Carbohydrate storage is necessary for providing glucose when we do not eat consistently throughout the day. The body stores carbohydrate as glycogen in both the liver and the muscle tissue. The liver breaks down glycogen and supplies the cells with glucose when blood levels dip too low. The liver supplies muscles with energy when they are depleted. However, once glucose is stored in the muscle, it must be used by the muscle. The amount of liver glycogen that will supply the brain and nervous system is used up every four to five hours, so the need for carbohydrate in the diet is continuous.

Glucose is a very versatile and important molecule in the body. The red blood cells, the brain, and the nervous system all use glucose as fuel. All other cells can use it as well. The body keeps blood-glucose levels within a narrow range under tight hormonal control. The hormones insulin and glucagon are important in blood-sugar metabolism. Insulin is secreted by the pancreas and circulates in the blood. Its role is to help glucose enter the cell, thus reducing blood-sugar levels. Glucagon has the opposite effect; it promotes the release and production of glucose by the liver and brings up low blood sugar.

CARBOHYDRATES AND THEIR EFFECT ON HEALTH

Carbohydrates are an essential part of a balanced diet. However, when they are eaten in abundance or are insufficient in the diet, health problems can occur.

Weight Gain

Do carbohydrates make a person gain weight? Actually, populations that consume high proportions of carbohydrates tend to have fewer weight problems. Simply put, if the body's energy requirements have not been exceeded, eating carbohydrate-rich food will not cause weight gain.

Weight gain due to excess calories occurs because of the fat-sparing effect of carbohydrate. Many more metabolic steps are required to convert sugar to dietary lipids than to convert dietary lipids to adipose tissue, or body fat. This sparing effect happens when the body continues to store its long-term energy, which consists of the dietary lipids in adipose tissue. However, if a person has eaten too much food and thus has excess unused calories, the body will store the unused blood sugars as fat. Increased body weight is due to low levels of exercise combined with excess calories from all energy-yielding nutrients plus alcohol.

Exhibit 4.12

Sugary food items like those in *Exhibit 4.12*, along with alcoholic beverages, are rich in calories but not in many other nutrients. When people consume these types of foods in excess, they are adding calories but not supplying the body with essential nutrients. Small amounts of sugar and alcohol generally are not harmful, but excessive amounts are.

Ketosis: Glucose in Short Supply

When a person's diet is low or completely lacking in carbohydrate, the body undergoes metabolic changes. Each cell requires a small amount of carbohydrate in the form of glucose in order to completely metabolize the lipids eaten or lipids resulting from weight reduction. When glucose is insufficient, the liver cannot fully break down the lipids being metabolized. As a result, ketone bodies, which are incompletely metabolized products of fatty-acid metabolism, build up in the blood and cause ketosis. The symptoms of ketosis include constipation, headache, bad breath, and dry mouth.

Many people follow low-carbohydrate diets to reduce their weight. The problem with extremely low-carbohydrate diets is not always in the actual weight-loss experience but in the aftermath of the weight loss. When people try to return to a more normal eating pattern, they might regain weight because they have not made permanent behavioral changes. Diets that include all macronutrients in reasonable quantities, accompanied by adequate regular exercise and behavior change, offer the best chance of long-term weight loss.

Diabetes: Types and Incidence

Diabetes mellitus is a disease characterized by **hyperglycemia**, or high blood-sugar levels. It is caused by genetic, metabolic, and other conditions, such as pregnancy. Three types of diabetes are commonly found in the United States: type 1, type 2, and gestational. Blood glucose is derived from dietary carbohydrate sources such as sugar, pasta, rice, grains, starch vegetables, and milk. When a person is diagnosed with any type of diabetes, eating a healthy, well-balanced diet is important for blood-sugar control and weight management. In addition to medical care, medication, and exercise, a person with diabetes must eat a balanced diet that controls all nutrients, but especially the type and amount of carbohydrate in their diet.

All types of diabetes are on the rise in the American population. According to recent government statistics, diabetes affects 25.3 million people in the United States. Of this number, more than 200,000 people under age 20 have diabetes. The majority of these young people have type 2 diabetes, which can be improved through proper diet and physical activity. This means that many people entering restaurants and food service operations can benefit from menus planned with diabetes-sensitive nutrition in mind.

TYPE 1 DIABETES

Type 1 diabetes is an autoimmune disease in which the pancreas stops producing insulin. A child or young adult must be genetically predisposed to develop it. In addition, something such as a viral infection must trigger the body's immune system to destroy the insulin-producing cells of the pancreas. About 5 to 10 percent of individuals have type 1 diabetes. Without insulin, large amounts of glucose build up in the blood and overload the body's ability to metabolize it. In addition, the increased blood glucose is circulated through the body and it spills into the urine.

Common symptoms of type 1 diabetes are hunger, thirst, weight loss, and frequent urination. People with type 1 diabetes also tend to develop complications that involve the cardiovascular system. Insulin must be taken each day to compensate for the body's inability to make this hormone naturally. Treatment also includes following a diet that controls carbohydrate intake and has adequate amounts of protein and fat. Other recommendations include eating less saturated fat and trans fat, achieving and maintaining ideal weight, getting daily exercise, and taking regular doses of insulin.

TYPE 2 DIABETES

The most common form of diabetes in the United States is type 2. It is found with higher incidence in certain populations, including African Americans, Latinos, Native Americans, Asian Americans, and Hawaiian and Pacific Islanders. It occurs at all ages but tends to reveal itself as people age. It occurs in people who are at healthy weight but who do not produce enough of their own insulin. However, this form of diabetes is more often caused by insulin resistance. Insulin resistance is a condition that develops when a person gains weight and produces too much insulin in response to high blood-sugar levels. Although the exact mechanisms are still being investigated, the constant flow of insulin causes the body to not recognize and utilize its own insulin well. When a patient is obese, initial treatment involves getting blood sugar under control with medication and then encouraging weight loss with proper diet and exercise. Exercise helps to sensitize the cells to insulin and improves diabetes control. Type 2 diabetes is treated with many different medications, including insulin when necessary (see *Exhibit 4.13*).

Exhibit 4.13

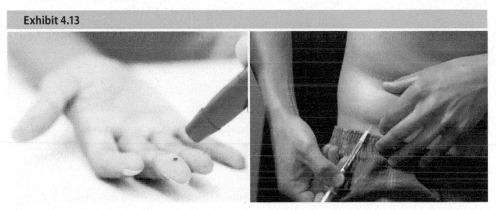

Overconsumption of carbohydrates, especially sweets, is harmful to diabetics, who must regularly monitor their blood-sugar levels and, sometimes, inject themselves with insulin.

Although the incidence of both type 1 and type 2 diabetes has increased recently in the United States, most of the increase has been seen in type 2 diabetes. Part of the increase has occurred in children, which is a new and alarming development. Studies have shown that the increase in the disease is due to an increase in adipose tissue (body fat) that has been linked to a combination of inactivity and poor dietary intake, including an abundance of calories from both carbohydrates and fats.

GESTATIONAL DIABETES

Gestational diabetes occurs when women who do not have a previously diagnosed case of diabetes demonstrate increased blood-glucose levels late in pregnancy, usually around 24 weeks. It is important for pregnant women with this type of diabetes to eat properly because failure to do so could harm the growing baby. With this type of diabetes, uncontrolled or excessive glucose can cause the baby to become too fat, resulting in a more difficult delivery. In addition, high blood-glucose levels may increase the baby's chance of obesity and type 2 diabetes. Some women who have gestational diabetes may go on to develop type 2 diabetes after pregnancy.

DIABETES: A DISEASE WITH COMPLICATIONS

Diabetes is considered a chronic disease with many different metabolic consequences. Individuals who develop diabetes must take good care of their health. No matter what kind of diabetes a person has, the treatment includes adherence to a healthy diet, good medical care, and regular exercise. Complications like blindness, amputation, kidney disease, and cardiovascular disease are all too common among people with diabetes.

It is important to keep blood sugar within the range actually needed by the body. One way to accomplish this is to follow a nutritious and balanced diet without excess fats and carbohydrates. Restaurant and foodservice professionals have an important role in helping customers meet this goal by developing and using healthy recipes, menus, and portions.

PROTEIN BASICS

Protein differs from carbohydrate and lipid in that protein is the only nutrient that provides nitrogen. Nitrogen is required for the tissues of the body to grow. Protein is a very important nutrient for health and in cuisine (see *Exhibit 4.14*).

Protein Structure and Sources

Proteins are compounds composed of long chains of varying amino acids, as demonstrated in *Exhibit 4.15*. The amino acids twist and fold to form three-dimensional shapes, giving complexity to protein structure and allowing it to carry out specific functions. When needed, protein can be utilized for energy and provides four calories per gram. The human body needs 0.8 gram of protein per kilogram of body weight per day, or about 0.36 gram per pound of body weight. The Food and Nutrition Board has set the AMDR for protein at 10 to 35 percent of daily calories (see *Exhibit 4.16*).

Exhibit 4.14

Exhibit 4.15

AMINO ACIDS AND PROTEINS

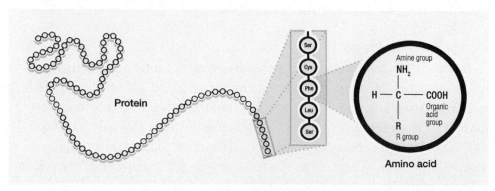

The chemical properties of amino acids help give shape to proteins and determine their specialized functions.

Exhibit 4.16

RECOMMENDED DIETARY REFERENCE INTAKES (DRI) FOR PROTEIN FOR PERSONS OF AVERAGE BODY WEIGHT

Age	Males (grams)	Females (grams)	Females pregnant or lactating (grams)
0–6 Months	9.1	9.1	NA
7–12 Months	11+	11+	NA
1–3 yrs	13	13	NA
4–8 yrs	19	19	NA
9–13 yrs	34	34	NA
14–18 yrs	52	46	71
19–30 yrs	56	46	71
31–50 yrs	56	46	71
51–70 yrs	56	46	NA
>70 yrs	56	46	NA

Adapted from *Dietary Reference Intakes for Energy, Carbohydrate, Fiber, Fat, Fatty Acids, Cholesterol, Protein, and Amino Acids (Macronutrients)*. ©2005 by the National Academy of Sciences.

Of the major food groups, those with significant amounts of protein are meats, poultry and fish, dairy, grains, and vegetables. Fruit contains very little of this nutrient. *Exhibit 4.17* provides the protein content of some common food items.

Exhibit 4.17

PROTEIN CONTENT OF SELECTED FOOD ITEMS

Food	Amount	Protein (grams)
Apple	1 raw with skin	0.4
Asparagus	4 spears	1.4
Bread	1 slice	3.6
Egg	1 large	6.3
Tofu	¼ block	6.6
Peanuts, dry roasted	1 oz	6.7
Beans, baked vegetarian	1 c	12.0
Fish, orange roughy	3 oz	19.3
Ground beef	3 oz	22.0
Chicken breast	1 breast	26.7

Source: U.S. Department of Agriculture

Exhibit 4.18	
Essential amino acids*	**Nonessential amino acids†**
Histidine	Alanine
Isoleucine	Arginine
Leucine	Asparagine
Lysine	Aspartic acid
Methionine	Cysteine
Phenylalanine	Glutamic acid
Threonine	Glutamine
Tryptophan	Glycine
Valine	Proline
	Serine
	Tyrosine

*Must be obtained from the diet.
†Can be made in the body.

THINK ABOUT IT . . .

Many people enjoy protein-rich food, such as meat and fish. If a person does not eat these types of food, how can he or she consume adequate protein?

What Are Amino Acids?

Amino acids are organic molecules made of carbon (C), hydrogen (H), oxygen (O), and nitrogen (N) atoms. There are 20 amino acids that can be synthesized by the genetic codes of plants and animals. Each amino acid has an identical unit (NH_2—CH—COOH) and a unique side chain with organic chains or rings of many types. It is the nature of the side chain that defines each specific amino acid. The NH_2 group of atoms is called an amine group. The COOH group is called an organic acid group. The CH is the carbon (and its hydrogen) to which the remaining atoms are connected in the side chain. *Exhibit 4.18* lists the amino acids used by the human body.

Protein Digestion and Metabolism

Although all food is chewed and softened by saliva in the mouth, the enzymes for protein digestion start their action not in the mouth but in the stomach. Here, pepsinogen, an inactive digestive enzyme for protein, is activated by the flow of hydrochloric acid in the stomach to its active form pepsin. At this point, pepsin starts to break down the peptide bonds to shorter chains of protein. The partially digested protein moves on to the small intestine, where the protein is broken down further by pancreatic digestive enzymes specific to peptide bonds between the amino acids. Finally, the protein is broken down into separate amino acids that can be absorbed by the villi of the small intestine and transported to the liver where they are metabolized.

Proteins and Nutrition

Proteins and amino acids generally are not used for energy as carbohydrates and fats are. Although protein contains fuel in the form of calories, these calories are not used as energy unless a person is in a physical state of starvation or has depleted his or her store of carbohydrates and fat.

The role of protein is important because it is part of muscles, skin, and even hair and nails. Its functions include growth and maintenance of cells, as well as formation of enzymes, hormones, and antibodies. Protein even plays an important role in regulating fluid and acid–base balance.

Protein and Nitrogen Balances

When a person's protein intake and protein usage are equal, he or she is in a state of protein balance. The body's protein balance is closely related to its nitrogen balance because nitrogen is a part of protein. The advantage of this relationship is that we can measure nitrogen in the body more easily than we can measure protein. Adults who are neither gaining nor losing weight are usually at equilibrium. That is, they are neither gaining nor losing nitrogen. However, during times of growth or development, such as pregnancy, people hold on to the protein and its nitrogen; this results in a state of positive nitrogen balance because there is more nitrogen being taken in than excreted. In the same way, a person who is suffering from a chronic illness or is starving has a negative nitrogen balance, or is excreting more nitrogen than he or she is retaining.

Keep in mind that consuming more protein than required does not make muscles larger. The only way to increase muscle mass is to exercise the muscles. When a person consumes more protein than needed, the body simply stores it as fat.

Nutritional Properties of Proteins

Remember that proteins are composed of amino acids. The body breaks down proteins into their amino acids and then reassembles the amino acids into the thousands of proteins that keep the body functioning. For this reason, from a nutritional viewpoint, the role of proteins centers on the properties of the amino acids.

Essential and Nonessential Amino Acids

As previously mentioned, proteins are made up of long chains of amino acids, and 20 of them are used in the human body. The human body is able to make 11 of the 20; however, the remaining 9 either cannot be made or the body does not make them in large enough quantities. From a nutritional viewpoint, these 9 amino acids are considered essential amino acids because people must obtain them from food.

When the body does not have enough of the required amino acids, it cannot form the proteins it needs to serve its functions. In addition, if there are inadequate proteins, then lipids cannot be transported to the cells.

High-Quality and Complete Proteins

A food that contains all nine essential amino acids is considered a high-quality protein, also known as a complete protein. *Exhibit 4.19* shows some food items that are complete proteins. On the other hand, a food that is missing one or more essential amino acids is considered an incomplete protein and is

Exhibit 4.19

EXAMPLES OF COMPLETE AND COMPLEMENTARY PROTEIN FOOD ITEMS

Complete protein food items		Vegetarian food items with naturally complete proteins	Complementary protein food items
Beef	Pork	Soy	Beans and rice
Chicken	Lamb	Quinoa	Whole-grain bread and peanut butter
Turkey	Eggs		Hummus and bread
Shellfish	Fish		Corn and lima beans
Dairy products			

therefore not high quality. It is important for people to consume all of the essential amino acids by eating a varied diet to ensure that these amino acids are present when the body needs them. People who consume animal sources of protein on a regular basis have little need for worry because these sources are always complete. However, those who consume mostly vegetarian sources of protein may be lacking in essential amino acids because these sources are usually incomplete, with a few exceptions.

Soy and quinoa have all nine essential amino acids; amaranth is almost as complete. If sufficient quantities of these food items are consumed, the body will have the essential amino acids it needs. Those who consume mainly vegetarian proteins should be sure to include complementary sources of protein in their meals. Complementary proteins are food items that provide all nine essential amino acids when combined, thus equaling a complete protein source. A good example of food items served together to make a complete protein is beans and rice; some others are shown in *Exhibit 4.19*. To avoid a protein deficiency, people should obtain all nine essential amino acids within a 24-hour period, not necessarily at each meal.

Soy Protein in the Diet

Exhibit 4.20

Soy, which is also called soybean, soya, or soya bean, is a legume that is native to eastern Asia but now is grown throughout the world. Soy beans (shown in *Exhibit 4.20*) are highly valued because soy is an inexpensive and high-quality vegetarian protein source.

Soy is a very good source of nutrients. It has high amounts of polyunsaturated fat, vitamins, minerals, and fiber, and lower levels of saturated fat than meat. In addition, it has isoflavones, which are chemicals found almost exclusively in legumes and thought to be helpful in reducing cholesterol and cancer.

The health benefits of soy are great enough that the FDA has authorized a health claim for food labels. This claim states, "25 grams of soy protein per day, as part of a diet low in saturated fat and cholesterol, may reduce the risk of heart disease." In order for this claim to be included on a product that contains soy protein, the product must have at least 6.25 grams of soy protein per serving.

Food Sources of Soy

Examples of soy products include the following:

- Edamame is the immature, green-colored soybean that is usually lightly boiled. It is the least processed form of soy.

- Tofu, or bean curd, is made from cooked and pureed soybeans.

- Soy milk is a liquid that resembles milk and is extracted from ground soybeans or made using soy flour. Soy flour consists of roasted soybeans ground up into a flour texture.

- Textured soy protein is made from soy flour that has been defatted. It is sometimes called textured vegetable protein (TVP). It is used not only as a vegetarian protein source in items like veggie burgers but also as a meat extender in meatloaf.

- Tempeh is made from whole, cooked soybeans that are formed into a cake.

- Miso is a fermented soybean paste usually used for seasoning or in soup.

- Soy burgers, sausage, hot dogs, cheese, and cold cuts are meatless or vegetarian protein sources that increase food choices for vegetarians. Processed soy products may have fewer nutritional benefits than their more natural counterparts (e.g., soybeans, tofu, and soy milk).

The protein and caloric contributions from some soy products are shown in *Exhibit 4.21.*

Excessive or Insufficient Protein in the Diet

The body needs a certain amount of protein on a regular basis. It can metabolize an amount above the minimum intake. However, when the minimum protein-intake amount is not met or the maximum protein-intake amount is exceeded, problems can occur.

Although there is no Tolerable Upper Intake Level (UL) established for protein, this does not mean that it is safe to consume excessive amounts of protein on a regular basis. Some scientific evidence points to harmful consequences when consuming protein in excess of 35 percent of energy intake. Problems caused by excessive protein consumption can include osteoporosis, kidney stones, and dehydration leading to kidney stress.

Exhibit 4.21

PROTEIN AND CALORIES IN SELECTED SOY PRODUCTS

	Soybeans	½ c serving ~7 g protein 190 calories
	Soy burger	1 each ~8 g protein 100 calories
	Soy milk	1 c serving ~8 g protein 110 calories
	Soy nuts	1 oz serving ~12 g protein 150 calories
	Tempeh	½ c serving ~18 g protein 200 calories
	Textured vegetable protein	¼ c serving ~14 g protein ~50 calories
	Tofu	½ oz serving ~18–20 g protein 50 calories

Source: U.S. Department of Agriculture

Exhibit 4.22

A lack of protein in the diet may lead to a protein deficiency. Protein deficiency can result in loss of muscle mass, hormonal irregularities, fatigue, insulin resistance, loss of hair or hair pigment, and loss of skin elasticity. Severe protein deficiency, which is seen only in instances of starvation, is fatal because the body does not have enough amino acids to construct its own proteins. Protein deficiency is uncommon in healthy individuals in the United States, where there are large amounts of protein food items available and intake of protein is usually more than adequate. Protein can be easily obtained through food. Besides meat, fish, and fowl (*Exhibit 4.22*), vegetables, especially legumes, are also sources of protein.

PROTEIN AND FOOD ALLERGIES

Along with many other health concerns, food allergies seem to be on the rise in the U.S. population. When a guest indicates that they have a food allergy, everyone in a restaurant or foodservice operation must pay attention, both in the front and back of the house. Managers should work diligently to ensure that the staff attends to each customer's requests. The goals are to avoid the allergen in any menu items that are prepared for the person and to avoid cross-contact of the allergen with the customer's food during or after preparation. In addition, the server needs to deliver the correct dish to the customer at all times.

Customers who have allergies trust an establishment to be very careful with their food. For people with food allergies, eating even a tiny amount of the allergen can cause a life-threatening reaction called anaphylactic shock. Protein is involved because the allergic reaction is to the protein portion of the food eaten. In addition, when the body forms an immune response to the food, it develops antibodies (also composed of protein) to that food. People with food allergies need to be very careful to avoid food with the allergen because repeat exposure may produce an even stronger reaction.

Eight foods that commonly cause allergies are peanuts, tree nuts, eggs, wheat, dairy, soy, fish, and shellfish. Although people can be allergic to many other foods, these eight cause most of the serious reactions that are seen by healthcare professionals. Restaurant and foodservice professionals should train their staff to listen carefully to customers as they communicate their dietary needs.

Anaphylaxis is a severe allergic reaction that can occur from a few minutes to several hours after exposure to the food allergen. This reaction can cause many different symptoms. Itching, shortness of breath, difficulty swallowing, and swelling of the lips or tongue are all signs that the person should seek immediate medical attention.

Manager's Memo

Each operation must decide how to handle special dietary requests, such as an order from a customer who has food allergies. Often the manager assumes the responsibility of ensuring that the customer has a safe experience in the restaurant or foodservice operation. If you are training or retraining employees on allergy awareness and procedures, information is available in the ServSafe materials. *ServSafe Manager* and the *ServSafe Coursebook* include information that educates managers and employees about how to prevent cross-contact with allergens in the kitchen and when serving food. Everyone in a restaurant or foodservice operation must be well trained on procedures for customers with food allergies. Accurate communication and coordination among waitstaff, chefs and cooks, and management are necessary to ensure the safety of your guests.

LIPID BASICS

Although restaurant or foodservice customers' eating habits are their own responsibility, providing a variety of nutritional menu items is the responsibility of chefs, menu planners, managers, and owners. Many customers desire food that enables them to follow nutritional guidelines for the amount and types of fat in their diet. Ensuring that the proper quantity and type of fat is used when preparing food not only provides tasty alternatives for customers, but it also is a good business decision. When customers recognize that an operation provides great-tasting, healthy cuisine, they are likely to visit again.

THINK ABOUT IT . . .

What fats are found in the fryers in restaurants and foodservice operations? How are restaurant managers and chefs responding to customer demands to lower amounts of trans fatty acids in the oils they use?

Lipids: Structure and Types

Lipids are a nutrient class that includes triglycerides, sterols, and phospholipids. Lipids differ in their degree of solubility in water. Triglycerides and sterols are insoluble in water, but phospholipids have both a water-soluble side and a fat-soluble side, which is an important property that allows them to form emulsions. About 95 percent of all lipids in the human diet are triglycerides, while phospholipids and sterols make up the other 5 percent of dietary intake.

CHOLESTEROL

Cholesterol is one of the sterols, which are hydrocarbons consisting of a steroid and an alcohol as well as carbon bonded to carbon in a closed ring. Cholesterol is an important sterol of the body and is a component of cellular membranes. It is a waxy substance found only in animal food such as meat, fish, poultry, and cheese. Cholesterol has multiple hydrocarbon rings and does not contain fatty acids. The amount of cholesterol varies from food to food. Eggs contain an especially high proportion of cholesterol.

In the body, cholesterol is a part of many substances, such as vitamin D and the hormones estrogen and testosterone. It is also the precursor, or originator, of the bile acids. Cholesterol is a natural component of the body, and the body can synthesize it when needed. Therefore, it is not required in the diet. *Exhibit 4.23* lists the cholesterol content of some popular food items.

The greatest concern involving cholesterol is the consumption of unnecessary amounts. Due to multiple factors, including genetics and excessive weight, cholesterol builds up in the body and may begin to negatively affect health. It may settle in the artery walls and create plaque

Exhibit 4.23

CHOLESTEROL CONTENT OF SELECTED FOOD ITEMS

Food item	Cholesterol (milligrams)
Beef liver, 3 oz	356
Large egg	213
Leg of roasted lamb, 3 oz	82
Roasted chicken breast, 3 oz	76
Lean roasted beef, 3 oz	74
Baked salmon, 3 oz	60
Cream cheese, 2 tbsp	32
Butter, 1 tbsp	31
Cheddar cheese, 1 oz	30
Milk (3.5 percent), 1 c	24
Ice cream, ½ c	22
Tofu, ¼ c	0

Source: U.S. Department of Agriculture

deposits, which are fatty deposits on the wall of a blood vessel. These are potential causes of cardiovascular disease. Although too much cholesterol in the diet is undesirable, saturated fat is even more serious, since the body absorbs more dietary cholesterol when saturated fatty acids are present.

Triglycerides

Fats are stored in the body in the form of triglycerides, which are molecules formed by one glycerol molecule and three fatty acids. Glycerol is a three-carbon alcohol that bonds with three fatty acids to produce a single structure. A fatty acid is an organic molecule found in animal and vegetable fats. It consists of a carbon-hydrogen chain with an organic-acid group (COOH) at one end, as shown at the right end of the molecule in *Exhibit 4.24*.

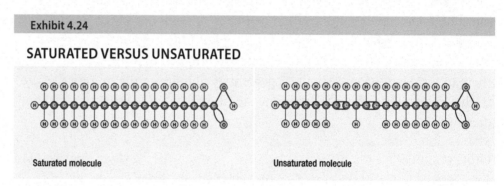

Exhibit 4.24

SATURATED VERSUS UNSATURATED

Saturated molecule   Unsaturated molecule

The saturated molecule on the left has all single bonds and all possible hydrogen atoms in the molecule. The unsaturated molecule on the right has two double bonds near the middle, and as a result, has four fewer hydrogen atoms than the saturated molecule.

Triglycerides contain fatty acids ranging from 4 to 24 carbons in length. Three types of fatty acids commonly found in food are saturated, monounsaturated, and polyunsaturated. Saturated fatty acids have no double bond present between the carbon atoms in their carbon chain; an example is shown in the left-hand image of *Exhibit 4.24*. Saturated fatty acids cannot accept or bond with any more hydrogen atoms because these fatty acids are already saturated with hydrogen. Unsaturated fatty acids contain one or more double bonds in the carbon chain; an example is shown in the right-hand image of *Exhibit 4.24*. A fatty-acid molecule is monounsaturated if it contains one double bond and polyunsaturated if it contains more than one double bond. The number and position of the double bonds in fatty acids is important to their chemical and physical properties. For example, the double bond gives greater fluidity to the molecule, making unsaturated and polyunsaturated fatty acids liquid at room temperature. In addition, the body can recognize them and use them in specific biochemical pathways.

Triglycerides in the diet are divided into fats and oils. Fats are triglycerides that are solid at room temperature and come from animal sources; oils are liquid at room temperature and originate from plant sources. Some of the more common fats are butter, sour cream, lard, cream cheese, and animal fat. Oils that are commonly used in cooking are soybean, corn, safflower, sunflower, canola, olive, sesame, and vegetable blends.

The majority of saturated fatty acids are found in meat and meat products such as bacon, sausage, tallow, and lard made from meat. These fatty acids are also found in milk and milk products such as butter, cheese, and cream cheese. Plant sources of saturated fat include small amounts in avocado. The tropical oils, including palm, palm kernel, and coconut, are concentrated sources of saturated fatty acids.

Fatty acids are mixed in nature. Triglycerides can contain all three types of fatty acids. Fatty acids are considered saturated when they contain a higher percentage of saturated fatty acids than any other type of fatty acid in their fatty-acid profile. Generally, fats and oils are referred to by the name of the fatty acid that has the greatest concentration in that food. Therefore, it is common practice to call corn oil polyunsaturated, olive oil monounsaturated, and butter saturated.

Studies involving cardiovascular health have shown that monounsaturated fats are beneficial to the heart. Olive oil and canola oil, for example, contain large amounts of monounsaturated fatty acids (Exhibit 4.25).

Exhibit 4.25

Oils from safflower, sunflower, soybean, and corn have large quantities of polyunsaturated fatty acids. Two essential fatty acids found in polyunsaturated oils are linoleic acid and alpha-linolenic acid. These acids will be discussed in greater detail later in the chapter.

Oils can be hydrogenated (made to chemically react with hydrogen) to make them more solid and to increase their shelf life. By hydrogenating oil, it becomes more saturated and has properties similar to those of saturated fat. An example of a hydrogenated product is shortening. The oil can be totally hydrogenated, such that it is entirely saturated, or partially hydrogenated, resulting in less unsaturated fat. Some soft tub margarines have partially hydrogenated fats added to solidify them.

Trans fats are formed when oils have been partially hydrogenated, allowing some of the double bonds to be broken and rebonded with hydrogen atoms. During this process, some of the hydrogen molecules are bonded differently. Trans fat formed by hydrogenation has been the focus of much attention because it acts similar to saturated fat and raises the body's LDL cholesterol levels. Dairy products and meats contain natural forms of trans fatty acids.

Phospholipids

Phospholipids have a structure similar to triglycerides; however, in place of one of the fatty acids, there is a phosphate group and nitrogen attached. Like cholesterol, phospholipids are part of the cell membrane. Phospholipids have a very important role in the body. They allow the cell membrane to be semi-permeable due to their arrangement in the membrane and their ability to link with both water and fat. Phospholipids are part of the bile and are important in emulsifying fat in the small intestine.

Lecithin is a phospholipid found both in the body and in foods such as egg yolks. Due to their lecithin content, egg yolks can be used as an emulsifier in the kitchen to hold oil and lemon juice or vinegar in an emulsion. Mayonnaise is an example of a familiar emulsion formed using egg yolks.

The Role of Lipids in the Body

Lipids provide nine calories of energy per gram. Adipose tissue is the largest storage area for energy in the body, in the form of fat. It is the body's preferred storage compartment. Although the body stores carbohydrates as glycogen, these are relatively small stores in comparison to the almost infinite supply of adipose fat that the body can store. Excess dietary intake from all nutrient sources—carbohydrates, protein, and lipids—can be stored as adipose tissue. This includes carbohydrates that cannot be stored as glycogen because the liver and muscle stores are full, as well as excess protein and fat.

The body's lipids are stored in many different places, varying from person to person based on gender, genetics, and total weight. There are adipose-tissue stores that surround the organs for cushion and protection, adipose-tissue stores under the skin for insulation, and adipose tissue in muscles. Apart from these functions, the body needs lipids in order to absorb fat-soluble vitamins, to spare body protein from being used for energy, to act structurally as a part of every cell membrane, to form the base for many hormones, and to act as lipoproteins.

Essential Fatty Acids

As much as people fret about fats, people cannot live without lipids because they are essential nutrients. As previously mentioned, linoleic acid and alpha-linolenic acid are two essential fatty acids necessary for normal growth and development. They are called essential fatty acids because they cannot be manufactured by the body and must be obtained from food. Linoleic acid is found in corn, safflower, soybean, cottonseed, and canola oils. Alpha-linolenic acid is found in canola, soybean, walnut, peanut, pecan, almond, wheat germ, and flaxseed oils.

A deficiency in these essential fatty acids may cause dermatitis, a condition that causes skin to become itchy and flaky. Increased fatty-acid deficiency can lead to diarrhea, infections, and a halt in growth and wound healing. People need very little oil to provide enough of the essential fatty acids, as demonstrated by the small Adequate Intakes listed in *Exhibit 4.26*. Since ample oils are usually used in cooking food, fatty-acid deficiencies are rare in the American population.

Exhibit 4.26

ADEQUATE INTAKES FOR LINOLEIC AND LINOLENIC ACIDS (GRAMS PER DAY)

Age (yrs)	Males		Females		Pregnant and lactating females			
	Linoleic acid	Linolenic acid	Linoleic acid	Linolenic acid	During	When	Linoleic acid	Linolenic acid
1–3	7	0.7	7	0.7	**Pregnancy**	First trimester	13	1.4
4–8	10	0.9	10	0.9		Second trimester	13	1.4
9–13	12	1.2	10	1.1		Third trimester	13	1.4
14–18	16	1.6	11	1.1				
19–30	17	1.6	12	1.1	**Lactation**	First 6 months	13	1.4
31–50	17	1.6	12	1.1		Second 6 months	13	1.4
>50	14	1.6	11	1.1				

Adapted from *Dietary Reference Intakes for Energy, Carbohydrate, Fiber, Fat, Fatty Acids, Cholesterol, Protein, and Amino Acids (Macronutrients)*. © 2005 by the National Academy of Sciences.

Cooking with Fats and Oils

Since fried food is popular, the restaurant and foodservice industry is unlikely to eliminate frying. Instead, chefs, recipe developers, and managers should choose healthy cooking oils that have little or no trans fatty acids. Healthier oils like canola and special oil blends will help customers avoid these harmful fatty acids.

By using healthy oils, cooks are not changing the amount of fat used, but they are changing the type of fat used. For example, pan-frying is not a low-fat cooking method, but using healthy oils such as canola, olive, or peanut provides a healthier ingredient than using butter or lard. It also enhances flavor. One of the challenges of following current guidelines when preparing food is that it is very difficult to replace saturated fat in some items because of the unique properties of saturated fat. Butter and other fats with high levels of saturated fats are ideal for baking because of their shortening effect, which is an interference with the formation of long gluten strands in wheat-based dough, giving it a crumbly texture.

Some margarine brands are now devoid of trans fatty acids but may have a small amount of palm oil or other saturated fat to make them appropriate for use as spreads and for baking and cooking. If substituted for shortenings or butter, these products may reduce the amount of saturated fatty acids while still allowing customers to enjoy pastries and cookies.

Manufacturers are currently producing low-trans-fat shortenings that have the qualities of trans fat shortening without the harm of trans fats. Unfortunately, even though they are reduced in trans fats, shortenings still have substantial amounts of saturated fat. When purchasing fats and oils for a restaurant or foodservice operation, managers should try to use only unsaturated products with few or no trans fats.

Oils deteriorate and need to be changed frequently. Oil used for deep-frying must be filtered regularly. When fats and oils deteriorate, they develop an off flavor and a bad taste called rancidity. Any fat can become rancid; however, this characteristic is much more common in unsaturated fats due to their double bonds. Hydrogenated fats and saturated fats are more resistant to rancidity because they have fewer double bonds. Oxidative rancidity occurs when oils are exposed to air and heat; they become rancid due to oxidation. The method for keeping most oils from going rancid is to store them in dark-colored, tightly sealed containers in a cool, dry, dark place; this retards their oxidation.

THINK ABOUT IT . . .

Which fat do you prefer with your bread: butter, margarine, or oil? What are the potential benefits and drawbacks of each type of fat?

Dietary Intakes of Lipids

Recent research supports a moderate intake of fat. Most evidence suggests that people do not like low-fat diets and that a moderate approach, with an emphasis put on a dietary intake of fat from healthy oils, is best. The Food and Nutrition Board has set the AMDR for lipids at 20 to 35 percent of total calories per day. Within this range, the type of fat matters more than the quantity of fat. The Food and Nutrition Board has indicated that even small quantities of saturated fats increase the risk of heart disease. The *Dietary Guidelines for Americans, 2010* and *ChooseMyPlate.gov* encourage the use of oils over solid fats. The same holds true for trans fatty acids: recommendations are to eat as few as possible. To follow these recommendations, restaurant and foodservice professionals as well as consumers should read labels to identify and avoid products that contain trans fatty acids.

The 2006 fat-consumption recommendations of the American Heart Association state that people should follow a diet with less than 7 percent of calories from saturated fat and less than 1 percent of calories from trans fat, and they should limit cholesterol intake to three hundred milligrams per day. (For the entire statement, see "Diet and Lifestyle Recommendations Revision 2006," a scientific statement by the American Heart Association published online at *www.americanheart.org* on June 21, 2006, in the *Circulation* newsletter.)

Margarine or Butter: Which Is Better?

When research indicated that trans fatty acids were harmful, people turned from eating margarine to eating butter in the belief that butter was better for them. The public perceived that butter was better for them because most margarine has partially hydrogenated fats, although in small amounts. What many people did not understand, however, is that butter is a very concentrated form of saturated fatty acids, which are linked to a higher risk of heart disease. For people trying to adhere to health guidelines, choosing butter less often and in smaller quantities is a realistic strategy to lower dietary saturated fat and cholesterol intake.

Exhibit 4.27

To create the characteristics of a spread, manufacturers add small amounts of either saturated fat or partially hydrogenated fats to margarine. If partially hydrogenated fats are included in a product's ingredient list, it means the product contains trans fatty acids. Otherwise, a small amount of saturated fat, like palm oil, has been used instead of hydrogenated fats to solidify it. Soft margarine with a small amount of added saturated fatty acids is lower in saturated fatty acids than butter (*Exhibit 4.27*).

Lipoproteins

At the end of digestion, dietary lipids make their way through the digestive and absorptive processes in the intestinal wall and are reformed into triglycerides. At this point, the lipid portion joins a protein to form a lipoprotein, a compound that is composed of proteins and various blood lipids from the diet or generated in the liver. Lipoproteins are the transport mechanism for fat in the body.

Lipoproteins and Health

When proteins are linked to lipids, including triglyceride, cholesterol, and phospholipids, they keep the fats in solution in the water environment of the body. These lipoproteins are important markers of health. They travel throughout the body and pass their contents of cholesterol, triglyceride, and phospholipids to cells. They also transport the fat-soluble vitamins. Two lipoproteins are important to understand because of their relationship to heart health: low-density lipoprotein (LDL), or bad cholesterol, and high-density lipoprotein (HDL), or good cholesterol.

LDL

LDL contains considerable amounts of cholesterol that it delivers to the cells. The cells take in this cholesterol, incorporate it into cell membranes, and make it into hormones and other important, complex substances. In the liver, receptor cells regulate cholesterol levels in the blood by binding with LDL. Saturated fatty acids block these receptors from working correctly, thus allowing the body's cholesterol levels to rise. This is part of the basis for recommendations to eat saturated fat in moderation. High saturated-fat intake can raise LDL cholesterol levels. LDL has been called bad cholesterol because it can increase the risk of cardiovascular disease. The American Heart Association's recommended blood-cholesterol levels are shown in *Exhibit 4.28*.

Exhibit 4.28

RECOMMENDED LDL AND HDL LEVELS (MILLIGRAMS PER DECILITER)

Cholesterol type	Recommended level
LDL "bad" cholesterol **(There are different goals for each level of risk for heart disease.)**	• People who are at low risk for heart disease: Less than **160 mg/dL** • People at intermediate risk for heart disease: Less than **130 mg/dL** • People at high risk for heart disease, including those who have heart disease or diabetes: Less than **100 mg/dL** • People at very high risk for heart disease: Less than **70 mg/dL**
HDL "good" cholesterol	• Women: **50 mg/dL** or higher • Men: **40 mg/dL** or higher
Total cholesterol	**Less than 200 mg/dL**

Source: "Numbers That Count for a Healthy Heart." www.americanheart.org. ©2006, American Heart Association.

HDL

HDL, which is made in the liver and intestines, is believed to be heart healthy. HDL has been called the good cholesterol because it lowers blood-cholesterol levels. HDL has more protein and is denser than other lipoproteins. It is also able to remove LDL from the blood and to reduce plaque in artery walls. A reduction in LDL not only brings down LDL cholesterol levels in the blood but also reduces total cholesterol. The body is very efficient at handling all types of cholesterol because it needs cholesterol for so many complex substances. If the control mechanisms set by the body do not respond properly, cholesterol can build up in vessel walls and cause strokes and heart attacks.

Are There Heart-Healthy Fats?

As mentioned earlier in this chapter, there are two essential fatty acids: linoleic and alpha-linolenic. These fatty acids are required by the body and must be included in the diet each day. Both are long-chain polyunsaturated fatty acids. Essential fatty acids are necessary for stimulating skin and hair growth, aiding with bone health, controlling metabolism, and aiding reproductive capacity. The requirements for both of these are small in relation to the amount of oil most people consume.

OMEGA-3 OR OMEGA-6 FATTY ACIDS

Why are fatty acids called omega-3 or omega-6 fats? Fatty acids differ by the length of their carbon chains, whether they are saturated or unsaturated, the number of double bonds (if present), and the position of the first double bond in the chain. The essential fat linoleic acid is an omega-6 polyunsaturated fatty acid. Nutritionists classify the fatty acids by numbering where the first double bond occurs in the molecule opposite the end that contains the acid group. In linoleic acid the first double bond occurs between the 6th and 7th carbons.

Alpha-linolenic acid, which is also an essential fatty acid, is an omega-3 fat. Omega-3 fatty acids have their first double bond between the 3rd and 4th carbon. In nutrition, the essential fatty acids are often referred to by their omega-3 or omega-6 designations because they enter different pathways in the body and cause differing results to health. Omega-3 fatty acids can help to reduce inflammation, thin the blood, and prevent stroke, while omega-6 fatty acids enter a pathway that balances this by constricting blood vessels, promoting blood clotting, and increasing inflammation. The body identifies the pathway by the position of the double bond in these fatty acids. Some dietary sources of omega fatty acids are shown in *Exhibit 4.29*. The reason everyone should consider eating some fatty fish with omega-3 fatty acids is discussed next.

Exhibit 4.29

DIETARY SOURCES OF OMEGA FATTY ACIDS

Omega-3 fatty acids

Cold-water oily fish   Flax   Canola oil   Green leafy vegetables   Walnuts

Omega-6 fatty acids

Cereals   Whole-grain breads   Most vegetable oils   Seasame seeds or oil   Soybeans

OTHER HEART-HEALTHY FATTY ACIDS

The other two fatty acids of particular interest are eicosapentaenoic acid (EPA), an omega-3 fatty acid, and docosahexaenoic acid (DHA). Both are polyunsaturated fatty acids that are so-called good fats. EPA and DHA are found in cold-water fish such as salmon, trout, bluefish, sablefish, mackerel, mullet, sardine, and tuna. The average intake of seafood in the United States is approximately 3.5 ounces per week per person. Fish such as tuna and salmon contain mercury in varying levels. Expert opinion is that Americans should increase their intake of all types of seafood to increase the EPA and DHA content of their diet. By varying the types of fish in the diet, people will also be able to keep their mercury intake lower.[2]

[2]DGA 2010, page 39.

METABOLIC EFFECTS OF ALCOHOL

Many adults choose to include alcoholic beverages in their diets. Recipes for some menu items include alcohol to add flavor and interest to the food. In addition, some food choices are enhanced by the addition or pairing of some alcoholic beverages with the meal. Americans, like other populations the world over, enjoy the chance to socialize and celebrate with a glass of wine, beer, or distilled spirits. Health surveys indicate that approximately 52 percent[3] of adults in the United States consume alcoholic beverages.

Alcohol, in the form of ethanol, is considered a non-nutrient, yet it contributes approximately 82 calories per day to the diets of adults in the United States.[4] A standard drink is defined as 5 ounces of wine, 1.5 ounces of distilled spirits, or 12 ounces of beer. Alcohol provides approximately 7 calories per gram, with the average alcoholic beverage providing about 14 grams or 0.6 ounce of pure alcohol[5]. Alcohol is rapidly absorbed through the stomach and the small intestine, and then it enters the blood. As the blood circulates to the liver, the liver metabolizes most of the alcohol until it is broken down to carbon dioxide and water.

Risks—and Possible Benefits—of Alcohol Consumption

One of the current health concerns regarding alcoholic beverages is that they provide extra calories and few nutrients. Extra caloric intake is a problem for people trying to control their weight. The body cannot store alcohol. Therefore, it metabolizes alcohol before processing calories from food, thus causing the body to store the calories from food rather than utilizing them.

Overuse of alcohol can lead to fatty liver disease and cirrhosis of the liver. Another health risk of drinking alcohol is increased incidence of cancers of the mouth, throat, esophagus, breast, and colon.

Women have less muscle mass, less body water, and fewer enzymes available to metabolize alcohol. Their bodies often suffer more from the effects of overconsumption than men's bodies do.

Recent studies suggest that moderate alcohol consumption improves cardiovascular health and increases life expectancy. Adults should discuss these studies with their doctors and make appropriate decisions about alcohol-related habits.

[3]http://www.cdc.gov/nchs/data/series/sr_10/sr10_249.pdf

[4]*Dietary Guidelines for Americans, 2010*, page 12, Table 2.2

[5]http://www.cdc.gov/alcohol/faqs.htm#standDrink

SUMMARY

1. **Identify the Acceptable Macronutrient Distribution Range (AMDR) and the Recommended Dietary Allowance (RDA) for carbohydrate, protein, and lipid.**

   The AMDR for carbohydrate for adults is 45 to 65 percent, protein is 10 to 35 percent, and lipid is 20 to 35 percent of daily calories. The RDA for carbohydrate is 130 grams. The RDA for protein is 0.8 gram per kilogram of body weight. The RDA for essential fatty acids for males is 17 grams of linoleic acid and 1.6 grams for linolenic acid per day; for females it is 12 grams of linoleic acid and 1.1 grams of linolenic acid per day.

2. **Identify the types of carbohydrates, their food sources, and their importance in the diet.**

   Carbohydrates are classified as either simple or complex. The simple carbohydrates are the sugars, which consist of monosaccharides and disaccharides. Examples of simple-carbohydrate food sources include honey and maple syrup. Complex carbohydrates—starch and fiber—are long chains of sugars bonded together. Examples of their food sources are potatoes and whole-grain cereals.

   Carbohydrates are essential nutrients. They provide energy to the body in the form of glucose. They also spare protein from being used for calories. Fiber provides a feeling of fullness and supports regularity.

   Weight gain due to excess calories occurs because of the fat-sparing effect of carbohydrate. Many more metabolic steps are required to convert sugar to dietary lipids than to convert dietary lipids to body fat. This sparing effect happens when the body continues to store its long-term energy, which consists of the dietary lipids in adipose tissue. However, if a person has eaten too much food and thus has excess unused calories, the body will store the unused blood sugars as fat.

3. **Identify the types of dietary fiber, their food sources, and their importance to health.**

   There are two types of fiber: soluble and insoluble. Soluble fiber lowers cholesterol absorption and keeps glucose levels from fluctuating. Insoluble fiber does not dissolve in water; it simply passes through the digestive tract and promotes regularity.

   Good sources of fiber are fruit, vegetables, and whole grains. Some particular foods that contain fiber are beans, broccoli, whole grains, nuts, and seeds.

4. **Explain diabetes and its causes and effects.**

   There are three types of diabetes: type 1, type 2, and gestational. The main effect of diabetes is an abnormally high blood-glucose level. Diabetes is caused by genetic, metabolic, and other conditions, such as pregnancy. It is also linked to obesity and overweight.

5. **Identify the dietary sources and functions of protein, and explain what essential amino acids and incomplete, complete, and complementary proteins are.**

   Protein is part of human muscles, skin, hair, and nails. It supports growth and maintenance of cells, as well as formation of enzymes, hormones, and antibodies. Protein also plays an important role in regulating fluid and acid–base balance. The major sources of protein are meat and meat products, dairy, grains, and vegetables.

Essential amino acids are amino acids that the body requires but cannot produce on its own. Thus, they must come from food sources. A complete protein is a food that contains all of the essential amino acids.

Incomplete proteins are foods that are missing one or more of the essential amino acids. When people do not get good sources of complete protein, they can combine incomplete proteins to receive all the amino acids they need. These combined proteins are called complementary proteins. Examples include peanut butter on whole-wheat bread or red beans and rice.

An excessive amount of protein can cause weight gain and loss of minerals. Insufficient protein consumption harms muscles, skin, hair, and basic body functions. Eventually, loss of protein will harm the major muscle: the heart.

6. **Identify the big eight allergens and their relationships to protein.**

   The big eight allergens are milk, soy, eggs, wheat, fish, shellfish, peanuts, and tree nuts. The allergens themselves are proteins.

7. **Describe the types and characteristics of lipids and their importance in health.**

   Triglycerides, which comprise 95 percent of the lipids in the diet, come from solid fats from animal sources and oils from mostly plant sources. A triglyceride is a molecule formed by one glycerol molecule and three fatty acids. Phospholipids such as lecithin and cholesterol make up the balance of fats found in the diet. Cholesterol is found only in animal food, such as meat, fish, poultry, and cheese. Cholesterol has a ring structure consisting of a steroid and an alcohol.

   A fatty acid is an organic molecule that consists of a carbon–hydrogen chain with an organic-acid group (COOH) at one end. Saturated fatty acids have no double bond present between the carbon atoms in their carbon chain, making them more solid at room temperature. A fatty-acid molecule is monounsaturated if it contains one double bond and polyunsaturated if it contains more than one double bond. The two essential fatty acids are linoleic acid (found in corn, safflower, soybean, cottonseed, and canola oil) and alpha-linolenic acid (found in canola, soybean, walnut, peanut, pecan, almond, wheat germ, and flaxseed oils). Omega-3 fatty acids help to reduce inflammation, thin the blood, and prevent stroke. Omega-6 fatty acids are converted by the body into chemicals that generally promote inflammation.

   Trans fats are formed when oils have been partially hydrogenated. During this process, some of the hydrogen molecules are bonded differently. Trans fatty acids are linked with increased heart disease because they raise blood-cholesterol levels.

   The current expert recommendation is to eat a moderate amount of fat, or 20 to 35 percent of an individual's daily caloric allowance. Most people do not like low-fat diets. The best approach is to use healthy oils and to reduce saturated fat to less than 10 percent of total caloric intake. It is advised to limit cholesterol to three hundred milligrams per day or less.

APPLICATION EXERCISE

REVIEW RECIPES AND MENU ITEMS FOR KEY NUTRITIONAL FACTORS

Managers can contribute to the success of their establishments by keeping up on health trends.

You should be able to analyze a menu and find foods that would be good sources of the nutrients discussed in this chapter.

1. Look at the menus for a few restaurants or foodservice operations in your area. Determine whether they have sources of whole grains on any part of the menu. What amount of whole grains do you find in the meals on the menu? If there are limited choices, how could you improve these menus to make them healthier?

2. What types of protein are served on the menu where you work or at other restaurants or foodservice operations in the area? Usually proteins make up a large portion of a serving on the restaurant plate. What size are the steaks and chops in the establishment? How many grams of protein and how many calories would each menu item provide?

3. One problem with eating out is that customers have no way of knowing if a restaurant or foodservice operation is interested in protecting their health. If you work in a restaurant or foodservice operation, does your restaurant still use trans fats? If you don't work in a restaurant, check with a friend who does. Go into the kitchen and see what fats are being used. Are any marked with trans fats on the label, or does the term *partially hydrogenated* appear in the ingredients list?

REVIEW YOUR LEARNING

Select the best answer for each question.

1. **Blood sugar is the common name for**
   A. fructose.
   B. glucose.
   C. galactose.
   D. sucrose.

2. **Which part of the grain of wheat is used to make white flour?**
   A. Endosperm
   B. Chaff
   C. Bran
   D. Germ

3. **The nutrient that provides nitrogen to the body is**
   A. carbohydrate.
   B. vitamin C.
   C. protein.
   D. lipid.

4. **Fiber is important in the diet because it**
   A. prevents regularity.
   B. keeps a person hungry.
   C. raises cholesterol levels.
   D. helps keep a person full or satisfied.

5. How many essential amino acids does the body need each day?

   A. 7

   B. 9

   C. 12

   D. 20

6. Which of the following is a symptom of type 1 diabetes?

   A. Cells do not need insulin.

   B. Insulin always needs to be injected.

   C. Cell receptors do not recognize insulin.

   D. The pancreas makes insulin in sufficient quantities.

7. For adults, the daily Recommended Dietary Intake of protein per kilogram of body weight is

   A. 0.3 gram.

   B. 0.5 gram.

   C. 0.8 gram.

   D. 1.0 gram.

8. People should have their LDL blood-cholesterol level checked because high LDL levels in the blood

   A. are linked to increased risk of heart problems.

   B. indicate that a person has a healthy heart.

   C. mean that a person is eating too little cholesterol.

   D. are proof that a person is overweight or obese.

9. Trans fats should be avoided because they have been found to

   A. raise blood HDL levels.

   B. raise blood LDL levels.

   C. lower blood triglyceride levels.

   D. raise HDL and lower LDL levels.

10. What is the American Heart Association's recommended daily dietary limit for cholesterol intake?

    A. One hundred milligrams

    B. Two hundred milligrams

    C. Three hundred milligrams

    D. Four hundred milligrams

5 Vitamins, Minerals, and Water

INSIDE THIS CHAPTER

- Vitamins, Minerals, and Health
- Functions of Selected Vitamins and Minerals
- Retaining Vitamins and Minerals When Cooking
- Supplementation of Vitamins and Minerals
- Water in the Diet

CHAPTER LEARNING OBJECTIVES

After completing this chapter, you should be able to:

- Distinguish between water-soluble and fat-soluble vitamins.

- Describe the functions, sources, and recommended intake amounts of vitamins and minerals in the body.

- Identify causes and implications of nutritional deficiencies.

- Identify the recommended sodium intake and the implications of high-sodium diets.

- Identify ways to retain the vitamin and mineral content of food when cooking.

- Determine when it is appropriate to take supplemental vitamins and minerals.

- Describe the recommended intake amounts and functions of water in the body.

KEY TERMS

CASE STUDY

Sarah is the manager of a college foodservice operation that serves one thousand students living in two dormitories on campus. Although she checks in on the operation on a daily basis, one day she decided to have her assistant relieve her for most of the day while she conducted in-depth observations of each production area. She made the following notes:

- Deliveries left longer at the dock than necessary in warm weather.

- Box of fruit left in storeroom; no one knows when it was placed there.

- Line cook boiling vegetables in deep water instead of using steamer. Check to see if steamer is functioning correctly.

- Vegetables cooked too soon for service and held too long.

- In salad preparation area, produce soaking in water while staff are on break.

After her day of observation, Sarah decided to talk to the entire staff about nutrient retention at the next regular staff training.

1. What nutrition information should Sarah provide her staff?

2. Why should Sarah and her staff be more careful to preserve nutrients for their customers?

Vitamins and minerals are measured in thousandths of a gram and millionths of a gram. To imagine how small one-millionth of a gram is, note that one-quarter teaspoon of sugar weighs about one gram and does not even come close to having a million granules.

VITAMINS, MINERALS, AND HEALTH

Vitamins and minerals are important in the human diet because they promote growth and optimum health. Both vitamins and minerals are essential for body functioning. Because some food items contain more vitamins and minerals than others, consuming a variety of nutrient-dense food items from each of the five food groups is necessary to obtain the vitamins and minerals needed for good health. This chapter focuses on individual vitamins and minerals and their roles in the body.

Vitamins

Scientists began discovering vitamins in the early 20th century. They assigned letters and numbers to unknown properties in food and later named them vitamins. The Polish scientist Casimir Funk originally used the term *vitamines*, a combination of the Latin word *vita*, meaning "life," and *amine*, for the type of organic chemical that scientists originally thought vitamins were. Vitamins are organic compounds, meaning they contain carbon and are made from plants or animals.

Vitamins are classified as either water soluble or fat soluble. Water-soluble vitamins are soluble (can dissolve) in water but not in fat, and generally they are not stored in the body. Fat-soluble vitamins are soluble in fat but not in water, and they can be stored in the body's adipose (fat) tissue. Now scientists know that there are thirteen vitamins: four fat-soluble vitamins and nine water-soluble vitamins (see *Exhibit 5.1*).

After identifying some vitamins, scientists conducted experiments to learn more about the new substances. This eventually led to the discovery of vitamins A and D, as well as the B-complex vitamins. Each vitamin's designated letter is based on its original discovery and chemical names. Vitamins may have more than one active form and therefore be assigned different chemical names. See *Exhibit 5.2* for information about the function of each vitamin and the related deficiency diseases.

Vitamins are called micronutrients because the body needs only a small amount of each one, while carbohydrates, fats, and proteins are called macronutrients because the body needs large amounts of them. To visualize the differences among grams, milligrams, and micrograms,

Exhibit 5.1

VITAMINS BY CATEGORY

Fat-soluble vitamins	Water-soluble vitamins
Vitamin A (retinol)	Thiamin B_1
Vitamin D (cholecalciferol)	Riboflavin B_2
Vitamin E (tocopherol)	Niacin B_3
Vitamin K (phylloquinone, menaquinone)	Pantothenic acid B_5
	Vitamin B_6 (pyridoxine, pyridoxal, pyradoxamine)
	Biotin B_7
	Folate B_9 or folic acid
	Vitamin B_{12} (cyanocobalamin)
	Vitamin C (ascorbic acid)

Exhibit 5.2

VITAMINS: PRIMARY FUNCTIONS AND DEFICIENCIES

Vitamin	Primary function	Deficiency
Vitamin A	Normal vision and normal cell development in the body	Night blindness, dry eyes, softening of the cornea
Thiamin	A coenzyme for energy metabolism, nervous-system function	Beriberi
Riboflavin	A coenzyme in energy metabolism, normal vision	Ariboflavinosis
Niacin	A coenzyme in energy metabolism	Pellagra
Pantothenic acid	Part of a coenzyme used in energy metabolism	Convulsions or anemia
Vitamin B_6	Part of a coenzyme used in amino-acid metabolism, helps make red blood cells, assists in the conversion of the amino acid tryptophan to the vitamin niacin	Anemia, nerve damage, seizures, skin problems, sores in the mouth
Biotin	Part of a coenzyme used in energy metabolism, used in cell growth, helps maintain a steady blood-sugar level, strengthens hair and nails	Changes in mental state, dry skin, fine and brittle hair, fungal infections, hair loss or total alopecia, muscular pain, skin rash, seborrheic dermatitis
Folate or folic acid	Part of a coenzyme used in the synthesis of new cells	Behavioral disorders, diarrhea, loss of appetite, sore tongue, headaches, heart palpitations, infant neural tube defects, irritability, low birth weight babies, megaloblastic anemia, premature babies, weakness, weight loss
Vitamin B_{12}	Part of a coenzyme used in the synthesis of new cells	Megaloblastic anemia, nerve-cell death, numbness or tingling of the extremities, pernicious anemia
Vitamin C	Antioxidant, collagen formation in the skin, helps immunity	Scurvy
Vitamin D	Maintains the normal levels of calcium and phosphorus in the blood	Osteomalacia, osteoporosis, rickets
Vitamin E	Antioxidant	Neurological disorders leading to poor transmission of nerve impulses, muscle weakness, and degeneration of the retina
Vitamin K	Blood clotting	Bleeding diathesis (causing problems with blood coagulation)

Exhibit 5.3

A varied diet helps people obtain all of the vitamins and minerals needed for optimal health.

think of the size of a meal that provides enough macronutrients versus the size of a vitamin tablet with 100 percent of the Daily Value (DV) for most vitamins. Vitamins are essential for life and must be obtained from food because the human body makes insufficient amounts of them, or none at all (see *Exhibits 5.3* and *5.4*). Unlike carbohydrates, fats, and proteins,

Exhibit 5.4

FOOD SOURCES OF VITAMINS

Vitamin	Vegetarian sources	Animal sources
Vitamin A	Dark orange and green vegetables, sweet potatoes, mangos	Fortified milk or dairy products, liver, eggs
Thiamin	Whole grains, enriched products, fortified products, nuts, legumes	Pork
Riboflavin	Whole grains or enriched grains	Milk and milk products
Niacin	Whole grains, enriched products, nuts	Milk, eggs, meat, poultry, fish
Pantothenic acid	Most	Most
Vitamin B$_6$	Green vegetables, green leafy vegetables, fruit, whole grains	Meat, fish, poultry
Biotin	Most; people make small amounts in the intestines	Most
Folate	Green leafy vegetables, legumes, seeds, enriched products	Liver
Vitamin B$_{12}$	None naturally; may be fortified in cereals	All
Vitamin C	Citrus fruit, peppers, strawberries, tomatoes, potatoes	None
Vitamin D	None, but made with the help of sunlight	Fortified milk, fatty fish, some fish-liver oils, eggs
Vitamin E	Green leafy vegetables, mayonnaise made with vegetable oil, nuts, peanut butter, sunflower seeds, sea buckthorn berries, seeds, vegetable oils (palm, sunflower, canola, corn, soybean, and olive), wheat germ, whole grains	Fish, only small amounts in some, not a good source
Vitamin K	Green, leafy cabbage-type vegetables, collards, spinach, also made by bacteria in the intestine	Minimal amounts in liver and eggs

vitamins and minerals contain neither energy nor calories. Instead, vitamins facilitate the operation of other nutrients. Some vitamins act as coenzymes because they are activators of other enzymes—body chemicals that catalyze, or speed up, a specific chemical reaction. Think of a coenzyme as a puzzle piece that completes the puzzle; it is specific to and combines with the target enzyme to enable certain important reactions to take place in the body.

Minerals

Minerals are chemical elements found in soil or ground water. We obtain them from both animal and vegetable food. Like vitamins, minerals are essential to a healthy body. For example, calcium is needed to build bones, to maintain bone health, to maintain blood pressure, and to aid muscle contraction. Sodium, potassium, and chloride are needed because they function as electrolytes and maintain fluid balance.

Minerals are divided into two main categories, major or trace, depending on the amount required by the body. Calcium, phosphorus, potassium, sulfur, sodium, chloride, and magnesium are considered the major minerals, of which the body needs one hundred milligrams or more per day. In contrast, the body needs trace minerals in very small amounts. For example, iron is needed in milligrams, while copper, chromium, and iodine are needed in micrograms. (See *Exhibit 5.5* for a complete list.)

With regard to the maintenance of the body, mineral activity is as important as vitamin activity. Minerals can compete for absorption in the small intestine. When this happens, there is a possibility of an imbalance.

This competition can also affect a mineral's bioavailability if a person takes too much of one, such as when taking supplements. Bioavailability is the degree to which the nutrients that people consume can be absorbed and become available for use by the body. Although many people do not get the daily recommended intakes of minerals, serious mineral deficiencies are usually caused by underlying medical conditions. *Exhibit 5.6* on the next page shows the functions and deficiencies of minerals in the body.

Minerals can be present in food but not necessarily available for absorption. Some food has chemicals that prevent the absorption of minerals. Two common examples are the oxalates in spinach that bind with the calcium and

Exhibit 5.5	
MINERALS BY CATEGORY	
Major minerals	**Trace minerals**
Calcium	Chromium
Chloride	Copper
Magnesium	Fluoride
Phosphorus	Iodine
Potassium	Iron
Sodium	Manganese
Sulfur	Molybdenum
	Selenium
	Zinc

Exhibit 5.6

MINERALS: PRIMARY FUNCTIONS AND DEFICIENCIES

Mineral	Primary function	Deficiency
Calcium	Bone health, maintenance of normal blood pressure, muscle contraction	Hypocalcemia, low blood calcium usually caused by other medical conditions, osteoporosis can result from chronic calcium and vitamin D deficiency
Chloride	Maintains fluid and electrolyte balance	Hypochloremia, usually caused by repeated vomiting in combination with low intakes
Chromium	Aids in carbohydrate metabolism	Impaired glucose tolerance, increased blood cholesterol and triglycerides
Copper	Part of various enzymes, used for electron transport	Deficiency is uncommon with exception of malnutrition
Fluoride	Bone and tooth health	Increased cavity formation
Iodine	Component of thyroid gland, a form of the hormone thyroxine regulates metabolic rate	Goiter (large growth on the thyroid gland), reproductive damage, hypothyroidism
Iron	Part of hemoglobin	Low iron stores, iron-deficiency anemia, can affect cognition and immune function in children
Magnesium	Part of bones and teeth, protein creation, muscle activity, activator of metabolism of macronutrients	Hypomagnesemia, low blood magnesium, occurs when other major minerals are deficient. Occurs with kidney disease and with alcoholism
Manganese	Cofactor for enzymes that facilitate metabolic processes and prevent damage by free radicals	Deficiency not seen in humans eating normal diets
Molybdenum	Purine degradation, formation of uric acid, enzyme reactions	Deficiency not seen in humans eating normal diets
Phosphorus	Part of bones and teeth	Hypophosphatemia, low blood phosphorus, occurs with underlying disease conditions
Potassium	Maintains fluid and electrolyte balance	Hypokalemia, low blood potassium, usually caused by vomiting and diarrhea, or use of diuretics (promotes urine formation), eventually irregular heartbeat
Selenium	Antioxidant, which protects substances from being oxidized and thus decreases the adverse effects of free radicals	Muscle pain, muscle weakness, and cardiomyopathy (structural change in the heart such as enlargement of the heart)
Sodium	Maintains fluid and electrolyte balance	Hyponatremia, low blood sodium, usually a result of vomiting, diarrhea, diuretics (promotes urine formation), or profuse sweating
Sulfur	Part of certain vitamins, part of sulfur-containing amino acids, determines shape of protein molecules	Deficiency not seen in humans
Zinc	Taste perception, coenzyme	Deficiency can result in delayed wound healing, impaired appetite, and diarrhea

the phytic acid of grains that can bind calcium and other minerals, preventing them from being absorbed. Some types of food encourage the absorption of minerals. For instance, when taken with plant proteins, vitamin C increases the absorption of iron. See *Exhibit 5.7* for a listing of good food sources for minerals.

Exhibit 5.7	
FOOD SOURCES OF MINERALS	
Mineral	**Food sources**
Calcium	Broccoli, Chinese cabbage, corn tortillas, dairy products, fortified fruit juice, greens, kale, legumes, milk, salmon, sardines, soy milk
Chloride	Baking soda, baking powder, bread, cheese, eggs, meat, milk, processed food, seafood, table salt, vegetables
Chromium	Brewer's yeast, cheeses, fish, liver, meat, nuts, poultry, whole grains
Copper	Cocoa, legumes, organ meat, nuts, seafood, seeds, wheat bran, whole-grain products
Fluorine	Fluoridated water, legumes, marine fish, organ meat, nuts, seeds, whole grains
Iodine	Iodized salt, seafood, vegetables, small amounts in milk
Iron	Cereals/breads, egg yolks, fish, fruit, greens, legumes, liver, meat, nuts, poultry, enriched or whole grains
Magnesium	Alfalfa, almonds, apples, brown rice, cocoa, figs, greens, lemons, legumes, meat, peaches, nuts, seafood, sesame seeds, soybeans, sunflower seeds, vegetables, whole grains
Manganese	Fruit, nuts, whole grains
Molybdenum	Bread, cereal, grains, nuts
Phosphorus	Cereals, eggs, fish, meat, milk, peas, poultry, whole grains
Potassium	Bananas, citrus fruit, legumes, meat, melons, milk, potatoes, tomatoes, vegetables, whole grains
Selenium	Dairy products, fish, organ meat, poultry, seafood, vegetables, whole grains
Sodium	Table salt, milk, processed food, spinach
Zinc	Enriched cereals, red meat, seafood, whole grains

DAILY INTAKE OF VITAMINS AND MINERALS

Individuals need to ingest the recommended vitamins and minerals each day in addition to carbohydrate, protein, lipid, and water. See *Exhibits 5.8* and *5.9* for the recommended daily amounts of vitamins and minerals and the Tolerable Upper Intake Levels. Without adequate food intake, children and adults develop deficiency diseases. People with nutritional deficiencies may experience weight loss, slowed growth, iron-deficiency anemia, or weakened immune function.

Exhibit 5.8

DIETARY REFERENCE INTAKES FOR VITAMINS

	Dietary Reference Intakes for Vitamins per Day						
	Male 9–18 yrs	Male 19–70 yrs	Male >70 yrs	Female 9–18 yrs	Female 19–70 yrs	Female >70 yrs	Male and female 19–70 yrs
	RDA/AI	RDA/AI	RDA/AI	RDA/AI	RDA/AI	RDA/AI	UL
Vitamin A (mcg)	600–900	900	900	600–900	700	700	3,000
Thiamin (mg)	0.9–1.2	1.2	1.2	0.9–1.1	1.1	1.1	ND
Riboflavin (mg)	0.9–1.3	1.3	1.3	0.9–1.0	1.1	1.1	ND
Niacin (mg)	12–16	16	16	12–14	14	14	35
Pantothenic acid (mg)	4–5	5	5	4–5	5	5	ND
Vitamin B$_6$ (mg)	1.0–1.3	1.3–1.7	1.7	1.0–1.2	1.3–1.5	1.5	100
Biotin (mcg)	20–25	30	30	2–25	30	30	ND
Folate (mcg)	300–400	400	400	300–400	400	400	1,000
Vitamin B$_{12}$ (mcg)	1.8–2.4	2.4	2.4	1.8–2.4	2.4	2.4	ND
Vitamin C (mg)	45–75	90	90	45–65	75	75	2,000
Vitamin D (mcg)	15	15	20	15	15	20	100
Vitamin E (mg)	11–15	15	15	11–15	15	15	1,000
Vitamin K (mcg)	60–75	120	120	60–75	90	90	ND

Adapted from Dietary Reference Intakes (DRIs), Recommended Dietary Allowances (RDA), and Adequate Intakes (AI)—Food and Nutrition Board, Institute of Medicine, National Academy of Sciences.
Key:
UL - Tolerable Upper Intake Levels
ND - Not Determined

Exhibit 5.9

DIETARY REFERENCE INTAKES FOR MINERALS

	Dietary Reference Intakes for Minerals per Day						
	Male 9–18 yrs	Male 19–70 yrs	Male >70 yrs	Female 9–18 yrs	Female 19–70 yrs	Female >70 yrs	Male and female 19–70 yrs
	RDA/AI	RDA/AI	RDA/AI	RDA/AI	RDA/AI	RDA/AI	UL
Major minerals							
Calcium (mg)	1,300	1,000	1,200	1,300	1,000–1,200	1,200	2,000–2,500
Chloride (mg)	2,300	2,000–2,300	1,800	2,300	2,000–2,300	1,800	3,600
Magnesium (mg)	240–410	400–420	420	240–360	310–320	320	350
Phosphorus (mg)	1,250	700	700	1,250	700	700	4,000
Potassium (mg)	4,500–4,700	4,700	4,700	4,500–4,700	4,700	4,700	—
Sodium (mg)	1,500	1,300–1,500	1,200	1,500	1,300–1,500	1,200	2,300
Trace minerals							
Chromium (mcg)	25–35	30–35	30	21–24	20–25	20	ND
Copper (mcg)	700–890	900	900	700–890	900	900	10,000
Fluoride (mg)	2–3	4	4	2–3	3	3	10
Iodine (mcg)	120–150	150	150	120–150	150	150	1,100
Iron (mg)	8–11	8	8	8–15	8–18	8	45
Manganese (mg)	1.9–2.2	2.3	2.3	1.6	1.8	1.8	11
Molybdenum (mcg)	34–43	45	45	34–43	45	45	2,000
Selenium (mcg)	40–55	55	55	40–55	55	55	400
Zinc (mg)	8–11	11	11	8–9	8	8	40

Adapted from Dietary Reference Intakes (DRIs), Recommended Dietary Allowances (RDA), and Adequate Intakes (AI)—Food and Nutrition Board, Institute of Medicine, National Academy of Sciences.

Key:

UL - Tolerable Upper Intake Levels

ND - Not Determined

There is neither an RDA/AI nor a UL set for sulfur because sulfur needs are met when enough protein is consumed.

Exhibit 5.10

FUNCTIONS OF SELECTED VITAMINS AND MINERALS

In order for restaurant and foodservice personnel to make informed decisions about recipes, portions, and menu choices, they must understand not only the importance of essential vitamins and minerals but also the functions of these substances in the body. It also will be helpful if they understand the food sources of the vitamins and minerals and the importance of retaining these nutrients in the food they prepare and serve to their customers (*Exhibit 5.10*).

Fat-Soluble Vitamins

Vitamins A, D, E, and K are fat-soluble vitamins. As a group, these vitamins are dependent on fat for absorption and utilization in the body. In order to circulate to the cells, vitamins A, D, E, and K use lipoproteins as their route of transportation in the body. They can be stored readily in liver and adipose tissue. Although they were discovered in the 20th century, these vitamins are still studied for their abilities to affect our health.

VITAMIN A

Vitamin A has multiple roles in the body. It is important in good vision, general growth and development, reproduction, bone health, and immune function. The main function of vitamin A is to promote good vision through the health of the retina, the light sensitive portion of the eye, and the cornea, the clear layer covering of the eye. That is why the active form of vitamin A is called retinol.

Its role in growth and development includes determining the specific function of cells, or cell differentiation. An example of this is the development of the mucous-forming cells and the cells that form the skin. Vitamin A is also essential for bone growth. A deficiency of vitamin A leads to poor bone growth, while a toxicity can cause bone fractures.

Vitamin A is a fat-soluble vitamin found in its active form in animal-based food such as liver, milk, and other dairy products. It is also found in plant sources as beta-carotene. Beta-carotene is an inactive form of the vitamin or precursor and is activated by the body. It is obtained from a variety of plant sources such as carrots, sweet potatoes, and other types of fruit and vegetables that are red, orange, or dark green in color. It gives carrots and sweet potatoes their orange color.

Beta-carotene is an antioxidant chemical that fights the excessive oxidation of molecules in the human body. Antioxidants serve an important function in the body. They protect cells from damage due to free radicals, or unpaired electrons, formed during the metabolic activity of the body. If left unchecked, free radicals can harm the cellular membranes and cause damage that leads to inflammation and disease.

A deficiency of vitamin A may lead to several deficiency diseases, including night blindness, or the inability to see clearly at night. Fortunately, this disease can be easily treated. Two more serious conditions that may arise from a deficiency of vitamin A are xerophthalmia, or dry eyes, and keratomalacia, or softening of the cornea, both of which could lead to permanent blindness. On the other hand, excessive amounts of vitamin A, which usually come from vitamin supplements, are toxic. Studies suggest that consuming too much vitamin A can lead to severe headaches, nausea, skin irritation, bone pain, bone fractures, and death.

VITAMIN D

A second fat-soluble vitamin required by the body is vitamin D. There are very few food sources of vitamin D. It can be found naturally in fatty fishes such as salmon and sardines. To ensure that it is available in the diet, milk and some breakfast cereals have been fortified with it (*Exhibit 5.11*). Its main function in the body is to regulate the blood's calcium levels to maintain bone health. Our bodies can make vitamin D from a compound that lies under the skin. Sunlight activates the natural production of vitamin D. When sunlight hits the skin, this compound is converted into a vitamin D precursor that is absorbed into the blood and activated in the kidney and liver.

Exhibit 5.11

Rickets, which causes bowing of the legs or knocked knees, is a disease that occurs in children due to a deficiency of vitamin D. In adults, a deficiency causes osteomalacia, or a softening of the bones that can lead to bone deformities. Osteoporosis, a bone-thinning disorder that strikes people as they age, is caused by a deficiency of vitamin D and calcium.

Vitamin D deficiency is a particular concern for people who do not receive enough exposure to the sun. In addition, for those who are exposed to the sun, extensive use of sunscreen blocks the activation of vitamin D. Consuming good sources of vitamin D is essential to offset the lack of sun exposure, and it also helps those who must limit their time in the sun.

VITAMIN E

Vitamin E is known as an antioxidant vitamin. It has a role in protecting cellular membranes and preventing damage from free radicals. Deficiencies of vitamin E are rare in healthy adults but occur in cases where malabsorption is present. As with all vitamins, getting adequate amounts of vitamin E is important. However, high-dose supplements are not recommended as they may negatively affect heart health.

Sources of vitamin E can be found in both plant-based and animal-based food. The oils are good sources of it and so is wheat germ. Many cooking oils contain added alpha-tocopherol, the active form of vitamin E, to delay rancidity that is caused by oxidation.

VITAMIN K

There are two forms of vitamin K—the plant form phylloquinone and the form found in animal-based food and made by intestinal bacteria, menaquinone. Food sources of vitamin K include plants such as leafy green vegetables, broccoli, and cauliflower. Oils such as soybean, olive, and canola are also good sources.

The primary function of vitamin K is to enable blood to clot, but it also plays a role in the health of bones. The body can make vitamin K in the intestines. However, the body does not make sufficient amounts, so vitamin K also must be obtained from food sources. A deficiency of vitamin K is unlikely unless a person has malabsorption as in celiac disease or cystic fibrosis.

Some adults must take medicines called anticoagulants or blood thinners that prevent clots. Elderly patients often take this type of medication. They must limit their consumption of dietary sources of vitamin K or they will reverse the medicine's effects and form harmful blood clots. In a dining situation, they may request no green vegetables and no salad when eating out to avoid more dietary vitamin K.

Water-Soluble Vitamins

The water-soluble vitamins should be consumed every day because the body more easily excretes them. In metabolic reactions, these vitamins are very interdependent. If one vitamin is missing, the others will not be able to participate in certain reactions.

THIAMIN, RIBOFLAVIN, NIACIN

The major function of thiamin, riboflavin, and niacin is to serve as coenzymes in metabolic reactions. Thiamin is essential in the metabolism of glucose to other products used by the body. It was one of the first vitamins to be discovered and synthesized. Good sources of thiamin are wheat germ, pork, legumes, whole grains, and nuts. Deficiencies of thiamin can be seen in people with alcoholism. With increased alcoholic intake, thiamin is poorly absorbed and easily excreted by the body. In addition, poor dietary intake may accentuate the problem.

Riboflavin and niacin accept and donate electrons, making them essential to the metabolic activities of the body. Riboflavin is found in small quantities in all plant-based and animal-based food, and the best sources are milk and milk products. A deficiency of riboflavin can lead to inflammation of the mouth, throat, and lips, along with the development of skin disorders. The body needs niacin in approximately two hundred enzyme reactions. It is found in meat, poultry, and fish as well as whole grains.

In the process of refining grains, these three B vitamins are removed. Some of the B vitamins are returned during the enrichment process. However, only reduced amounts of thiamin, riboflavin, niacin, folic acid, and the mineral iron are restored, leaving enriched bread with less of these nutrients than that found in whole-grain products.

VITAMIN B₆

The primary role of vitamin B_6 is to act as a coenzyme in amino-acid and protein metabolism. It also has a role in blood-cell synthesis, carbohydrate metabolism, and production of the chemicals that carry nerve impulses in the body. Vitamin B_6 is found in ready-to-eat cereals as well as meat, fish, and poultry. Severe deficiency of this vitamin is uncommon. Low dietary intakes can negatively affect the body's immune function. Toxic amounts from supplements can cause damage to the nervous system.

FOLATE

Folate is an important B vitamin required in the development of red and white blood cells. Folate deficiency results in megaloblastic anemia, which is associated with abnormally large red blood cells. Folic acid is used in supplements and enriched flour because folic acid is better absorbed than the natural folate found in food.

VITAMIN C

Sailors are sometimes referred to as limeys because they used to suck on lemons or limes to ingest vitamin C in order to avoid the illness later named scurvy. Hundreds of years ago, the lack of fresh fruit and certain vegetables in the diets of sailors caused this vitamin deficiency. Scurvy causes swollen gums, loose teeth, a rash that looks like red spots, and hair loss. The functions of vitamin C include acting as an antioxidant and assisting the body in the absorption of iron from plant sources.

Minerals and Blood-Pressure Regulation

Minerals play an important role in the regulation of blood pressure. It appears that deficiencies of the minerals potassium, calcium, and magnesium may contribute to the incidence of hypertension, or high blood pressure. Also, for people who have a genetic tendency toward high blood pressure, excessive sodium intake may increase the likelihood of developing this condition. Table salt is a combination of the minerals sodium and chloride. Salt has approximately twenty-three hundred milligrams of sodium in each teaspoon, making it an important source of sodium in the diet. The National Institutes of Health publishes the Dietary Approaches to Stop Hypertension (DASH) eating plan as a heart-healthy guide. The DASH plan is a diet that is low in sodium but high in other minerals to help normalize blood pressure. It is available at *www.nhlbi.nih.gov/health/public/heart/hbp/dash/new_dash.pdf*.

Restaurants and foodservice operations should review their recipes to see if they are adding excessive amounts of salt or using products that are extremely high in sodium. Sodium is an essential nutrient, but public-health experts encourage Americans to reduce their intake to prevent hypertension. Under some menu-labeling laws, some restaurants and foodservice establishments are required to provide nutrition information to the public upon request. This nutrient information must contain the amount of sodium in each standard menu item. It makes sense for managers and chefs to bring sodium levels down by substituting food items that are flavorful but low in sodium. Recommended sodium levels are lower than they have been in the past, and it will take time for both customers and chefs to adjust to less salt. *Exhibit 5.12* shows some low-sodium types of food that are rich in other nutrients.

Exhibit 5.12

HEART-HEALTHY FOOD ITEMS

According to the Dietary Guidelines for Americans 2010, individuals should lower their sodium intake to twenty-three hundred milligrams, or less than one teaspoon of salt per day. In addition, as mentioned in chapter 3, people who are more than 51 years of age, of African-American descent, or affected by hypertension, diabetes, or chronic kidney disease should not consume more than fifteen hundred milligrams or slightly less than 0.75 teaspoon of salt per day.

Mineral-Related Health Issues

Based on the functions of the different minerals previously described, it is clear that all minerals are important for health. Several particular health issues related to minerals merit further discussion.

MINERALS AND BONE HEALTH

As the body constantly builds up and breaks down bone, minerals work to maintain bone health. Calcium is well recognized for its role in healthy bones and teeth; it is also the most common mineral in the body. Phosphorus and magnesium are also present in the bones. Osteoporosis, which affects millions of Americans, is a disease that causes bones to become porous so that they fracture easily. When an elderly person seems to be getting shorter, osteoporosis is a possible cause.

Osteoporosis has several risk factors:

- **Gender:** Females are more likely to develop osteoporosis than are males.
- **Age:** The risk of osteoporosis increases with age.
- **Race:** Caucasian and Asian women are at a higher risk.
- **Family history:** A family history of osteoporosis increases risk.
- **Frame size:** People with smaller frames have a higher risk.
- **Medications:** Some medications can increase risk.

People can prevent osteoporosis by taking some simple actions. Do weight-bearing exercise such as jogging or walking, and decrease or eliminate smoking and the consumption of alcoholic beverages. Consume the recommended amounts of calcium and vitamin D. Any calcium supplements should contain vitamin D, as it enables calcium to pass through the intestinal wall and into the bloodstream.

MINERALS IN THE BLOOD

Iron, zinc, and copper are important minerals that form hemoglobin. Hemoglobin is the active molecule in red blood cells; it is a protein in the body that carries oxygen through the blood. Iron-deficiency anemia, which is the most common nutritional deficiency in the world, occurs when there is a lack of iron in the diet or a problem with absorption of iron in the body, resulting in low levels of hemoglobin. The symptoms of iron-deficiency anemia include weakness, irritability, headaches, pale skin, and sensitivity to cold temperatures. Iron deficiency is more common in women and children than in men.

Iron comes in two forms in the diet: heme and nonheme. Heme iron is iron from animal sources, while nonheme iron comes from vegetarian sources. The body more easily absorbs heme iron than nonheme iron.

RETAINING VITAMINS AND MINERALS WHEN COOKING

Restaurant and foodservice managers should ensure that the cooking methods used at their establishments help retain the food's vitamins and minerals. If the water used to boil a green vegetable has turned green, there is a good chance that some vitamins were lost. Minimizing cooking time helps preserve vitamins and minerals, especially water-soluble vitamins. Steaming, shown in *Exhibit 5.13*, is the best process for preserving the vitamin content of vegetables; microwaving and stir-frying are other good methods. Even rinsing or soaking produce can result in lost vitamins, because the water-soluble vitamins are leached out.

Minerals and fat-soluble vitamins are not as fragile as water-soluble vitamins. However, restaurant and foodservice professionals should avoid soaking produce because it will leach out minerals like potassium. Also, storing food for extended periods of time, or simply exposing it to air or light, can destroy the vitamins. For example, light exposure destroys riboflavin, which is found in milk products.

Exhibit 5.13

Exhibit 5.14

SOME FOOD ITEMS WITH KNOWN PHYTOCHEMICALS

Yellow and orange vegetables	
Cruciferous vegetables (broccoli, cauliflower, and cabbage)	
Citrus fruit	
Onions	
Garlic	
Green tea	
Wine	
Soybeans	
Leeks	
Chives	

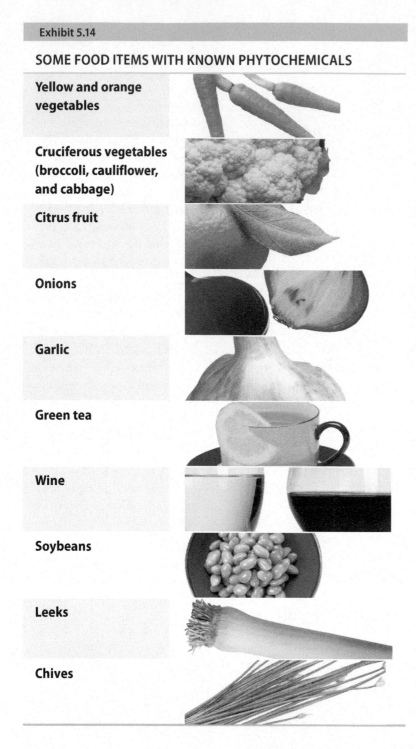

SUPPLEMENTATION OF VITAMINS AND MINERALS

Although it is possible to obtain all necessary vitamins and minerals by following a healthy diet, Americans spend billions of dollars on vitamin and mineral supplements each year. There are some instances that require vitamin and mineral supplements; however, for healthy adults who are free of chronic disease, nothing more than a multivitamin is usually warranted.

Phytochemicals

It is best to obtain essential vitamins and minerals from food because food usually contains fiber and other substances such as phytochemicals. Although humans technically do not require phytochemicals in their diets, these substances may enhance the quality of life. Phytochemicals have a strong antioxidant effect and thus help protect the body from cancer and heart disease. Phytochemicals are found in food. For example, the isoflavones in soy are phytochemicals. When removed from food and offered in supplements, however, phytochemicals often show no positive effects. In fact, studies have shown some negative effects.

Cruciferous vegetables such as broccoli, cauliflower, and cabbage are rich in phytochemicals. *Exhibit 5.14* provides additional examples of food items that are known sources of various phytochemicals. Generally speaking, most fruits and vegetables contain at least one phytochemical.

Taking Vitamin and Mineral Supplements

Sometimes healthy people choose to take multivitamins as "insurance" to make sure they obtain all the vitamins and minerals they need each day. Supplements often occur in the form of a tablet, which usually contains synthetic forms of single or mixed vitamins and minerals. Vitamin tablets should be taken with a meal or snack to increase absorption. Otherwise the vitamins or minerals will likely be excreted in the urine and wasted.

There are times when the supplementation of vitamins and minerals is necessary. The major health conditions that call for vitamin supplementation, mineral supplementation, or both are discussed below. Although this is not a complete list, it provides an overview of the types of medical conditions that make supplementation necessary.

PREGNANCY AND BREAST-FEEDING

During pregnancy and breast-feeding, women need higher than normal amounts of some vitamins and minerals. For example, the B vitamin folate (or folic acid) is important for the prevention of neural-tube defects in infants. Spina bifida and cleft palate are examples of birth defects that result from inadequate folate intake during pregnancy.

Folic acid is added to prenatal vitamins for women whose intake is suboptimal and therefore puts the fetus at risk. The mineral iron is usually supplemented during pregnancy and breast-feeding as well. In addition, breast-feeding mothers may give their infant vitamin D supplements due to low supplies in breast milk.

IRON-DEFICIENCY ANEMIA

Individuals with iron-deficiency anemia lack sufficient iron in their blood. When a person is diagnosed with this disease, his or her physician may prescribe a daily iron tablet. Iron supplements should be taken only if prescribed by a physician, as excess iron can be harmful.

LOW-CALORIE DIETS AND CHRONIC DIETING

People who diet frequently or otherwise restrict their food consumption may also be restricting their vitamin and mineral intake. These people will benefit from a multivitamin that supplies the necessary vitamins and minerals that come from the food items they are not eating. Those who follow diets that eliminate an entire food group should also consider taking a multivitamin.

OSTEOPOROSIS

Calcium and vitamin D supplements are prescribed to people who have osteoporosis. They may also be prescribed to individuals who have a family history of osteoporosis in an effort to help prevent the disease.

VEGANS

Vegans are people who eliminate all animal products from their diet. They should supplement vitamin B_{12} because it occurs only in animal products. Vegans might also need to supplement vitamin D, iron, and zinc. See chapter 9 for more information about vegan and other vegetarian diets.

THINK ABOUT IT . . .

Animal products provide vitamins and minerals. Vegans obtain some of these essentials via supplements. They also eat food that is high in the vitamins and minerals that are also found in animal products. What types of food should vegans add to their diets?

LACKING INTRINSIC FACTOR

Intrinsic factor is a protein needed for bodily absorption of vitamin B_{12}. In the aging process, a person may lose the ability to produce intrinsic factor and become deficient in vitamin B_{12}. Some types of abdominal surgery may also impact the body's ability to process this vitamin. In these instances, an individual should obtain a B_{12} injection from a doctor for direct absorption into the bloodstream.

Potential for Toxicity

When people consume more calories than they need, the calories are stored as fat. In a similar way, more does not necessarily equal better when it comes to vitamins and minerals. In fact, excess amounts of vitamins and minerals can be toxic and thus detrimental to health. For example, vitamin A toxicity can cause a skin rash as well as hair loss, bone problems, birth defects, and even death.

It is difficult to get too many vitamins and minerals from whole unprocessed food. Fortified food can add to total vitamin and mineral intakes if eaten regularly. However, toxic amounts of vitamins and minerals are usually the result of the daily consumption of high-dose vitamin or mineral supplements. Usually, a toxic level of a vitamin or mineral is the result of supplementation in excess of 100 percent of the DV for that nutrient. This can happen either because the supplement contains more than 100 percent of the DV or because the supplement was taken more than once each day.

The best guide to follow when consuming vitamin and mineral supplements is the UL or Tolerable Upper Intake Level that is issued by the Food and Nutrition Board. This was discussed in chapter 3 and is shown in *Exhibits 5.8* and *5.9* earlier in this chapter. The UL values answer the question as to how much is too much with regard to vitamins and minerals. The UL is the highest level of daily nutrient intake that poses no risk of adverse health effects to almost all individuals. Some vitamins and minerals are beneficial up to a certain dosage, but at a higher level they are toxic and potentially harmful to the body. Because the fat-soluble vitamins are stored in adipose tissue, they are more likely to be toxic at excessive levels. Vitamin B_6, niacin, and vitamin C are potentially harmful water-soluble vitamins when consumed in excess. For example, high doses of vitamin C have been reported to help precipitate kidney stones. Keeping supplement intakes below the UL for each vitamin and mineral listed will decrease the risk of toxicity.

WATER IN THE DIET

Water is essential to the human body because it is involved in almost all of the chemical reactions that make the body work. The body needs a certain amount of water every day in order to function properly. Food and drink are the primary sources of water.

Water is the most abundant and important macronutrient in the body. It makes up about 60 percent of body weight. Water has many important roles in the body. It not only keeps people hydrated, or supplied with an ample amount of water, but also helps regulate body temperature, transports nutrients, makes up part of all cells, hydrates the skin, lubricates joints, and facilitates digestion, absorption, and excretion. Thirst is the mechanism that tells people they need water.

A lack of water in the body causes dehydration, or a deficiency of water in the body's cells and fluids. On the other hand, excess water can cause water intoxication, a condition in which there is too much water and not enough electrolytes in the body and which causes a shift in the amount of water in the cells. A rapid weight loss might be a sign of dehydration, whereas a rapid weight gain could indicate water intoxication. Both dehydration and water intoxication can be life threatening.

Water Requirements

According to U.S. dietary surveys, the daily Adequate Intake (AI) for water is 3.7 liters for men and 2.7 liters for women. These amounts account for water from all sources: food, beverages, and drinking water (*Exhibit 5.15*). Individual fluid needs vary according to physical-activity levels and prolonged exposure to high temperatures. More water is necessary for athletes during training and events because they need to reduce body temperature and make up fluid lost through sweating. Most people get enough water by letting thirst be their guide.

Exhibit 5.15

Restaurant and foodservice professionals should make liquids available at each meal. Drinking water can be included at the table with each individual place setting. Contrary to popular belief, beverages with caffeine are considered hydrating. Studies show that people who drink moderate amounts of coffee and tea do not get dehydrated. Beverages that contain alcohol, however, may actually increase a person's daily need for fluids because alcohol is dehydrating, meaning that it reduces the water available to the body by chemically causing fluid excretion. Additionally, alcohol contains calories but no other nutrients.

Hard and Soft Water

Hard water is water that contains large amounts of minerals such as calcium, magnesium, and sulfur. Soft water is water that contains minerals in smaller amounts. The distinction is mostly related to the interaction of soap with these minerals. Softened water is hard water that has had these minerals removed through a chemical process in a purification facility or water softener; it usually contains extra sodium or other minerals instead of the ones that make the water hard.

SUMMARY

1. **Distinguish between water-soluble and fat-soluble vitamins.**

    Water-soluble vitamins dissolve in water but not in fat, and generally they are not stored in the body. Fat-soluble vitamins are soluble in fat but not in water, and they can be stored in the body's fat tissue.

2. **Describe the functions, sources, and recommended intake amounts of vitamins and minerals in the body.**

    Both vitamins and minerals are essential to life, growth, and body maintenance. These substances either come from food or are produced within the body. The functions of specific vitamins and minerals are explained throughout the chapter.

    Food should be the source of our nutrients. The fat-soluble vitamins have both plant and animal sources. For example, vitamin A comes from dairy products and the precursor beta-carotene comes from orange vegetables like squash and carrots. Many of the B vitamins, such as thiamin, riboflavin, and niacin, are found in enriched and whole-grain products. Vitamin B_{12} is found only in animal products. Calcium is found in good amounts in milk. Potassium is found in both fruits and vegetables, with bananas and potatoes being good sources. For a full list, refer back to *Exhibits 5.4* and *5.7.*

    The UL is the DRI value that will indicate if a person needs to reduce the amount of vitamins and minerals they are consuming. Consuming too many vitamins and minerals can be harmful to health. Whole food and fortified food can contribute to total vitamin and mineral consumption. Toxic amounts of each are usually the result of taking high-dose supplements every day.

3. **Identify causes and implications of nutritional deficiencies.**

    Nutritional deficiencies occur when people ingest less than the recommended amounts of vitamins, minerals, or other nutrients. Iron-deficiency anemia and osteoporosis are examples of deficiencies of iron and calcium, respectively. Nutrient deficiencies can lead to stunted growth, weight loss, a weakened immune system, and disease.

4. **Identify the recommended sodium intake and the implications of high-sodium diets.**

   The recommendation for sodium for healthy adults is twenty-three hundred milligrams per day. People who are over 51 years of age, of African-American descent, or affected by hypertension, diabetes, or chronic kidney disease should consume no more than fifteen hundred milligrams daily. High sodium intake increases the risk of developing hypertension, or high blood pressure.

5. **Identify ways to retain the vitamin and mineral content of food when cooking.**

   The best way to retain vitamins and minerals is to cook food for a short time. Steaming, microwaving, and stir-frying are three good cooking methods to preserve vitamins and minerals. To prevent leaching of vitamins or minerals, do not soak vegetables. Instead, rinse them thoroughly and drain.

6. **Determine when it is appropriate to take supplemental vitamins and minerals.**

   There are some circumstances in which an individual should take a vitamin or mineral supplement to get sufficient levels of a nutrient. Examples of these circumstances are pregnancy and breast-feeding, iron-deficiency anemia, vitamin B_{12} deficiency, and osteoporosis.

7. **Describe the recommended intake amounts and functions of water in the body.**

   Water keeps the body hydrated, regulates body temperature, transports nutrients, makes up part of all cells, hydrates the skin, lubricates joints, and facilitates digestion, absorption, and excretion. It also participates in the body's chemical reactions.

   Dehydration causes a deficiency of water in the body's cells and fluids. Over-hydration causes water intoxication, a condition in which there is too much water and not enough electrolytes in the body and which causes a shift in the amount of water in the cells. Both dehydration and water intoxication can be life threatening.

   The AI for water each day is 3.7 liters for men and 2.7 liters for women. These figures include water from all sources: food, beverages, and drinking water. Individual fluid needs vary according to physical activity and exposure to high temperatures.

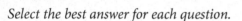

APPLICATION EXERCISES

Exercise 1

Select a meal from a restaurant and decide what portion sizes should be served for each item. Then navigate to the MyPlate Web site at *www.choosemyplate.gov*. Enter the items in the portions you have selected to determine how many vitamins and minerals a person will ingest with this particular meal. What percentages of the vitamin and mineral DRIs does the meal provide?

Exercise 2

Make a list of food items that you think could improve the number and amounts of vitamins and minerals on the menu at the restaurant you chose for Exercise 1. What would the new menu items cost the operation? What staff changes or other operational changes would need to be made in order to produce and serve the items? How do you think customers would react to your changes? How would these items sell?

REVIEW YOUR LEARNING

Select the best answer for each question.

1. **What deficiency disease occurs in children who lack vitamin D?**
    A. Xerophthalmia
    B. Osteoporosis
    C. Rickets
    D. Scurvy

2. **According to the Dietary Guidelines for Americans 2010, the maximum daily recommended sodium intake for a healthy adult is**
    A. 1,000 milligrams.
    B. 1,300 milligrams.
    C. 2,000 milligrams.
    D. 2,300 milligrams.

3. **The primary function of the three B vitamins, thiamin, riboflavin, and niacin, is to**
    A. serve as a coenzyme in energy metabolism.
    B. act as an antioxidant to combat cell damage.
    C. synthesize DNA inside the body's cells.
    D. enable blood clotting in small wounds.

4. **The primary function of vitamin C is to**
    A. synthesize protein.
    B. act as a coenzyme.
    C. act as an antioxidant.
    D. enable blood clotting.

5. **What substance can bind calcium and make it unavailable for absorption?**
    A. Purine
    B. Tocopherol
    C. Oxalate
    D. Manganese

6. **What is a good source of vitamin B_{12}?**
    A. Corn
    B. Rice
    C. Tofu
    D. Meat

7. Which mineral performs functions that include blood-pressure regulation, muscle contraction, and nerve transmission?
   A. Calcium
   B. Fluoride
   C. Manganese
   D. Phosphorus

8. The primary function of water in the body is to
   A. synthesize collagen.
   B. release free radicals.
   C. maintain body temperature.
   D. act as a coenzyme for energy metabolism.

9. What is one way to retain the vitamin and mineral content of food during cooking?
   A. Extend cooking time.
   B. Minimize cooking time.
   C. Avoid microwaving food.
   D. Soak vegetables before cooking.

10. What is the most common nutritional deficiency in the world?
    A. Scurvy
    B. Osteoporosis
    C. Iron-deficiency anemia
    D. Degeneration of the retina

PART TWO
Establishing Nutrition Programs

CHAPTERS

6 Market and Menu Assessment

INSIDE THIS CHAPTER

- Assessing Nutrition Trends and the Restaurant and Foodservice Market
- Analyzing the Target Market
- Conducting a Thorough Analysis
- Setting Nutrition Goals and Putting the Plan into Action
- Conducting a Nutrition Analysis
- Reviewing the Analysis

CHAPTER LEARNING OBJECTIVES

After completing this chapter, you should be able to:

- Identify and recognize the importance of nutrition trends.
- Analyze the target market for a nutrition program.
- Use competitive analysis to determine how the competition addresses the target market.
- Use SWOT analysis to determine how an operation might address a target market.
- Examine menu items using nutritional analysis of standardized recipes.

KEY TERMS

CASE STUDY

Erik, the manager of an independent family-style restaurant, recently read some interesting newspaper articles about health trends in the United States. He also noted that his customers are requesting greater flexibility in their menu options.

Erik worries that he will not be able to compete with neighboring restaurants. He is not sure what he should do or what areas he should focus on to protect and grow his business in light of these changes.

1. What business issues should Erik be concerned about?

2. Where should Erik go to get answers to his questions and concerns?

3. How will Erik know when he has made the right decisions for his establishment?

ASSESSING NUTRITION TRENDS AND THE RESTAURANT AND FOODSERVICE MARKET

To address the overall health of the U.S. population, this book has included statistics from the Dietary Guidelines for Americans 2010. These guidelines were summarized in chapter 3. In general, the U.S. population would benefit from access to healthier menu options. According to the Dietary Guidelines, the overall environment in the United States is **obesogenic**, or providing conditions that lead to obesity, and public-health authorities have indicated that Americans' lifestyles must change in order to improve their health.

Current dietary recommendations for the public include increasing nutrient-dense food and decreasing calories, sodium, added sugars, and solid fats for Americans aged two and older. Since the public has been made aware of these recommendations, Americans have been seeking alternative dietary choices to maintain or improve their health. The sodium reductions recommended in the Dietary Guidelines, which were discussed in chapter 5, are particularly difficult for the public to adhere to when eating out. Although guests can skip higher-fat items and eat lighter desserts, they have difficulty reducing sodium without the help of chefs taking a moderate approach to the use of salt.

There are other reasons to consider new choices when dining out. Greater numbers of people are being diagnosed with food allergies. These individuals want the freedom to eat at establishments outside their homes and the assurance that their food will be prepared to their specifications. For these reasons, it seems that the need for improved and expanded menu options will continue to grow for some time to come.

The Dietary Guidelines were written with the idea that the sectors of influence, such as the restaurant and foodservice industry, must assist people in their efforts to access healthy food when dining out. Additionally, some local, state, and federal legislation requires that some restaurants post calorie levels for standard menu items. These establishments would also be required to provide additional nutrition information on-site when their customers request it. Due to the large numbers of people who may be interested in following a healthy diet, restaurants and other foodservice operations may want to consider changing the nature of the plate to accommodate this trend.

It is a good idea for restaurants and foodservice operators to weigh the potential impact of adopting a nutrition program for their establishments. A **nutrition program** is defined in this book as a set of goals and actions with the objective of achieving a nutritional standard. One way that a nutrition program can be measured is with regard to sales and profit. The act of improving a menu by adding whole grains and increasing the amounts of fruit and vegetables, for example, can be considered a nutrition program if the effort increases customer satisfaction and adds to an establishment's ability to compete. A nutrition program for allergens ensures that a customer who requests an allergen-free menu item (*Exhibit 6.1*) receives it correctly each and every time, thus reducing liability issues and winning repeat customers. This chapter includes an example of how to evaluate the need for nutrition programs and how to use nutrition analyses to set nutrition program goals.

Exhibit 6.1

ANALYZING THE TARGET MARKET

When considering the development of a nutrition program, a manager must first assess the current situation and the environment in which the restaurant or foodservice operation exists. An effective manager will conduct an assessment of the establishment's target market, or the specific groups of customers that an operation seeks to serve.

No operation can be all things to all people. Managers use a variety of strategies to identify and segment a target market. Doing so allows managers to determine what group or groups of customers they would like to serve. Having this information in turn allows managers to target their approach when designing a nutrition program.

The process of selecting a target market can be thought of as a series of decisions that focus on markets with the most potential. To select a target market, establishment managers narrow the field of "potential customers" to a field of "customers to target." They can target customers by doing the following:

- **Identifying all potential customers in an area:** Those who may have an interest in a specific operation's products and services.

- **Identifying all potential customers who are financially able to purchase their products and service:** It is important to recognize that, in many cases, potential customers might be willing but unable to buy an establishment's products and service.

- **Identifying the recognizable characteristics of their targeted customers:** The specific target market or markets that managers plan to address.

For instance, an operation may be considering the introduction of vegan and vegetarian options as part of a nutrition program. First, it would want to ensure that there is an interest in vegan and vegetarian food in the overall market. Second, the establishment would need to consider how much of the total market can afford the items. This is especially important if the establishment is a fine-dining restaurant with high price points. Finally, the manager of the establishment would want to consider the characteristics of the customers likely to purchase vegan and vegetarian items, in order to tailor the marketing and menu approaches to draw in these customers.

In terms of profitability, a market segment would likely make a good target market if it meets several characteristics:

- Large enough
- Steady or growing in numbers, not declining
- Not filled with too many competitors
- Not blinded by loyalty to existing competitors
- Able to be attracted with the marketing budget available
- Profitable enough to pursue, given the costs the operation must incur and the revenues it can reasonably expect to obtain

In terms of an operation's capability, a customer segment will likely make a good target market for the establishment when it meets these criteria:

- The establishment has the capability to offer more value than competitors can offer (e.g., healthier food, better variety).
- Addressing this market fits well within the operation's image.
- The operation has the financial and human resources needed to enter and survive in the market segment.
- The operation has the marketing budget needed to reach the segment with its marketing message.

As part of identifying the recognizable characteristics of their targeted customers, managers use demographic and psychographic information. This information allows managers to begin grouping potential customers into categories, or market segments.

Demographics

Managers often segment their customers based on demographic variables. Demographic variables are sets of statistical data about customers in the target market. Examples of demographic variables are shown in *Exhibit 6.2.*

Age and income are two demographic areas that are important to nearly all restaurant and foodservice operations, not just those creating nutrition programs. Do most people eat the same thing as adults as they did when they

Exhibit 6.2

DEMOGRAPHIC FACTORS

Age	Education	Ethnicity	Geography	Home ownership
Household size	Income level	Nationality	Occupation	Race
Religion	Sexual orientation	Spending patterns	Stage in family life cycle	

Exhibit 6.3

TYPICAL AGE-LEVEL CATEGORIES

Category	Age
Child	0–9
Youth	10–19
Young adult	20–34
Early middle age	35–49
Late middle age	50–64
Retiree	65 and over

were five years old? Although some adults may still enjoy some of the same types of food they ate as a child, it is likely that their culinary preferences and needs have changed over the years, and they will continue to change with age.

Managers should be familiar with this concept and how it can affect their business. Restaurant and foodservice managers need to understand the various population trends regarding age as well as the needs of different age groups, such as those shown in *Exhibit 6.3*.

For example, the number of retirees in the United States is expected to rise dramatically over the next 20 years. In general, this trend is due to the aging of the baby boom generation coupled with advancements in healthcare and improvements in the overall quality of life.

As a group, retirees have unique needs. Since health concerns are important to this group, specialized menu selections such as low-caloric, low-sodium, or low-fat items are an increasingly popular draw. In addition, portion sizes are often made smaller to suit this category. Even though many retirees may have large amounts of discretionary income, many also need or choose to be careful with their money. As a result, many of them prefer establishments that offer low-cost, high-quality meals.

Psychographics

In addition to segmenting a market based on demographics, it can be useful to group potential customers by other traits. Psychographic characteristics of a customer relate to that customer's personality, values, attitudes, interests, or lifestyle. In many cases, the psychographics of a target market are more important than its demographics. Psychographics are important to managers because psychographics describe the human characteristics of restaurant and foodservice customers. Psychographics can be important in developing a nutrition program. For instance, if a restaurant seeks to emphasize locally grown, organic produce as part of its nutrition program, it will need to reach customers who value this type of food. Establishing such a restaurant in an area where this psychographic segment is small may not ensure success for the operation.

Exhibit 6.4

CONDUCTING A THOROUGH ANALYSIS

After a manager has determined his or her target market for the nutrition program, he or she should complete assessments of his or her establishment. A competitive assessment might involve analyzing current economic conditions, labor-market changes, and current culinary trends that may impact the establishment. It will also involve surveying the competitive landscape. A second assessment will examine the strengths and weaknesses of the operation, and it might determine current employee skill level, historical and current food sales, and cost information.

Competitive Analysis

One of the most important external factors facing an operation is that of the competition. A competitive analysis is a formal or informal process of assessing competitors in a specified geographic area or industry segment that examines the products and services offered by these establishments and their relationship to the target market. For example, managers may assess establishments in a specific geographic area as part of a competitive analysis (*Exhibit 6.4*).

One of the manager's primary objectives should be to foster and maintain a competitive advantage within the marketplace. Performing a competitive analysis in the early stages of creating a nutrition program can help to achieve this primary objective. Managers may examine the particular menu items that the competition offers, the prices of menu items, the services and service style of menu items, the look and feel of the competition (atmosphere and ambience), the demographics of the competition's customers, and much more. Managers should carefully determine what competitive factors they wish to analyze before beginning this process. With a well-focused survey of the competition, restaurant and foodservice professionals will better be able to position their own establishments within their target markets.

For example, to begin the planning process for a nutrition program centered on specialty diets, including vegetarian or vegan and gluten-free meals, managers should analyze some of the following items:

- How many restaurants are in the vicinity?
- How many fine-dining, casual, fast-casual, or quick-service restaurants in the area serve vegetarian, vegan, and gluten-free menu items?
- How many items appear on the competition's menus?
- What establishments other than restaurants offer vegetarian food and gluten-free items for purchase?
- What are the main ingredients that appear on the food menus?
- What are the prices for the food items on the menu?

Manager's Memo

Managers should always observe and evaluate their competition. As a manager, it is important to concentrate not only on your own establishment but also on the developments and changes of other area restaurants. Becoming familiar with other operations and their products and services will better assist you in the planning of your own establishment's programs. Competitive analysis is just one component in the assessment process.

- How are the menu items organized, and what items are emphasized on the menu?
- What suggestions does the server make during the order-taking and sales process (*Exhibit 6.5*)?

Exhibit 6.5

After gathering survey information about the competition, managers should organize the data. This helps managers to recognize trends in the information that may be beneficial when developing a nutrition program. Competitive analysis will allow a manager to know where best to target his or her resources by identifying areas where the market may be underserved or where the competition's pricing is too high.

SWOT Analysis

After examining the competitive landscape, managers should focus on assessing their own operation's position with the market. A SWOT analysis looks at an operation's strengths, weaknesses, opportunities, and threats (see *Exhibit 6.6*). A correctly completed SWOT analysis can be used to identify strengths and to capitalize on opportunities for the establishment, while improving on weaknesses and hopefully eliminating threats. While the focus of a SWOT analysis is primarily an internal one, managers should also be aware that some threats and opportunities may come from external sources.

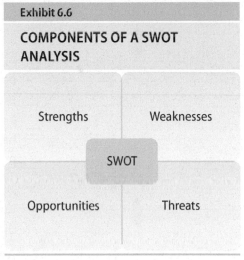

Exhibit 6.6

COMPONENTS OF A SWOT ANALYSIS

Strengths	Weaknesses
SWOT	
Opportunities	Threats

STRENGTHS

In this part of a SWOT analysis for a nutrition plan, an owner or manager indicates all of the strengths of their operation as related to the nutrition plan. These are areas in which the business already excels. Examples of strengths might include a diverse menu, well-trained staff, good relations with vendors, high food quality, and service that consistently exceeds customer expectations.

WEAKNESSES

This part of the SWOT analysis identifies any weaknesses in a business. This analysis is done so that the weaknesses can later be eliminated or turned into strengths. Some examples of weaknesses are a menu with a large number of high-calorie or high-fat entrées, few vegetarian entrées, limited vendor options, undifferentiated products, poor-quality products, or poorly trained staff.

In addition to weaknesses, there may be certain barriers to success—things outside of the restaurant establishment that might cause a weakness. For example, if the items to be produced are overly expensive because of limited vendor resources, the establishment will not easily be able to prepare a cost-effective product.

Some barriers can be overcome by proper planning and execution. For example, to overcome the expense example above, managers may seek to do more business with specialty vendors in an effort to receive some volume discounts.

OPPORTUNITIES

In this section of the SWOT analysis, the nutrition program developer should address realistic opportunities to either increase revenue or decrease costs. Examples of such opportunities include expanding menu options, revising high-calorie recipes without reducing quality, or tapping previously untapped target markets. One way to determine opportunities is to look at strengths with an eye for building on them and to look at weaknesses to see if eliminating them can create opportunities.

THREATS

Threats can come from a variety of sources. Identifying possible threats to a business is important to ensure that the threats are addressed or controlled before they can do much damage. Examples of possible threats that could be included in the SWOT analysis include an increased number of competitors, a price war with a competitor, rising costs of locally sourced products, bad press related to food allergy issues, or evolving demographics of potential customers.

To conduct a successful SWOT analysis, owners and managers must be realistic about the strengths and weaknesses of their operations as well as the opportunities and threats they face.

Clay's Country Kitchen: An Example of Planning in Action

The following is an example of a situational analysis in which a manager thinks through a data set to make his decision. The SWOT data that follow come from a small, family-style restaurant, Clay's Country Kitchen. The owner, Gabriel, and the manager, Elias, want to continue with successful existing menu items, but they want to capitalize on health trends to increase sales and profitability. The owner asks Elias to perform a SWOT analysis. The results of this analysis appear in *Exhibit 6.7*. Questions to ask about the results appear in *Exhibit 6.8*.

When undertaking a SWOT analysis, remember that one of the main challenges for a given establishment is maintaining objectivity. Managers like Elias must be careful not to project their desires when recording and analyzing the facts about their establishments.

THINK ABOUT IT . . .

What are some ways that you as a manager can avoid excessive subjectivity in the SWOT analysis? How might subjectivity jeopardize the success of the assessment process and the overall success of the program?

Exhibit 6.7

SWOT ANALYSIS: CLAY'S COUNTRY KITCHEN

Strengths
- More than 50 food offerings are on the menu.
- All menu items run below 25 percent when comparing food cost to selling price.
- Sixty-five percent of customers surveyed are satisfied with the menu selections.
- Kitchen labor turnover is at a five-year low.

Weaknesses
- Thirty-five percent of customers surveyed are not satisfied with the menu selections.
- Several menu item descriptions do not reflect the standardized recipe used in the kitchen.
- Menu has not been revised in the past five years.
- Majority of the items on the menu are prepared using the fryer and the convection oven.

Opportunities
- Current food distributor has just introduced a new line of fresh and organic food products.
- Production and availability of gluten-free and vegan products are up.
- A local culinary school recently added a course in nutritional cooking to the curriculum, meaning an increased potential for hiring employees who understand the importance of applying nutrition principles.
- Construction of a new 30-family condominium complex has begun across the street.
- A national POS (point-of-sale) system manufacturer has introduced new software that can assist with nutrition information for food items.

Threats
- A new competitor that has similar pricing structure and menu offerings has opened nearby.
- A new gourmet supermarket offering fresh and organic produce and food products, as well as an entire department devoted to prepared and catered foods, has opened down the street.
- The city's food sales tax is scheduled to increase in six months.

Exhibit 6.8

IMPORTANT SWOT ANALYSIS QUESTIONS

	Strengths	Weaknesses
Opportunities	How do I use these strengths to take advantage of these opportunities?	How do I overcome the weaknesses that prevent me from taking advantage of these opportunities?
Threats	How do I use my strengths to reduce the likelihood and impact of these threats?	How do I overcome the weaknesses that will make these threats reality?

ANALYZING STRENGTHS

The first strength identified by the manager of Clay's Country Kitchen is that the restaurant currently has 50 menu offerings. This gives the operation both the ability to adjust and improve menu items and the ability to build flexibility into the menu. This information might be used to justify adding gluten-free side dishes or offering appropriate substitutions to current menu items. Gluten-free options appeal to customers with celiac disease, who avoid gluten in the diet.

The expanded menu might also appeal to a broader audience and might accommodate a new section for vegetarians. The facility already has walk-in coolers and storage areas large enough to accommodate large quantities of ingredients, so space is not an issue.

However, purchasing special ingredients like gluten-free products might affect Clay's second strength: food cost to sales price. The new gluten-free items might have to be priced higher since food costs are currently at 25 percent when compared to selling price.

Elias realizes that his third strength is a good customer base. He also notes that, according to the customer survey data, the business has grown through word of mouth. The fact that the restaurant has adequate sales and is profitable gives Elias the confidence to make some menu changes. He thinks he can monitor customer satisfaction with new menu items. He has the survey history of what customers have demanded in the past and what changes they have responded to both positively and negatively.

Exhibit 6.9

Finally, the data show that the restaurant enjoys a low turnover rate. The stable workforce and employees' positive morale make changing menus, including an associated retraining, potentially easier. This satisfied workforce can be considered a strength (*Exhibit 6.9*).

ANALYZING WEAKNESSES

The data revealed some weaknesses that the manager should consider along with any menu change. The first identified weakness came from a group of comment cards. Thirty-five percent of the customers were not happy with the menu offerings. Many of them indicated that they were disappointed with the lack of healthy menu options for children. In addition, guests noted that side dishes supported vegetarian selections, yet no entrées were designed to accommodate a vegetarian or vegan diet.

A second weakness is the need for retraining a complacent staff on standardized recipes, which are recipes that give a known quality and quantity at a known cost. Standardized recipes are sets of instructions to produce and serve a food or beverage item that will help ensure that quality and quantity standards will be consistently met. The manager noticed that menu items did not match the standardized recipe descriptions.

The restaurant achieved lower food costs by receiving vendor discounts tied to the volume and predictability of Clay's order over the past five years—a period when there were no menu changes. New menu items may require Clay's to engage with different vendors, which may result in higher per-unit pricing for smaller purchases.

The last weakness is that a healthier menu might require equipment that the kitchen does not currently have. Moving to a healthier menu will likely require more prep space and alternative cooking equipment. Up-front costs will probably increase, but the benefits should accrue in the long term.

ANALYZING OPPORTUNITIES

At this point Elias, the manager of Clay's Country Kitchen, reviews his data for opportunities. He realizes that he must act quickly because his current supplier is offering an incentive to those who order its new fresh and organic line of food. The manager realizes that if he agrees to purchase these new food items now, he can get them at a reduced price. This will help with food costs incurred by the plan to increase fruit and vegetables on the menu, as Elias will not need to change or add a new food distributor; neither will he need to add to the number of food deliveries per week.

A headline in a trade magazine reinforces the manager's view that both whole grains and gluten-free products are a growing part of the consumer-products industry. For this and other reasons, his idea of using more whole grains and adopting gluten-free menu items seems sound.

The culinary school data show an unexpected opportunity. It occurs to the manager that the new curriculum will provide a source for potential new employees who have the needed skills to assist in the development of the new nutrition program for Clay's.

Capturing more market share is possible, even likely, for Clay's because of the customer base from the new condominium complex. The manager realizes he should not take this for granted.

As he continues reviewing the opportunities, Elias reasons that the new POS system will allow the restaurant to post nutrition information on the menu and thus help Clay's maintain a competitive advantage over restaurants that have less-desirable menu items.

Exhibit 6.10

ANALYZING THREATS

Competition is a big factor in determining what menu changes Clay's Country Kitchen should make. Elias identified a nearby restaurant that offers a menu similar to that of his establishment: comfort food, fried food, and a children's menu containing hot dogs, macaroni and cheese, and French fries. The gourmet supermarket is also a serious competitor because that business also handles catering, as well as meals to go (*Exhibit 6.10*). Knowing this information underscores the potential for Clay's to develop a catering and prepared-food line.

The changes to food offerings will allow Clay's to adjust their selling prices upward. Then the restaurant will not have to make further price adjustments down the road due to a planned city sales tax increase.

It is important to remember that sometimes factors derived from data can be perceived as both an opportunity *and* a threat. In addition, threats can become opportunities if properly handled. Unfortunately, the reverse can also happen.

As shown earlier in *Exhibit 6.8*, the next steps for the manager would be to take a look at the strengths and determine how he can use them to capitalize on the opportunities identified, to eliminate the weaknesses, and to reduce the threats. The manager may also use the information gained from the SWOT analysis to review his target market and to adjust it as necessary.

SETTING NUTRITION GOALS AND PUTTING THE PLAN INTO ACTION

Now that the manager of Clay's Country Kitchen has conducted a SWOT analysis and has reviewed the data it generated, he can move on to define his goals and plans for a nutrition program.

Setting Organizational Goals

As his next step, Elias weighs the cost and benefit considerations of implementing his plan for a nutrition program. The costs of making the menu changes he envisions are the purchase and installation of a new grill, the addition of a small steamer for vegetables, the purchase of value-added products and ingredients, and the training or retraining of employees to use equipment and to adapt or change menu items. He is unsure about the number of new customers that will be attracted by the healthier options and gluten-free menu items, but he thinks that traffic from the new housing development may offset the costs if Clay's can bring in more families during slow periods.

Given all of the considerations of the SWOT, the manager has decided to implement a nutrition program and to revise and update the menu. The goals for the program are to improve nutritional aspects of the entire menu so that low-calorie, low-sodium options comprise at least 25 percent of the menu, to raise customer satisfaction to 93 percent, to eliminate incidents of food allergies, and to increase overall sales for the establishment by 10 percent over three months.

Exhibit 6.11

The revisions and updates to the menu will include the following:

- A vegan entrée section
- Additional gluten-free items
- Additional whole-grain breads and buns (*Exhibit 6.11*)
- More fresh fruit and vegetable ingredients
- Healthful improvements to the children's menu section
- Nutrition information printed on the menu

Elias will also need to develop and document a plan and a time frame in which to meet all of these goals.

Putting the Plan into Action

Next, Elias will begin to implement his plan. His first step will be to conduct a nutrition analysis of his existing recipes. A **nutrition analysis** is the process of determining the nutritional content or composition of a food. Based on his findings, Elias will have some decisions to make about changes to his menu. Some items may need to be replaced, while others may need to be slightly modified. The rest of this chapter is devoted to this analysis.

Elias will also need to make other changes to fully implement his nutrition plan. These include the topics listed below, which will be covered in later chapters:

- Review and modify the types of food offered (chapter 7).
- Review and modify cooking and preparation methods (chapter 8).
- Implement a food-allergy program (chapter 9).
- Train staff on the new recipes, preparation methods, and processes (chapter 10).
- Implement a marketing program to announce his new menu (chapter 11).
- Evaluate and modify, as needed, his nutrition plan (chapter 11).

CONDUCTING A NUTRITION ANALYSIS

The manager of Clay's Country Kitchen is not alone in conducting a nutrition analysis of his menu items. Various local, state, and federal laws require some operations to provide nutrition information to their customers. Chapter 12 provides more details regarding this area.

Even when not legally required, some operations may still choose to include nutrition information for their customers. Managers may do so due to customer demand or because they feel that including this information keeps their operation competitive.

Restaurant or foodservice operations that are required by law to label standard menu items will want to conduct a reliable nutrition analysis of their recipes in order to learn the nutrient values of the food they serve. A restaurant or foodservice operation should receive at least the following information from a nutrition analysis of their menu items:

- Total number of calories
- Calories from fat
- Total carbohydrates
- Sugars
- Protein
- Total fat (including saturated fat, trans-fatty acids, cholesterol)

- Sodium
- Dietary fiber
- Vitamins
- Minerals

Types of Analysis

There are two basic ways to determine the nutrient composition of food: laboratory analysis or calculation. Based on its business model, each restaurant or foodservice operation decides which method best meets its needs. Regardless of the method chosen, the nutrition analysis should be as accurate as possible because the restaurant is legally responsible for the quality of the information.

LABORATORY ANALYSIS

A laboratory analysis is done on carefully prepared samples of the standardized recipe or typical food that would be served to the customer. The samples are prepared using the standardized recipe, and then they are properly packaged following the directions given by each laboratory and sent directly to the company doing the analysis. The laboratory performs the nutrient analysis by incinerating the sample of food and using chemical extraction and laboratory equipment to reveal the nutrient composition and content. This method provides accurate results if the samples are prepared correctly and sent immediately to the laboratory for testing. It is usually the more expensive of the two methods presented here.

ANALYSIS BY CALCULATION

Nutrition analysis by calculation is based on information gathered from previous laboratory analyses of many different samples of food. These analyses are stored in software databases. The nutrient values in the databases are used to approximate the nutrient content or composition of the food items that will be used in an operation's recipes. When using the calculation method, the recipes for the menu items are entered into the calculation software. For calculations to be accurate, each menu item must have a standardized recipe. This includes food items such as sauces, toppings, glazes, and garnishes. These items will be analyzed in the correct proportions along with the food they enhance.

The software can then generate the nutrition analysis for the menu item. A restaurant or foodservice operation can purchase a software program that provides access to a nutrient database and then complete its own nutrition analysis. Alternatively, the operation may choose to hire a consultant who will do these calculations for them. Nutrient databases usually have the U.S. Department of Agriculture's National Nutrient Database for Standard Reference as a basis, plus many other sources of nutrient information from food companies and food producers. The goal is to match the food to its source, or to a source that is very close in nutrient composition, and utilize that data in the calculations.

There may not be a known nutrient composition for every food item that an operation may use. This is because some food items have not been analyzed in the laboratory. Experienced professionals try every avenue to get the most reliable data for an operation. However, it is not always possible to find every value needed, and some substitutions will be made to arrive at reasonable nutrient values.

Although the need for obtaining nutrient values may seem to be the most important part of nutrition labeling, the planning goes far beyond the actual nutrition analysis. Since an operation will need to be responsible for the information it is using to label its food, it must also guarantee that the food is the same each and every time it is served, within reason. This makes the standardized recipe a very important part of this process.

The Importance of Standardized Recipes for Nutrition Analysis

Almost every operation that has survived a competitive market uses recipes to ensure that their signature dishes can be repeated day in and day out for their customers. Customers are known to return for their favorite dishes and expect to receive the same food item they savored previously. A recipe is defined as a written log or record of the ingredients and methods used to prepare a given dish. Many restaurants and foodservice operations have recipes; however, they are not always standardized. In order to achieve an accurate nutrition analysis, a restaurant or foodservice operation should adopt the use of

RESTAURANT TECHNOLOGY

A restaurant or foodservice operation may want to invest in a software program that will allow them to enter their recipes and complete the nutrition analysis on their own. Most of these programs are Web-based and do not need to be updated because the information is constantly revised when new data are available. Many restaurants or foodservice operations will want to hire a registered dietitian (RD) as a consultant to help them with their nutrition analysis or other nutrition services.

standardized recipes. Standardized recipes are the key to providing the same portioning and ingredients each and every time the recipe is made to ensure that the nutrients contained therein always occur in the same amounts.

Standardized procedures and recipes lead to other benefits, such as decreasing waste and reducing food costs. A standardized recipe is adapted to a professional kitchen and is specific to the ingredients, equipment, and personnel in an operation. It is important for managers to note, however, that training staff to follow standardized recipes is just as important as establishing the recipes in the first place. If recipes are not followed, there is no guarantee that the food the waitstaff is serving matches the nutrient analysis. Each restaurant is responsible for adhering to its stated calorie labeling as well as to the balance of the nutritional information made available to the public. Restaurants and foodservice operations will have a better experience if they plan for this standardized approach.

The restaurant and foodservice industry has used standardized recipes for a long time. Some classic dishes, such as chicken tetrazzini (shown in *Exhibit 6.12*), can be adjusted to meet dietary recommendations. The exhibit shows both an example of a standardized recipe and the accompanying nutritional analysis.

As shown in the example, a standardized recipe has the following characteristics:

- Usual or identifiable name
- Set portion size
- Set yield or the amount produced
- Detailed ingredient listing with weight or volume of each ingredient
- List of equipment needed to prepare the recipe
- Set method of preparation or technique
- Set temperature and amount of preparation and cooking time

Consistent portion sizes, yields, and ingredients ensure that the nutrient analysis is a true reflection of the food served. Yield is used to calculate the nutrients per portion. In addition, recipes should include an internal temperature the food should reach to ensure food safety as well as a holding temperature for items that will be held until service.

In an effective operation, dishes are made to order on the line using standard preparation and cooking techniques. The process is repeated each time an item is prepared, but the technique is altered slightly with each chef or cook. In this case, the restaurant or foodservice operation may need to observe the preparation and measure the amount of each ingredient used in the process to develop a standardized recipe. This will be an important step in ensuring reliable nutrition analysis and protecting the restaurant if its nutrition facts are questioned.

Exhibit 6.12

SAMPLE STANDARDIZED RECIPE: CHICKEN (TURKEY) TETRAZZINI

UTENSILS NEEDED: Stock pot, cutting board, French knife, wire whip, mixing bowl, gallon/quart/cup measures, measuring spoons, plastic gloves, clean foodservice cloths, 2 steam table pans (12" × 20" × 2.5")

YIELD: 48 servings
OVEN TEMP: 350°F (176.6°C)
BAKING TIME: 30 minutes
SERVING SIZE: 1/24 pan
SERVING TOOL: Spatula/spoon

Ingredients	Weight/ volume	Procedure
Spaghetti, whole grain	6 lb	1. Cook spaghetti in salted water. Rinse and drain. *Do not overcook.*
Margarine, soft tub	1 lb	2. Cook onions and celery in margarine until transparent.
Celery, cut fine	2 qt	3. Make roux by adding flour, salt, and pepper. Cook 5 minutes.
Onions, cut fine	2 qt	4. Add chicken (turkey) stock and cook until thick, stirring as necessary.
Flour, bread flour	1 lb	5. Add cubed chicken (turkey) and mushrooms; mix.
Salt	1 tsp	6. Add spaghetti; mix well.
Pepper, black	1 tsp	7. Add green pepper just before panning.
Chicken (turkey) stock	2 gal 2 c	8. Divide evenly into two 12" × 20" × 2.5" pans.
Chicken (turkey), cooked and cubed	12 lb 8 oz	9. Mix topping. Top each pan with 1 qt topping.
		10. Bake at 350°F (176.6°C) for 30 minutes. Internal temperature should
Mushrooms, fresh/chopped	2 c	reach 165°F (73.9°C) for 15 seconds.
Green pepper, chopped	3 c	11. Serving: Divide into servings by cutting pan contents 6 (length) × 4 (width).
Topping		
Bread crumbs, fine	1 qt	*Example*:
Sharp cheddar cheese, grated	1 qt	Holding Temperature: Hold prepared product at 135°F (60°C) until service.

SPECIAL INSTRUCTIONS:

Do not overcook spaghetti. See recipe for chicken stock if none is available.

Nutrition Analysis: Chicken (Turkey) Tetrazzini

1 Portion equals 1/24 of hotel pan 12" × 20" × 2.5"

Total calories	560.0
Calories from fat	145.0
Total fat (g)	16.0
Saturated fat (g)	5.0
Trans fat (g)	0
Cholesterol (mg)	88.0
Sodium (mg)	570.0
Total carbohydrates (g)	60.0
Sugars (g)	5.0
Dietary fiber (g)	6.0
Protein (g)	45.0

Vitamins and minerals (select grouping from those analyzed)

Vitamin A (RAE)	130.0
Vitamin C (mg)	10.0
Iron (mg)	4.0
Calcium (mg)	125.0

Food items that are added during preparation or plating must also be included in the nutrition analysis, as is the case with the topping in the chicken tetrazzini recipe. An item such as a marinade, topping, or filling may not seem important, but it often increases calories, sodium, etc. These items also need to be analyzed for their nutrient contributions. In the case of marinades, a determination is made regarding what part of the marinade is still left on the food. In the case of a sauce that is added to finish a dish, the sauce recipe will need to be analyzed and the portioning of the sauce determined to get a better idea of how many calories are actually in the item.

Standardizing recipes and ensuring that the back-of-the-house staff follows them are critical. Subsequent chapters discuss how to ensure that staff members adhere to the consistent practices with regard to cooking and preparation. Additional information and details about standardizing recipes can be found in ManageFirst *Principles of Food and Beverage Management.*

REVIEWING THE ANALYSIS

Regardless of the method used to determine the nutrition analysis, managers need to review the data (*Exhibit 6.13*). Reviewing the data involves making sure that all ingredients were included, the correct food items were selected to make the analysis, and the yield and portion sizes were correct. This involves cross-checking the input data with the results.

Restaurant and foodservice managers who hire a consultant should plan to review nutritional-analysis results and ask questions. Those who hire a laboratory should ensure that someone will be available after the work has been done to review the results and to provide answers to managers' questions.

Reviewing the Analysis: Clay's Country Kitchen

To continue the scenario at Clay's Country Kitchen, Elias, the manager, begins to look at the results from the nutrition analysis he has received from his consultant. He realizes right away that some of the items on the current menu have high amounts of calories, total fat, saturated fats, cholesterol, and sodium. He expected that would be the case for many items. At the same time, he was surprised to see that some entrées and side dishes were not high in calories. However, sodium levels on most items exceeded the recommendations from the consultant. Reducing sodium levels will be a challenge.

In his next steps, Elias will need to determine what menu items will be revised or replaced by comparing the nutritional analyses against the goals of his nutrition plan. Then he will also need to develop standardized recipes for the new items. Elias also will need to examine the ingredients and preparation processes for items he plans to keep but that need to be slightly revised. The next chapters will examine food choices and preparation processes in detail.

Exhibit 6.13

SUMMARY

1. **Identify and recognize the importance of nutrition trends.**

   Nutrition trends can impact customer preference. Managers can gauge the importance of health trends to their businesses by paying attention to and understanding the importance of the following: customer requests, demographics, news stories on health and fitness, information from trade organizations, government reports and regulations, and experts' market predictions.

2. **Analyze the target market for a nutrition program.**

   An operation cannot be all things to all people, so managers will need to determine their target market. They do so by narrowing down the larger population by asking who is interested in the product, who can afford the product, and what are the characteristics of people in that market. Managers use demographic and psychographic data to classify customers in their target market.

3. **Use competitive analysis to determine how the competition addresses the target market.**

   After managers determine their target market, they should evaluate how the needs of that market are being met by the competition. Managers will want to compare menu offerings, price points, and other data to understand how their competition addresses the target market. Doing so will allow managers to identify underserved portions of the market.

4. **Use SWOT analysis to determine how an operation might address a target market.**

   A SWOT analysis is one way to review potential risks and rewards when implementing a nutrition program. In examining how an operation relates to a target market, a SWOT analysis can be used to identify and capitalize on strengths and opportunities while improving weaknesses and eliminating threats.

5. **Examine menu items using nutritional analysis of standardized recipes.**

   Managers seeking to implement nutrition programs may undertake a nutrition analysis of their menu items. Nutrition analyses are now part of legal compliance for some operations.

   Nutrition values for specific food items can be determined via two types of nutrient analysis: laboratory analysis and calculation. Restaurant and foodservice managers can accomplish nutrition analysis either in-house or by hiring a laboratory or consultant. Regardless of the method employed, managers must enforce the use of standardized recipes to ensure that what the customers receive is the same as what was analyzed.

APPLICATION EXERCISES

Exercise 1

Perform a SWOT analysis on the menu from the restaurant or foodservice operation where you work, or choose another establishment you are familiar with. Investigate the following possibilities:

- Children's menu
- Vegetarian or vegan choices
- Gluten-free menu items or options

Organize your data into strengths, weakness, opportunities, and threats so that you can use this information for the next exercise.

Exercise 2

Using the data you collected in Exercise 1, design an improved menu section for one of the following, and use the data to explain your choices:

- Children's menu
- Vegetarian or vegan choices
- Gluten-free menu items or options

REVIEW YOUR LEARNING

Select the best answer for each question.

1. **SWOT stands for strengths, weaknesses, opportunities, and**
   A. target markets.
   B. triumphs.
   C. threats.
   D. triage.

2. **People with celiac disease must avoid**
   A. glucagon.
   B. avidin.
   C. biotin.
   D. gluten.

3. **What is the name of the group or population on which a restaurant or foodservice operation chooses to focus?**
   A. Engineered market
   B. Balanced market
   C. Target market
   D. Local market

4. **Why might the same ideas derived from a data set appear under both opportunities and threats in a SWOT analysis?**
   A. Opportunities do not last long.
   B. It is important for the data to be balanced.
   C. Threats tend to continue once you identify them.
   D. Threats can turn into opportunities, and vice versa.

5. **The best reason for a restaurant or foodservice operation to conduct a competitive analysis is to**
   A. ensure that food costs go down.
   B. put competitors out of business.
   C. gain access to insurance carriers and discounts.
   D. assess the operation relative to its competitors.

6. **Which is an example of a psychographic variable?**
   A. Age
   B. Occupation
   C. Lifestyle
   D. Nationality

7. **According to the Dietary Guidelines for Americans 2010, Americans should reduce the amount of _____ in their diets.**
   A. green vegetables
   B. saltwater fish
   C. dietary fiber
   D. added sugar

8. **What is a nutrition program?**
   A. An analysis of strengths, weaknesses, threats, and opportunities
   B. A set of goals and actions to achieve a nutritional standard
   C. An analysis of the nutrient contents within a given dish
   D. A set of recipes for a given menu

9. **What action is critical in analyzing the target market for a restaurant?**
   A. Focusing on consumers outside the market
   B. Determining which consumers cook at home
   C. Ignoring characteristics of the target market
   D. Identifying customers who can pay for services

10. **Calorie counts are more accurate when food is prepared using a standardized recipe because these recipes are**
    A. tastier than other types of recipes.
    B. derived from secret family recipes.
    C. made by the same person each time.
    D. formulated to include portion size and yield.

FIELD PROJECT

Recipe Analysis

Gather two recipes from your home or a professional kitchen and analyze them using recipe analysis software. There are many free online versions and you can find them by querying "free recipe analysis software" in the search engine of your choice. Follow the directions for the software, inputting the name and quantity, weight, or volume of each ingredient.

1. How easy are the free online software programs to use?

2. For each recipe, record the following:
   a. Total calories
   b. Calories from fat
   c. Total fat
   d. Saturated fats
   e. Trans fats
   f. Cholesterol
   g. Sodium
   h. Total carbohydrates
   i. Sugars
   j. Dietary fiber
   k. Protein
   l. Vitamins and minerals

3. Compare the sodium level of one portion of the recipe to the Dietary Guidelines for Americans 2010 given in chapter 3. How different are they?

4. Compare the saturated fat and cholesterol levels to the Dietary Guidelines. What do you notice?

7

Marketable Food: Growing, Handling, Processing, and Packaging

INSIDE THIS CHAPTER

- Consumer Interest in Food Production
- Food-Production Methods
- Harvesting and Transporting Food
- Processing and Packaging Food
- Receiving and Storing Food

CHAPTER LEARNING OBJECTIVES

After completing this chapter, you should be able to:

- Distinguish among organic, certified organic, and conventional production of food.

- Define *genetically modified organism* and *agricultural biotechnology*.

- Describe the steps involved in harvesting and transporting food.

- Explain food additives, food irradiation, freeze-drying, and *sous vide*.

- Identify the characteristics of enriched food and fortified food, and explain their roles in nutrition.

- Define *processed food* and *processed packaged food*, and describe the nutritional differences among the various types of processed food.

KEY TERMS

agricultural biotechnology, p. 151

certified organic, p. 149

chemical loss, p. 152

conventional food, p. 148

crossbreeding, p. 150

enrichment, p. 157

food additive, p. 154

food irradiation, p. 156

fortification, p. 157

freeze-drying, p. 156

genetically modified organism, p. 150

herbicide, p. 149

hybrid plant, p. 150

organic food, p. 149

packaged processed food, p. 154

pesticide, p. 149

physical loss, p. 152

processed food, p. 153

recombinant DNA technology, p. 150

selective breeding, p. 150

sous vide, p. 156

sustainability, p. 148

transgenic organism, p. 150

CASE STUDY

Two chefs are discussing their efforts to put fresh, local food and ingredients on their menus. Chef Teri works in a small, locally owned restaurant in the southern United States with a flexible menu and a number of devoted customers who pay higher prices for the opportunity to enjoy seasonal and fresh food. The region's growing season is long, and many small, local farms produce organic food that is available for much of the year.

Chef Barb works for a large chain operation in a midwestern city. The chain has fixed menus and high-volume purchasing. This chef has more limitations on what she can buy and where she can get fresh food. The growing season is short in this area, and transporting some food is inevitable.

Both chefs plan to use their buying power to influence food purchases and how they are handled on delivery. Their goal is to bring their customers nutritious food at affordable prices.

1. What is the main difference between the types of food each of these chefs might purchase?

2. What can each chef do to ensure that she is using the best possible food sources?

3. In what ways are the nutrients in food preserved or lost during local and long-distance transit?

CONSUMER INTEREST IN FOOD PRODUCTION

Studies by the restaurant industry over the past ten years have indicated that consumers are interested in issues such as sustainability, the use of organic food, and the procurement of food from local sources. Many customers want to know where and how their food was grown and how far it has traveled to its destination. Chefs are interested in these issues as well. In a recent survey conducted by the National Restaurant Association, more than sixteen hundred chefs ranked local produce as the top food trend.

Restaurant and foodservice professionals should be aware of their clienteles' interests, and they should educate themselves about the types of products available to meet those interests. In addition, managers should be prepared to answer questions about the food they purchase for their operations.

The challenge for restaurants and foodservice operations is to purchase the highest-quality products from sources that provide a variety of choices at fair prices. This chapter defines certain farm practices and traces the movement of food from growth to storage at the restaurant or foodservice operation (see *Exhibit 7.1*). It also includes information about processed food and additives.

FOOD-PRODUCTION METHODS

Each day farmers and ranchers create new and interesting approaches to growing food with the goal of achieving sustainability. The Environmental Protection Agency (EPA) defines sustainability as practices that meet current resource needs without compromising the ability to meet future needs. Meeting this goal requires innovative approaches to growing quality products and to increasing the food supply without damaging the environment and consuming valuable resources.

There are many opinions about how the agricultural industry should grow food and care for farm animals. Each method is dynamic and ever-changing as new research and development occurs. It is important to remember that food is grown for profit. Supporting farmers and businesses that produce food is integral to sustainability because without financial success there is little incentive to produce food. As farming practices continue to change and grow in new directions, consumers are likely to judge each method with respect not only to nutrition and wholesomeness but also to environmental impact. The overall success of sustainability relies on the success and satisfaction of farmers and the farm community.

Conventional Farming

Many restaurant and foodservice operators rely on conventional food products, which are defined as food products grown using approved agricultural methods. In the United States, such methods are studied and regulated by the U.S.

Exhibit 7.1

STAGES OF FOOD'S JOURNEY

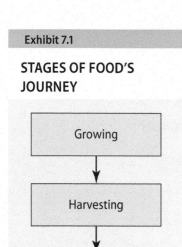

- Growing
- Harvesting
- Transporting
- Processing
- Receiving
- Storing
- Preparing
- Cooking

Exhibit 7.2

Some customers are concerned about these issues when purchasing food or eating out.

Department of Agriculture (USDA). The approved methods allow for the use of certain fertilizers, pesticides (chemicals formulated to kill insects), herbicides (chemicals formulated to kill weeds), hormones, and medicines that are deemed safe. Although each farm is different, most modern farms have provided increased agricultural production by use of pesticides and herbicides. The majority of the food sold by supermarkets and foodservice vendors comes from conventional producers. (See *Exhibit 7.2*.)

Organic Farming

Organic food is defined as food that has been produced without synthetic fertilizers, sewage sludge, irradiation, and genetic engineering. According to the USDA, *organic* is a labeling term indicating that the food or other agricultural product has been produced through approved methods that integrate cultural, biological, and mechanical practices that foster cycling of resources, promote ecological balance, and conserve biodiversity.[1] Animals raised organically are given organic feed and access to the outdoors (*Exhibit 7.3*). In addition, they are not given any hormones or antibiotics.

Many farmers produce food organically but do not apply for USDA certification and therefore do not use the *certified organic* label. Farmers who want their food to be labeled certified organic must submit a plan for their operation. The plan specifies practices and substances used in production, methods of isolating organic from non-organic substances, record-keeping methods, and a commitment to allowing inspections. In addition, farmers pay fees to support

[1] *USDA National Organic Program/Background Information. USDA 2002. Retrieved September 11, 2011.* www.ams.usda.gov/nop.

Exhibit 7.3

THINK ABOUT IT . . .

Why might some farmers produce organic food yet not apply for the USDA certification? What advantages and disadvantages might come with seeking certification?

Exhibit 7.4

USDA CERTIFIED ORGANIC LABEL

KEEPING IT SAFE

Restaurant and foodservice professionals who wish to address sustainability may choose to increase their use of food from organic farms or from local sources. This can be a challenge for some operations due to the need to ensure that food is purchased from reputable suppliers. From a manager's point of view, food safety is a primary concern when making food purchases.

Managers can ask to inspect a new supplier's operation, to check its business references, and to review its hazard analysis and critical control points (HACCP) plan. In addition, a manager might contact state and local authorities to ensure that a prospective supplier meets state and local safety requirements. It is generally best to use suppliers that meet these requirements and comply with good manufacturing practices (GMP) or good agricultural practices (GAP) or both.

this process. If a farm sells less than $5,000 worth of organic products per year, it is exempt from certification and can label its products organic, but it cannot use the organic seal (see *Exhibit 7.4*).

A common misconception about organic food products is that they contain more nutrients than conventionally grown food does. Although some studies have shown that organic food has a higher level of nutrients, other longitudinal studies contradict this result. Another myth is that organic food products are produced by small operations and conventional food products are made by large producers. Actually, both large and small producers grow organic and conventional food products, and the finished food products are quite similar nutritionally.

Genetically Modified Food

Understanding genetically modified food and the genetic engineering of plants requires basic knowledge of how traditional plants and animals are bred. In traditional **crossbreeding**, different varieties of plants or animals exhibiting favorable characteristics are bred to produce offspring with the best qualities of each variety. **Hybrid plants** are a common example of crossbreeding. This is a long and arduous process, as half the genes come from one plant and half the genes come from the other. Farmers may want to improve only one or two characteristics of a given plant, but they end up with *all* characteristics and have to breed the plants again and again in order to end up with a plant that has only the traits they seek. The process of reproducing the best plants of the harvest or the best animals of the herd is called **selective breeding**.

Genetically modified organisms are plants or animals whose genetic makeup has been altered using **recombinant DNA technology**. As the name suggests, this technology allows the DNA, or genetic code, of two organisms to be combined, as shown in *Exhibit 7.5*. This results in a permanent change to the genetic code of the receiving plant or animal, as well as its offspring. **Transgenic organisms** are those in which the DNA of one species is implanted in another. For example, the DNA from a bacterium may be added to a plant. Genetic modifications to plants are done by scientists on a cellular level.

There are multiple reasons why a scientist or food producer may choose to modify an organism genetically. Genetically modified plants may be able to resist challenges to plant growth such as pests, weeds, or fungi, and resist the chemicals that kill pests. They may be bred to have enhanced nutritional value. They may be more tolerant of extreme heat, cold, or drought. In the United States, the use of genetically modified plants has decreased the use of pesticides, prevented the loss of topsoil, and reduced the use of fossil fuels. Genetically engineered animals could have new traits that allow them to be grown faster, to live in areas previously not viable due to drought or heat, and to be more disease resistant.

Although some people believe that changes in plants or animals are achieved quickly with this technology, many genetically modified organisms have taken years to develop. These plants and animals are also the most highly regulated. Three agencies have jurisdiction over the development and use of these products: the USDA, the EPA, and the Food and Drug Administration (FDA).

From a nutritional standpoint, genetically modified food products are comparable to conventional food products. Some, however, may have been modified to increase the presence of certain micronutrients. Golden rice, which was modified to increase vitamin A and iron levels for areas of the world where these nutrients are needed, is one example.

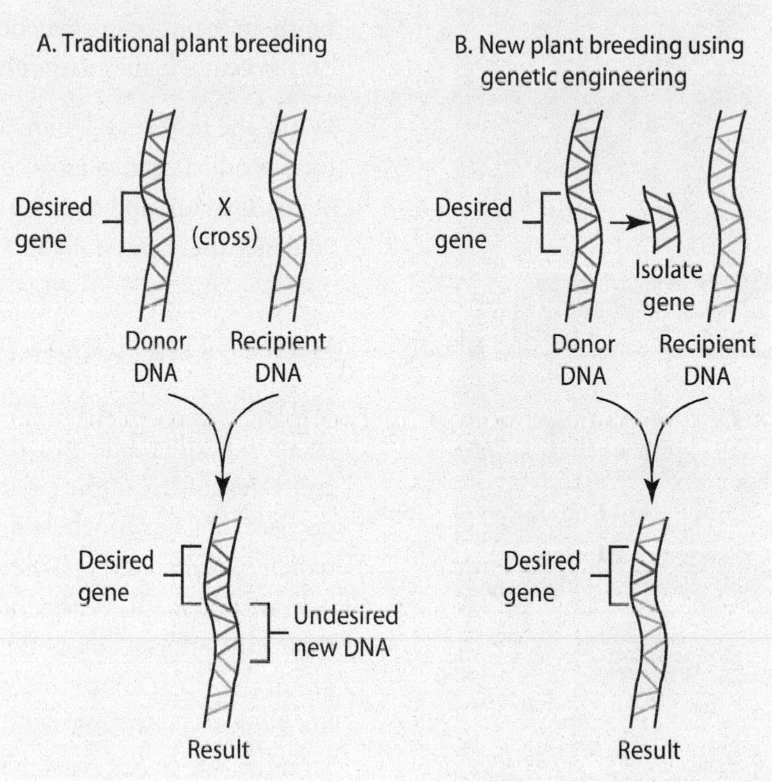

Agricultural biotechnology changes living organisms in order to produce something of use, such as plants or animals, microorganisms, or products. This definition includes not only genetic modification but also the use of biological organisms in the production of wine, cheese, and yogurt, for example. In a general sense, humans have been modifying the genes of plants and animals for generations by using crossbreeding and selective breeding, which are considered natural methods of biotechnology.

Exhibit 7.5

PLANT BREEDING VERSUS GENETIC ENGINEERING

A. Traditional plant breeding

B. New plant breeding using genetic engineering

Consumer Concerns

Consumers worldwide have raised objections to the use of genetically modified organisms in food, and some countries do not allow them in food at all. There are several reasons for these concerns. Consumers worry about the long-term environmental and health effects of eating these food products. Some are concerned that a genetically modified organism could have a gene from another organism that they should not eat for allergenic, moral, or other reasons. Since genetically modified plants may be selected over existing plants grown in some areas of the world, some consumers are concerned about the economic impact of these products. Additional consumers dislike not knowing when they are eating genetically modified organisms.

Exhibit 7.6

HARVESTING FOOD

As a more specific example, if a plant, such as a soybean plant, is bred to be resistant to a specific herbicide, then fields may be sprayed with that herbicide to kill weeds. This leaves the soybean plants intact, but they now may have herbicide on them. Consumers may be concerned as much with the chemicals that remain on the beans as they are with the genetic modification of the soybeans.

While the European Union and Japan require labeling of genetically modified food products or products containing genetically modified organisms, the United States, Canada, and many other nations do not. However, there is no conclusive evidence that genetically modified food products are harmful to human health.

HARVESTING AND TRANSPORTING FOOD

Harvesting, as shown in *Exhibit 7.6*, is the process of gathering crops to bring them to market. Like growing, this stage of the food system is largely removed from the control of the typical chef or restaurant or foodservice manager. But decisions related to where and how food products are harvested, as well as which of these food products are eventually used, can impact the health of an operation's guests. As a general rule, freshly harvested food products are at their nutrient peak and best overall condition. Similarly, fish, meat, and poultry are in their best condition at the time they are killed or caught. The challenge for food producers and food processors is to preserve the quality of food so it remains safe to eat, palatable, and nutritionally rich as it travels from field to foodservice operations.

Washing, trimming, cutting, and some degree of preservation is often necessary after harvest. With each stage of handling, food experiences nutrient loss. Peeling, trimming, cutting, and other physical actions can cause nutrient loss. For example, **physical loss** is caused by removing the tough fiber and vitamin-rich stems of broccoli when packaging frozen florets. Alternatively, there may be a **chemical loss** (reduction of nutrients due to destruction or transformation of the chemical composition of food), such as a lower level of a nutrient in a canned or frozen product when compared to its fresh counterpart. A general rule for fresh fruit and vegetables is that the longer the food is allowed to grow until it is ripe and the sooner it is eaten after harvest, the more nutritious the food item will be. One reason is that after harvest, micronutrients like vitamin C begin to deteriorate. Exposure to sunlight, heat, and oxygen during long periods of storage further contributes to nutrient loss.

Transportation is required to move food products from where they are harvested to where they are used. Depending on how far apart these locations are, many different forms and steps of transportation may be required. For example, fresh raspberries from Chile that are purchased by an operation in January might have been harvested some time ago. They will have gone through many transportation steps to get to their final destination. For instance, the items might have been carried by hand in the field, carried on a wagon to the farm's processing center, taken by truck to the nearest airfield, and flown to their final destination. From the airplane, they are driven to a local distributor, and finally they are taken to the grocery store, restaurant, or foodservice operation.

Using and serving local produce is a good way to serve food products that experience little loss of quality or nutrients. Since the produce does not have to travel far to market, it can grow for a longer period of time and be used and consumed more quickly. Even in large cities, access to fresh food products harvested the same day is available to consumers and food professionals. Of course, this is only possible when the food is in season (that is, currently being harvested). Purchasing produce from local sources, and in season allows the customer to taste foods at their peak flavor and nutrient content, and can help support local farmers and the community.

PROCESSING AND PACKAGING FOOD

Depending on the location of the operation, time of year, budget, and consumer needs, fresh, local produce may be challenging or impossible to serve. When fresh food is unavailable or too expensive, food that has undergone minimal processing such as freezing, canning, drying, and juicing can contribute significant nutrients to the diet and meet nutrient needs (*Exhibit 7.7*). While it may sound odd that a canned tomato can have as many or more nutrients than a fresh one, consider that many food manufacturers locate their processing facilities close to where the food is grown. This means that a tomato can be harvested and canned on the same day.

Exhibit 7.7

Alternatively, a fresh tomato, especially in an out-of-season location, may have to be picked before fully ripe, treated with ethylene gas to force-ripen it, and shipped many miles over several days before reaching the consumer. From a culinary perspective, various food products respond differently to processing, and many food items are able to retain excellent quality and flavor. The kitchens of even the best restaurants contain canned tomatoes; frozen berries, corn, and peas; and dried mushrooms and beans.

Processed Food, Processed Packaged Food, and Processed Produce

Processed food is food that has undergone any type of planned or deliberate change before being delivered for consumption. The International Food Information Council (IFIC) describes the continuum of processing as ranging from minimal processing to complex processing. An example of minimally processed food would be washed produce stored in a clean package. Further processing would apply to packaged processed food such as frozen food, canned food, and jar baby food. Packaged processed food also includes products that consumers themselves process further—for example, biscuit and pancake mixes made at home.[2] Processing can be valuable when it makes food safer.

Manufacturers may process food to preserve it for transportation. For instance, processed produce can be washed and packaged in modified atmosphere packaging (MAP) in order to delay deterioration via microbial spoilage and to extend shelf life. All fruit and vegetables will deteriorate in a few days without care. Speaking in general terms, the more processing food undergoes, the less nutritional value it contains. This is one of the arguments for purchasing fruit and vegetables as close to home as possible.

Food can be processed either minimally or substantially. Eating frozen vegetables or packaged whole grains is not the same as eating highly processed candy containing refined sugar and artificial coloring. Some minimally processed food, such as canned food, may have higher amounts of sodium, so it is important to make informed decisions about which processed food you eat and how much you eat. However, a healthy diet can contain food that is fresh, frozen, canned, juiced, or dried.

Food Additives

Food additives are ingredients other than the ingredients of the original food that are put into food to perform specific functions, such as improving flavor, color, and texture; retaining nutritional value; preventing spoilage; and extending shelf life. Some additives perform functions that are often taken for granted. Additives can help keep food wholesome and appealing while it is transported to market. Simple ingredients like vitamin C or ascorbic acid may be added to prevent browning, while other additives may be chemicals designed for special functions, such as fillers, binders, colors, preservatives, flavoring, flavor enhancers, stabilizers, and emulsifiers.[2]

Without additives, many food items would be less attractive, less flavorful, less nutritious, more likely to spoil, and more costly. Additionally, people would not be able to enjoy the same variety of safe and tasty food items year-round, and many convenience food items would not exist.

Most people's diets include some additives. However, managers and other culinary professionals should be aware of what additives are in the food they purchase. *Exhibit 7.8* lists the different types of additives and their functions. Additives can substantially change the original food and, in turn, its reception by consumers. For example, adding an ingredient with sodium to increase

[2]*International Food Information Council. 2010.* Understanding Our Food Communications Tool Kit. www.foodinsight.org

Exhibit 7.8

FOOD ADDITIVES AND THEIR FUNCTIONS

Additive	Function
Antioxidants	Antioxidants slow the oxidation process that turns fats rancid. Some fats, especially vegetable oils, do not become rancid as quickly because they contain naturally occurring antioxidants, such as tocopherol.
Benzoates	Benzoates are used as preservatives in acidic food items such as fruit juices and syrups, pie fillings, pickles, pickled vegetables, and sauces. Benzoates occur naturally in cranberries.
Colorants	Food colors (or colorants) fall into three groups; natural pigments extracted from plant materials, inorganic pigments and lakes (metals combined with organic colors), and synthetic coal-tar dyes.
Emulsifiers	Emulsifiers enable the formation of water-fat mixtures; they are a common ingredient in baked items because they help integrate the fat. Examples of some emulsifiers are gums, egg yolks, albumin, casein, and lecithin. All these substances help disperse oil in water uniformly. Emulsifiers also interact with fats to modify their crystal structure, which reduces viscosity or increases aeration (as in whipped cream). Emulsifiers interact with starch to reduce stickiness and to slow the staling of bread. They interact with gluten and thereby improve the baking quality of wheat flour, resulting in better texture and volume in packed goods.
Gums	Gums are substances that form a sticky mass in water. Gums help to keep emulsions from separating into constituent parts and are widely used in salad dressings, processed cheese, and confections.
Monosodium glutamate (MSG)	MSG is probably one of the best-known and widely used flavor enhancers. MSG occurs naturally in food items and is often added to canned soups and meat. MSG gives some people headaches.
Nitrates	Nitrates are natural constituents of plants and, together with nitrites, are used in the pickling of meat. Nitrate is converted into nitrite in the process.
Nitrites	Used in canned meat, nitrite is the essential agent in preserving meat by pickling. It inhibits the growth of *Clostridium botulinum* and therefore prevents botulism. Nitrites also preserve the desirable color and flavor of these products.
Phosphates	Phosphates are used widely within food processing and have several applications. For baked goods, phosphates are used as leavening agents. Phosphates are also used in the tenderizing of meat and in the processing of meat and seafood to improve texture.
Stabilizers	Stabilizers help maintain the structure of emulsions. They are often used in meringues and marshmallows to produce body and mouth feel.
Thickeners	Thickeners add body to a food product without imparting flavor. Modified starches are used as thickeners in commercial baking, as they work well with acidic ingredients, tolerate high temperatures, and do not cause pie fillings to "weep" during storage.

THINK ABOUT IT . . .

Think about some of the food items that you buy regularly. Which ones are most likely to contain additives? What functions do you think those additives serve?

flavor or to cure a food may make the food less desirable to people who are trying to lower their sodium intake. The problem with additives is that some are eventually found to have a negative impact on the body and must be removed from the market. In the past, coloring additives such as red #2 and green #1 were removed from use in foods.

Food Irradiation, Freeze-Drying, and *Sous Vide*

Food irradiation, which is the process of treating food with ionizing radiation, can reduce or eliminate bacteria and parasites that cause foodborne illness. Irradiation also inhibits sprouting and mold growth and can sometimes be used in place of fumigation with chemicals to eliminate insect pests. This process neither changes the nutritional value of the food nor makes the food radioactive or dangerous to eat. Food that has been irradiated is stored, handled, and cooked in the same way as untreated food.

Another food-processing method is **freeze-drying**. This process removes all the moisture from food to prevent spoilage. In freeze-drying, a machine first freezes the food. Then the air pressure within the machine is lowered so that the ice changes directly into water vapor. When the food is sufficiently dry, it is packaged in waterproof pouches. Freeze-dried food retains its nutrients and can be stored for a long time. The food is restored to its original form with the addition of water.

Sous vide, the French term for "under vacuum," is a food-preparation method that utilizes vacuum packaging. Restaurants, foodservice operators, and food manufacturers alike use this method of cooking, which reduces food shrinkage and preserves nutrients and flavor. In this process, fresh ingredients are used to create a dish. The food is vacuum-packed in a pouch and cooked slowly in a vacuum.

If this process is used by a restaurant, the food will be served when it is fully cooked and ready. However, if it is part of a food-manufacturing process, the food will be chilled or flash-frozen when it is fully cooked. *Sous vide* is a carefully controlled process because it carries the risk of pathogens that grow without oxygen, such as *Clostridium botulinum*. Restaurants and food processors using this food-preparation method must pay careful attention to HACCP guidelines and monitor temperatures.

Food Enrichment and Fortification

In the process of milling flour, the bran and the germ are removed, leaving the starchy endosperm and protein in the white flour. This yields a versatile product that can be used for baking cakes and pastries but lacks the nutrition of whole-grain flour. In the middle of the last century, when nutritional deficiency diseases were still common in the U.S. population, the FDA took action by adopting federal standards of identity for flour and initiating an enrichment program.

Enrichment means restoring nutrients that are removed when food is processed. Originally flour was enriched with thiamin, riboflavin, niacin, and iron (*Exhibit 7.9*). In 1996 the FDA required that folic acid be added in order to reduce the incidence of birth defects. The enrichment of flour restores only part of the whole grain's original nutrients, however. Eating whole grains is the only way to receive all of the benefit of nutrients from the grain.

Fortification differs from enrichment in that fortification means adding nutrients that the food did not have originally. Examples include the fortification of salt with iodine, orange juice with calcium, milk with vitamin D, and processed cereals with a range of vitamins and minerals. All of these fortifications increase the value of the food because they contribute nutrients that are difficult for the population to receive without their addition.

Exhibit 7.9

RECEIVING AND STORING FOOD

The steps of receiving, storing, and preparing food also affect the nutritional value of food products. By the time food is received, deterioration is accelerating. However, the use of proper procedures can minimize the loss of nutrients. Many of the principles of safe storage are reviewed in the *ServSafe Coursebook*.

Receiving

Once the food enters the establishment, the role of the restaurant or foodservice professional in maintaining the nutritional value of the food is critical. Long storage times and high temperatures can compromise both the safety and the nutritional value of food products. Frozen products should be received frozen to ensure they are safe to eat. Refrigerated items like meat, fish, and poultry must be received at 41°F (5°C) or lower. Some food products like onions, potatoes, and dry goods can be received at room temperature and should be clean and dry. Fruit and vegetables should be free from insect infestation, mold, cuts, discoloration, dull appearance, wilting, wrinkling, and unpleasant odors or tastes. A general rule is that the produce should feel heavy for its size.

Manager's Memo

It is clear that some consumers are interested in knowing where their food is grown, how far it travels, and how it is prepared. Managers and chefs can communicate this information through descriptions on their menus. If you have purchased from a well-known local farm, they may allow you to use their name on the menu. If you have organic produce, highlight those dishes on a special card or menu for the evening. Think about using the name of heritage plants or animals. These descriptions may differentiate you from your competitors, and they communicate your contributions to sustainability. Remember that descriptions must be accurate and adhere to the truth-in-menu laws and regulations.

Exhibit 7.10

Storage

Over time, the nutritional value and safety of food deteriorate because the food can dry out, become susceptible to rot, or grow mold or fungus. The best way to prevent such deterioration is to maintain a low inventory of food products that are susceptible to these processes. As a general rule for these items, managers should order only what they need in the short term and, when possible, opt for frequent, small deliveries (*Exhibit 7.10*) rather than large, infrequent orders.

Fruit that is nearly ripe or fully ripe may be shipped in an open package to avoid the buildup of ethylene gas, which the fruit produces as it ripens. This will help to reduce over-ripening. If fruit needs to be encouraged to ripen, an apple, which provides abundant ethylene gas, may be added to the package. Fruit may also be placed in a closed package to encourage ripening.[3]

It is critical to maintain proper storage temperatures for all food—low room temperature for dry goods, 41°F (5°C) or lower for refrigerated goods, and frozen food should remain frozen.

SUMMARY

1. **Distinguish among organic, certified organic, and conventional production of food.**

   Conventional food products are those grown using agricultural methods approved by a national governing agency. In the United States, these methods are studied and regulated by the USDA. Organic food is food that has been produced without synthetic fertilizers, sewage sludge, irradiation, and genetic engineering. Farmers who want to use the certified organic label must be certified by a USDA-accredited certifying agent, and they must maintain records of their operation.

2. **Define *genetically modified organism* and *agricultural biotechnology*.**

   Genetically modified organisms are plants or animals whose genetic makeup has been altered using recombinant DNA technology. This technology allows the DNA, or genetic code, of two organisms to be combined. This results in a change to the genetic code of the receiving plant or animal and its offspring. Agricultural biotechnology is the application of technology to living organisms in order to produce something of use.

3. **Describe the steps involved in harvesting and transporting food.**

   Harvesting food involves gathering it (for example, in the field) for market. This is often followed by light processing, such as washing, trimming, or

[3]*Bennion, M., and Schuele, B.* Introductory Foods, *12th ed. Pearson. Prentice Hall, Upper Saddle River, NJ.*

preserving. Transporting food can involve several steps, such as being carried by hand in the field, carried on a wagon to the farm's processing center, taken by truck to the nearest airfield, and flown to its final destination. From the airplane, it may be driven to a local distributor and finally taken to the grocery store, restaurant, or foodservice operation.

4. **Explain food additives, food irradiation, freeze-drying, and *sous vide*.**

Food additives are put into food to perform specific functions, such as improving flavor, color, and texture; retaining nutritional value; preventing spoilage; and extending shelf life. Additives are used to keep food fresh and appealing while it is transported to market.

Food irradiation is a process that helps to reduce or eliminate pathogens in food using ionizing radiation. Irradiation can inhibit sprouting and mold growth and can be used in place of chemicals to eliminate insect pests. Irradiation neither changes the nutritional value of the food nor makes the food radioactive.

Freeze-drying removes all the moisture from food to prevent spoilage. Food that has been freeze-dried can be stored for a long time and restored to its original form with the addition of water.

Sous vide is a food-preparation method that utilizes vacuum packaging. This method reduces food shrinkage and preserves nutrients and flavor. It is used by restaurants, foodservice operations, and food manufacturers. *Sous vide* is a controlled process due to the potential for pathogens. When using this process, managers should pay close attention to their HACCP plan.

5. **Identify the characteristics of enriched food and fortified food, and explain their roles in nutrition.**

Enrichment means restoring nutrients that are removed when processing food. This generally applies to grain products. Flour is enriched with thiamin, riboflavin, niacin, folic acid, and iron. Fortification differs from enrichment in that fortification adds nutrients to food that did not have them originally, such as adding iodine to salt. Fortification increases the value of food because it contributes nutrients that a given population is unlikely to receive without this addition.

6. **Define *processed food* and *processed packaged food*, and describe the nutritional differences among the various types of processed food.**

Processed food is food that has undergone any type of planned or deliberate change before it is delivered for consumption. Processed packaged food includes products that the consumer will process further, such as biscuit and pancake mixes.

In general, the more processing a food undergoes, the less nutritional value it has. However, some types of processing, such as the use of preservatives or special packaging such as modified atmosphere packaging, can maximize a food's nutritional value. Additionally, enrichment and fortification improve the nutrient content of food. Some additives used to flavor or cure may increase the amount of sodium in the food and make it less desirable, however.

APPLICATION EXERCISES

Exercise 1. Food Additives in Your Diet

a. Take the food-additive challenge: For one week, keep track of the food you eat and list all items that contain food additives. This will include collecting candy-bar wrappers, containers, etc., and checking their contents. Be sure to use containers as references because some words are difficult to remember—and to spell.

b. Once you have all the week's additives recorded, look them up on the Web site below and categorize them. Then read about each one. Once you finish your reading, you will know the functions of some of the food additives you eat each day.

The Center for Science in the Public Interest lists food additives and their effects on the body at *www.cspinet.org/reports/chemcuisine.htm*

Exercise 2. Community-Supported Agriculture

a. In each U.S. state there are community-supported agriculture (CSA) organizations with farms. Check the Internet to find out if there are any near you. Call them to determine the price of a share for a box of produce each week. How much higher or lower would this cost be than your current cost for produce for the week?

b. Would you consider joining a CSA? Why or why not? What might be good about the system? What might be difficult?

c. Would a CSA be an appropriate supplier for a restaurant or foodservice operation? Why or why not? What might be good about the system? What might be difficult?

REVIEW YOUR LEARNING

Select the best answer for each question.

1. **Which vitamin was added to the enrichment process for flour to reduce the risk of birth defects?**
   A. Niacin
   B. Thiamin
   C. Folic acid
   D. Citric acid

2. **Which process is used to replace a nutrient removed in processing?**
   A. Hydrogenation
   B. Fortification
   C. Enrichment
   D. Irradiation

3. **What type of farming permits the use of pesticides, synthetic fertilizers, and herbicides in the growing process?**
   A. Experimental
   B. Conventional
   C. Integrated
   D. Organic

4. **A process that adds nutrients that do not exist in the original food is called**
   A. additives.
   B. enrichment.
   C. fortification.
   D. pasteurization.

5. In order to improve color or flavor, or to prevent spoilage, food manufacturers use
   A. herbicides.
   B. additives.
   C. pesticides.
   D. fumigants.

6. The difference between *sous vide* and traditional cooking techniques used by restaurants, foodservice operations, and food manufacturers is that *sous vide* involves
   A. less preparation.
   B. a vacuum seal.
   C. more heat.
   D. sodium.

7. To maintain quality and safety, refrigerated meat and poultry should be received at a temperature of
   A. 41°F or lower.
   B. 43°F or lower.
   C. 45°F or lower.
   D. 47°F or lower.

8. What farming system focuses on maintaining productivity without damaging valuable resources?
   A. Organizational
   B. Conventional
   C. Sustainable
   D. Reliable

9. The formation of ethylene gas is a concern when storing
   A. milk.
   B. meat.
   C. fruit.
   D. butter.

10. Which is most likely to result in a chemical loss of nutrients in food?
    A. Exposure to oxygen
    B. Growing bacteria
    C. Over trimming
    D. Ripening

FIELD PROJECT

The Cost of Eating Organic Produce

a. Compare the prices of the following organic and conventional food items at your local grocery store: potatoes, apples, celery, carrots, and salad greens.

b. Once you get both totals, determine the difference in cost. Using your eating habits as a basis, what would this cost be for a month? What would the cost be for a year?

c. Write arguments both for and against purchasing either all organic or all conventional produce.

8

Cooking for Health: Culinary Skills in Action

INSIDE THIS CHAPTER

- Cooking Healthfully *and* Tastefully
- Adapting Recipes for Improved Nutrition
- Organizing and Disseminating Standardized Recipes
- Ensuring That Recipes Are Used
- Teaching Portion-Control Principles
- Observing and Evaluating Employee Performance

CHAPTER LEARNING OBJECTIVES

After completing this chapter, you should be able to:

- Explain how cooking and cooking methods affect nutrition.

- Explain the difference between the center-of-plate concept and the MyPlate model.

- Describe how to modify and adapt recipes according to the latest dietary recommendations, and explain the importance of adopting standardized recipes.

- Identify effective ways to organize and store recipes and to make recipes accessible to staff.

- Explain how to train staff to use scales and measuring tools.

- Describe the importance of evaluating the effectiveness of employee training on measurement tools and procedures as well as providing feedback to employees.

KEY TERMS

CASE STUDY

Gwen is the manager of a university campus foodservice operation. She has been assigned the task of incorporating food items that come from local sources within two to three hours from campus. In an effort to help the extended university community, she will contract with local farmers and vendors who can supply the quantities of food needed on a regular basis. The project, which was initiated jointly by students and staff, will result in more fresh produce during the growing season. Increasing the amounts of fruit and vegetables on the foodservice menu meets current national nutrition goals. Gwen is visiting her units one by one to gather some information and to develop a plan to revise the menus to accommodate the new influx of fruit and vegetables.

1. What nutrients will potentially increase as a result of additional servings of fruit and vegetables on the university foodservice menu?

2. What will Gwen have to consider as she changes vendors and menus?

3. What are the challenges of changing to local and fresh sources? How does the location of an operation affect menu items when the operation purchases local and fresh food items?

COOKING HEALTHFULLY *AND* TASTEFULLY

As people become more health conscious, they often request more nutritious options at the dining table. Chapter 6 reviewed steps that restaurant and foodservice professionals can take to ensure that their operations are choosing and serving wholesome, nutritious food. Professionals must also recognize, however, that if their operations do not serve menu items that taste good, their customers will begin to look elsewhere for their meals, regardless of the operation's focus on healthy alternatives.

Chefs and cooks need to combine culinary skills with an understanding of nutrition in order to provide guests with tasty food that is low in solid fat, salt, and added sugars. They must also understand the elements that contribute to the flavor of food.

Cooking with health in mind involves the following:

- Healthy ingredients and cooking methods
- Increasing amounts of fruit, vegetables, and whole grains used in entrées, soups, salads, and side dishes
- Using salt with care and purpose
- Using fat only where it makes the best contribution to flavor
- Using less added sugar, such as in desserts

In addition to cooking healthfully, plating of menu items and overall presentation are equally important. They require consideration of color, balance, texture, and architecture.

Appealing to the Senses

Flavor is perceived through all the senses (see *Exhibit 8.1*). Skilled chefs with nutritional sensitivities build flavor in layers by using fat-free marinades, dry rubs, **infused oils** (oils that have been heated with seasonings to enhance flavor), salsas, vinaigrettes, citrus, reductions, and smoking. Building flavor means using a balance of tastes and smells that complement each other. Asian and Latin American cuisines have been balancing flavors for a long time. Here are some examples of popular flavor combinations:

- Sweet and sour: chicken with pineapple and tomatoes
- Hot and sour: Asian hot and sour soup
- Acid and fat: salmon with lemon sauce
- Acid, fat, and piquant: chipotle barbecue pork
- Acid, fat, piquant, and sweet: chipotle honey barbecue pork

Each bite of food should be enjoyable and memorable. The chef or cook should combine tastes (sweet, sour, salty, bitter, and umami) to develop certain flavors that tantalize the appetite. The diner should experience a wonderfully delicious *and* healthy meal.

A skilled chef or cook can modify a recipe to meet nutritional guidelines, as well as the particular customer's needs, while preserving the essence of the dish being prepared. This requires knowledge of healthy cooking techniques, such as preparing a low-fat meatloaf starting with a traditional high-fat meatloaf recipe. Accomplished cooks know how to substitute ingredients, such as using a leaner cut of meat, using egg whites instead of whole eggs, decreasing the amount of salt, and increasing spices. All of this may be done to maximize flavor.

APPEARANCE

The adage that people eat with their eyes is nowhere more applicable than in healthful cooking. Healthy food can be very visually appealing. What could be more enticing than a whole grilled fish stuffed with herbs, lightly steamed pencil asparagus, or a ripe fanned half pear? As a general rule, colorful food is nutritious food. A colorful array of fresh fruit and vegetables, rich brown grains, and pink or pale lean cuts of meat are not only visually attractive but also indicative of wholesome ingredients, proper cooking techniques, and valuable nutrient content. Making healthy food appealing goes a long way toward encouraging guests to eat more healthfully.

Maintain Nutrients with Careful Preparation and Cooking

Most restaurants and foodservice operations have an opportunity to use a variety of fresh, flavorful ingredients, emphasizing whole grains, fruit and vegetables, lean meat, poultry, fish, and seafood. Professionals should select small quantities of flavorful vegetable fats, such as olive oil and nut oils, rather than saturated fats (solid fats), such as butter, shortening, and lard. Chefs and cooks must know how to prepare and cook food with methods that preserve nutrients, maximize quality, and maintain yield. A list of healthy cooking techniques is included later in this chapter.

Exhibit 8.1	
PERCEIVING FLAVOR	
Aspects of the Flavor Experience	
Sight	• Color • Visual texture • Consistency • Visible steam
Smell	• Greatest sensitivity to taste comes when breathing out with the mouth shut. • Taste and smell function together to translate the wide range of flavors found in food and beverages (see chapter 2). • Wine tasting has a narrow taste spectrum and broad smell spectrum.
Touch	• Mouthfeel • Texture • Temperature: greatest flavor sensation between 70°F and 105°F (21°C and 41°C)
Taste	• Approximately ten thousand taste buds interpret sweet, sour, bitter, salty, and umami (savory). • **Maillard reaction**: the interaction between an amino acid and a sugar to form browning and a variety of flavors
Sound	Sounds of preparation, cooking, and eating (snap, pop, crunch, sizzle)

A skilled chef or cook knows how to work with all forms of food: fresh, frozen, canned, dried, and juiced. In addition, it is important to realize that light, heat, acidity, and alkalinity can change, diminish, or destroy the nutrients in food. Chapter 5 discusses how simple exposure to air or light can destroy vitamins in food. One example is riboflavin, a B vitamin found in milk. Riboflavin is destroyed by light. To limit the exposure of milk to light, it is sold in opaque jugs or cardboard cartons that help preserve its riboflavin content. Water-soluble vitamins and minerals can be lost due to leaching if they have been soaked in water. For this reason, fruit and vegetables should be washed and rinsed quickly and carefully to retain their vitamins and minerals.

In addition to careful preparation, minimal cooking time helps preserve vitamins and minerals, especially water-soluble vitamins. Steaming is the best process for preserving the vitamin content of vegetables; microwaving and stir-frying are other good methods.

Portion Size and Plating

In designing a healthy menu item, it may become necessary to rethink the center-of-plate concept commonly taught in culinary and hospitality schools and used by chefs worldwide. The center-of-plate concept is that a meal should be focused on an expensive centerpiece item, usually a protein-rich food such as meat, poultry, or fish, and that the rest of the meal's components should be treated as accompaniments. A traditional center-of-plate menu offering might include a 14-ounce strip steak (the center-of-plate item) accompanied by French fries and a vegetable. The center-of-plate concept focuses on protein items to the detriment of the rest of the meal.

While the meal with the large steak may appeal to some customers, it is at odds with the recommendations of the Dietary Guidelines for Americans 2010. These guidelines would recommend a three-ounce portion of meat, poultry, or fish. A three-ounce portion of meat is about the size of a deck of cards. Restaurant and foodservice professionals can choose smaller cuts of meat and balance the plate with more vegetables, fruit, and whole grains. To implement a nutrition program that focuses on smaller portions and fewer calories, managers may need to rethink the center-of-plate concept and instead adopt a whole-plate approach. The new MyPlate is a better model on which to base a healthy, balanced plate (*Exhibit 8.2*). More information can be found in chapter 3. Menu items should reflect the percentages provided for carbohydrate, protein, and fat discussed in that chapter.

THINK ABOUT IT . . .

Consider your favorite recipe, prepared either at home or in a foodservice operation. What changes might you make to the preparation and cooking methods to ensure that the meal retains a maximum amount of nutrients?

Exhibit 8.2

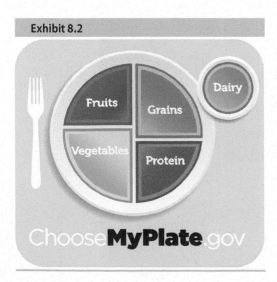

Visual Cues and Plate Size

People tend to judge the size of food portions by how much of the plate the food covers. Food that covers most of the plate is typically judged as a normal-size portion. Food that covers very little of the plate is typically judged as a skimpy portion. To help customers appropriately judge the amount of food they are eating, use plates and bowls of appropriate sizes.

In addition, certain presentation techniques will help a customer judge portion size. For example, a three-ounce chicken breast that is sliced and fanned out on the plate will cover more of the plate than will a three-ounce chicken breast presented in its usual form. Other food-presentation techniques add height and perceived size to a menu item. If the operation is increasing the amount of vegetables and whole-grain food used, these items can be added to the three-ounce portion of meat to produce a portion of food that customers perceive as having a value appropriate to what they are paying.

ADAPTING RECIPES FOR IMPROVED NUTRITION

An easy way to prepare healthful meals is to start with wholesome, healthy ingredients and then prepare them with methods that reduce the use of solid fat, salt, cholesterol, and added sugar. When eaten in excess, these food components cause negative health effects.

Solid Fat

As earlier chapters have discussed, excess fats such as cholesterol and saturated fat increase the risk of heart disease by increasing LDL blood-cholesterol levels. When blood cholesterol levels are increased, people are at risk for cardiovascular disease, including heart attack and stroke.

Sodium

Adding table salt when preparing food or eating at the table usually represents only a small part of a person's sodium intake. The larger part of sodium intake comes from processed food such as yeast breads, precooked chicken dishes, and pizza. Although it is important for people to select processed food with less sodium, the judicious use of salt in cooking is necessary to reduce dietary sodium intake.

According to the Dietary Guidelines for Americans 2010, the estimated average intake of sodium for Americans aged two years and older is thirty-four hundred milligrams—more than twice the Dietary Reference Intake recommendation of fifteen hundred milligrams for African-Americans and people who suffer from hypertension, diabetes, or kidney disease. The current average is also significantly higher than the recommended intake for the rest of the population, which is twenty-three hundred milligrams or less.

Both commercial entities and foodservice operations should pay attention to this issue because when people develop hypertension, they often require one or two medicines to reduce their blood pressure, and many of the medicines used to treat blood pressure have unpleasant side effects. Reducing salt in all types of food products will help to reduce hypertension in the American population.

Added Sugars

Added sugars in the diet are an issue for the entire population because they directly contribute to dental cavities. In addition, people who consume too much sugar increase their risk of becoming overweight or obese and developing type 2 diabetes. The largest sources of added sugar in the American diet are soda, energy drinks, and sports drinks.

Adding Nutrients to Make Meals Healthy

Cooks and chefs should also make concerted efforts to adapt recipes to contain more vegetables, fruit, and whole grains. These ingredients can be part of the entrée, or they can be added to appetizers, soups, salads, sides, and desserts. By increasing quantities of these items, you also increase the amount of fiber in the diet.

Improving a menu for both health and taste generally means introducing new recipes, adjusting existing recipes, changing cooking techniques, adding ingredients, and replacing ingredients when necessary. Any or all of these may be necessary to arrive at a menu that will incorporate the desired healthy aspects.

Some Food Science

In making recipe and cooking changes, it is important to apply food-science principles. For example, when reducing fat in a brownie recipe, it is necessary to analyze how fat functions in the recipe. Fat can provide moisture, flavor, color, richness, body, and mouthfeel. It is not sufficient simply to remove the fat from the recipe; it must be substituted with an ingredient that can function in the way that the fat did. Here are some examples of common ingredients and their functions in recipes:

- **When the ingredient is for leavening:** Leavening refers to increasing the volume or lightening a baked product by capturing gases generated by the chemical reaction of sodium bicarbonate (baking soda) and an acid such as buttermilk, or by the addition of baking powder to a product. Leavening in yeast products occurs when yeast and carbohydrates ferment to produce carbon dioxide. Leavening can also be accomplished by whipping or beating a food substance such as an egg white to incorporate air into a food product. An example would be the use of whipped egg whites in angel food cake.

- **When the ingredient is for tenderizing:** Solid and liquid fats are used to tenderize food. Sugar, milk, and egg yolks are also tenderizers.

- **When the ingredient is for flavoring:** Fats, sugar, eggs, fruit, and artificial flavorings all provide flavor. Salt rounds out flavors. Citrus and vinegars intensify flavor and salty tastes.

- **When the ingredient is for structure:** Egg whites are used to give food body and volume. Egg albumen gives strong structure to cells that capture air during baking. Starches such as potato starch, cornstarch, arrowroot, rice, flours, grains, and cereals have properties that thicken liquids.

Modification by Changing Cooking Techniques

An easy technique to employ in modifying recipes is to use alternate cooking techniques (see *Exhibit 8.3*). Chefs and cooks can replace methods such as deep-frying and pan-frying, which result in significant fat absorption, with

Exhibit 8.3	

COOKING METHODS USED TO REDUCE FAT

Method	Description
Baking	Same as roasting but for nonmeat items. Food is placed directly in a baking dish and cooked in the oven. High heat creates the Maillard reaction of browning.
Barbecuing	Food is cooked on a grate over indirect heat. Dry barbecuing has dry herbs and spices applied to the exterior of the meat. Wet barbecuing has basting with a barbecue sauce.
Braising	This slow and flavorful method of cooking is used with tougher or less fatty cuts of meat and with fruit and vegetables. It can be made lower in fat by choosing a leaner meat or trimming excess fat. The meat is seared using the dry-sauté method, and then a flavorful liquid with aromatic vegetables is added when cooking the meat. The whole food item is used, half submerged in the braising liquid, covered, and allowed to cook very gently for a long period of time until tender. When cooking is completed, the meat is removed and the braising liquid is degreased to remove excess fat, or the liquid can be left overnight to chill and the hardened fat layer removed. If there are vegetables in the sauce, they can be puréed and used as the thickener for the sauce.
Broiling	Food is cooked on a perforated pan over a catch pan with high direct heat from above in a broiler. Classically, fat is used when broiling lean poultry and fish to aid in browning, but it drips off prior to serving. Used on tender cuts of meat trimmed of visible fat, vegetables, fruit, and pizza. The high heat and quick cooking retains vitamins and minerals.
Dry-sautéing	Food is cooked at high heat in a nonstick sauté pan with very little or no fat. The pan is prepared by heating the pan to a high heat, wiping the surface with oil, removing excess, and repeating the procedure until the pan is glazed. Meat, fish, and eggs do well with this method, but starchy food and tofu do not. Afterwards, the pan is deglazed with stock, wine, or water. The pan is not washed with soap but rubbed with salt and rinsed to retain the nonstick surface. If necessary, pan spray or oil in a spray bottle (atomized oil) can be used to touch up the surface.

(Continued)

COOKING METHODS USED TO REDUCE FAT (*continued*)

Method	Description
En papillote	Food baked and steamed in a greased paper or parchment bag is named for the French term for "in parchment." The dish, usually both meat and vegetables, is cooked and often served in the bag. Because the greased bag retains the moisture and reduces the harsh heat of the oven, the dish is aromatic, moist, and flavorful.
Grilling	Food is cooked on a grate over direct or indirect heat. (Sometimes "grilling" is mistakenly used to refer to cooking in oil on a flat surface also called a grill.)
Oven-frying	Oven-frying food can be done to lower fat but get the crispy crust of fried food. The food is breaded and then baked or broiled at high heat.
Pan-steaming	Food is cooked in a pan on the range or in a microwave dish with a small amount of boiling liquid.
Poaching	Food is cooked gently, just below a simmer, in liquid such as stock, wine, juice, or water. Often used to cook fruit, meat, or fish. This is a gentle cooking method that keeps food tender and moist. The poaching liquid often is reduced and used as a sauce. The related shallow-poaching method uses less liquid and is for single servings of tender cuts of meat or fish.
Roasting	Same as baking but for roasting meat, vegetables, and poultry. Food is placed on a rack over a catch pan and cooked in the oven. The high heat and quick cooking retains vitamins and minerals and also creates the Maillard reaction of browning.
Smoke-roasting	Also known as pan-smoking. Aromatics like woods, teas, and herbs impart great flavor to food. The food is smoked on the range, then finished in the oven. The advantage of this method is that little or no salt is required for seasoning to achieve good taste. To give more flavor before smoking, the items can be marinated.
Sous vide	*Sous vide* is French for "under vacuum." This method involves slow cooking of food in vacuum-sealed plastic bags. It requires special equipment to vacuum seal the bag and cool the packaged food properly. The packaged food is cooked slowly to the desired temperature, in a controlled temperature water bath or steam. It can be held at that temperature until service or cooled quickly and reheated at a later date. The advantage of this cooking method is that the food is extremely flavorful, tender, has little waste and weight loss, and has maximum vitamin and mineral retention. A significant advantage for restaurant operations is that the food cannot overcook, which is extremely important for reducing food waste. Banquet chefs find this method helpful when preparing meals for large crowds because the food can be made ahead and reheated for service. *Sous vide* also can be used to marinate single-service food items to be cooked quickly at a later time. Under correct conditions, vacuum sealing extends the shelf life of the product.
Steaming	Food is cooked in a perforated basket over boiling water with no fat. This method is especially good for vegetables, and it avoids the problem of leaching out the vitamins and minerals when vegetables are boiled.
Stewing	Identical to braising, except the meat, vegetables, or fruit are cut into pieces that are fully immersed in the flavorful liquid.
Stir-frying	Food is cooked over extremely high heat with a small amount of fat in a wok or sauté pan and stirred constantly. Using a round-bottom wok is superior to using a flat-bottom sauté pan because the round bottom uses much less fat. If the wok is seasoned, even less oil is needed.
Sweat	Food items, particularly vegetables, are cooked in a small amount of fat over low heat. The food is covered with a piece of foil or parchment paper and the pot is covered to allow the food to cook in its own juices.

methods like stir-frying, which allows the fat to cook the food and then drip away, as shown in *Exhibit 8.4*. They may also choose to use methods that avoid fat altogether. As an illustration, consider the popular dish of buffalo chicken wings. The wings are traditionally dredged in flour, deep-fried, and tossed in a mixture of butter and hot sauce. By roasting them in a hot oven rather than deep-frying them, cooks can obtain a similar but lower-fat result.

If none of these alternate cooking techniques work for the recipe, chefs and cooks should search for a new food product that does work. New food products and applications are developed regularly. It is the responsibility of restaurant and foodservice professionals to keep up-to-date on these developments and to contribute to them by experimenting with various modifications.

Exhibit 8.4

Modification by Replacing Select Ingredients

Another way to modify recipes successfully is to replace some of the ingredients rather than eliminating them. Sometimes replacements can result in a similar product that appeals to consumers; other times, the results are awful. The best strategy is to use recipes or formulas from a trusted source and to experiment with different combinations. *Exhibits 8.5* and *8.6* (on the next page) list some common substitutions for ingredients that are often reduced or eliminated from recipes.

Exhibit 8.5

COMMON INGREDIENT SUBSTITUTIONS

Item	Substitute
Salt	Herbs, spices, and acid items
Refined sugar	Commercially available sugar substitutes, fruit juices, purées, and dried fruit
Fat	Fruit purées in baked goods, liquid in savory preparations, strained yogurt, starch, and commercially available gels and gums

Not all substitutions result in a healthier product. For example, using honey in place of refined table sugar simply results in the substitution of one sugar for another. Nutritionally, these two ingredients are quite similar. Also, substitutions do not always work on a one-to-one ratio. For example, most artificial sweeteners are many times sweeter than sugar. Careful attention to the manufacturer's directions is necessary to prevent using too much sweetener, since the end result would be unpalatable.

There are different ways to substitute recipe ingredients. Restaurant and foodservice professionals must remember that food substitutions must be done in such a way that all of the functions of the replaced food item are fulfilled. Here are some guidelines that will help in making decisions about which ingredients to substitute.

Exhibit 8.6

RECIPE SUBSTITUTIONS TO LOWER FAT

Traditional food item	Possible alternative food item (if it meets the recipe's needs)
Whole milk	2-percent or skim milk
Eggs, whole or yolks	Egg whites or a commercial egg substitute, fruit or vegetable purée
Butter	Trans-fat-free margarine, olive oil, nut oils, avocado
Coconut and palm oil	Canola oil, soybean oil, safflower oil, grapeseed oil, applesauce, low-fat plain yogurt
Cheese	Low-fat varieties
Yogurt	Low or no fat
Bacon	Turkey bacon
Sausage	Turkey sausage, seasoned ground turkey, soy crumbles
Ground beef	Ground sirloin, ground turkey breast, ground soy
Chocolate	Cocoa
Cream	Canned evaporated skim milk

Choosing Healthier Fats

As discussed in chapter 4, fats and oils contain saturated, monounsaturated, and polyunsaturated fatty acids, which are found in various amounts in all the fats used for cooking. The fats that cooks use are usually named for the fatty acids that are present in the largest quantities. For example, the solid fats, such as butter, lard, shortening, and sour cream, contain high proportions of saturated fats and are referred to as saturated fats. However, all three types of fatty acids are distributed in differing amounts in all fats and oils. *Exhibit 8.7* shows these amounts.

Trans-fatty acids are found naturally in meat and milk and are produced when oils are hydrogenated in order to solidify them. These fats have been found to increase the level of LDL cholesterol in the body. Recommendations include keeping trans-fatty acids as low as possible in the diet. It is important for restaurants and foodservice operations to review all the ingredients in their recipes and to remove sources of trans-fatty acids produced by hydrogenation. Look for *partially hydrogenated fats* on the labels. Managers may want to speak with vendors about products that can replace hydrogenated fats on grills and in the deep-fryer. The food products that contain these fats include snack-food items, some margarine, and many prepared desserts. The trans-fatty acids found in milk, meat, and poultry can be limited by using low-fat dairy products and lean cuts of meat.

MARGARINE VERSUS BUTTER

Margarine is made from vegetable oils that are solidified either by hydrogenated fats or by a saturated fat. Soft margarines solidified with partially hydrogenated fatty acids contain small amounts of trans-fatty acids in each serving. Due to current food-labeling regulations, trans-fatty acids in food do not have to be declared on the nutrition facts label unless they occur in quantities of 0.5 gram or more per serving. This means that soft margarines can contain small amounts of trans-fatty acids and still show "0 trans fats" on the label. Stick margarines usually contain more hydrogenates (hydrogenated fats) and therefore more trans-fatty acids than soft margarines do.

Exhibit 8.7

PERCENT OF SATURATED, MONOUNSATURATED, AND POLYUNSATURATED FATTY ACIDS BY WEIGHT

1. Animal Fats

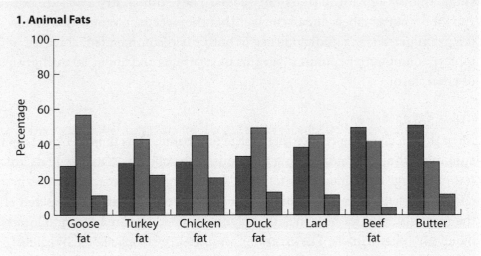

2. Oils

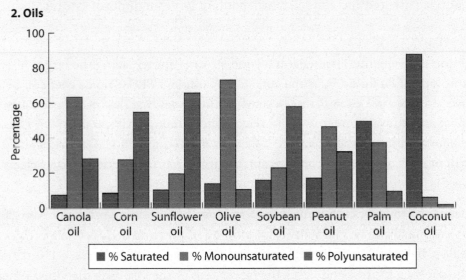

USDA Composition of Foods Raw, Processed, Prepared, USDA Nutrient Database for Standard Release 24.
USDA Nutrient Data Laboratory: *www.ars.usda.gov/nutrientdata*

Since trans-fatty acids are known to increase bad-cholesterol levels and to decrease good-cholesterol levels, food companies have been trying to reduce the amounts of trans-fatty acids found in their products. Soft margarines can be used in cooking to reduce the use of butter and thus to reduce saturated fats. Stick margarines are usually not recommended for more healthful cooking because they contain either more trans fats or more saturated fats to solidify them.

Butter is derived from milk fat that is churned commercially until a yellow creamy solid fat is produced. It has a rich flavor and is the choice of most chefs. However, butter has a high amount of saturated fat and contains a small amount of natural trans-fatty acids. These trans-fatty acids are not shown on butter labels due to the fact that they occur in quantities under 0.5 gram per serving. Judicious use of butter is recommended, since a tablespoon of butter contains 7 grams of saturates and about 30 milligrams of cholesterol.

OTHER SATURATED FATS

Most skilled chefs can reduce their usage of saturated fats in food by changing cooking techniques and by using more oils than solid fats. Saturated fats are found in large quantities in butter, lard, shortening, sour cream, and cream cheese. Oils contain more monounsaturated and polyunsaturated fats and are the most desirable for heart health. Polyunsaturated fats are known to lower blood-cholesterol levels. The exception would be the tropical oils, like palm, palm kernel, and coconut oil, which contain large amounts of saturated fats.

LEANER CUTS OF MEAT

Using high-quality, lean meat is a good strategy for replacing the large amounts of fat found in prime cuts. For example, USDA Choice beef can be used in place of USDA Prime beef. Marbling is fat that lies intramuscularly in meat and adds to tenderness and flavor when cooked. Although USDA Choice is a leaner grade of beef because it has less marbling than USDA Prime, it is still of high quality and contains sufficient fat to broil or grill. USDA Select beef is lean because it has the lowest amount of marbling.

Leaner or tougher cuts of meat require moist-heat cooking methods. Moisture in lean meat can be maintained by cooking in parchment, foil, or vegetable leaves. Basting lean meat with stock both prevents it from drying out during the cooking process and keeps the fat content of the resulting dish low. When meat is sautéed, brushing a little oil on it and cooking it in a nonstick pan is a healthier method than placing the meat into a puddle of oil.

Finally, when making substitutions to reduce fat in a dish, chefs and cooks must remember why the fat is in the dish in the first place. Not all fats can be reduced, removed, or replaced. For example, butter, rendered bacon fat, duck fat, and goose fat have flavors that are appealing to consumers and cooking properties that are difficult to imitate. A pie crust can be made easily with lard or shortening. When substituting vegetable oil for shortening, however, it is considerably more difficult to obtain a comparable result. Because oil is a liquid, it mixes well with flour and covers the grain. With the addition of water to mix the crust, gluten strands easily develop and make the dough tough.

Modification by Adding Select Ingredients

Many people think that healthy cooking is simply about removing undesirable ingredients from a menu item. However, healthy cooking also can be about adding healthful ingredients. Most people in developed countries do not get sufficient fiber from their diets. Adding fresh fruit and vegetables, whole grains, and legumes to dishes is a good way to make food that is nutritionally sound, contains more fiber, and is of interest to customers from a culinary perspective. This strategy also saves money, as these types of food are usually cheaper per pound than meat, fish, poultry, cheeses, and other ingredients. For example, adding an interesting preparation of amaranth, quinoa, or millet to a menu will accomplish all of the above goals. Using these and other nutritious but nonstandard ingredients can also expand the creativity of a chef.

A successful recipe adaptation yields a dish that is not only nutritionally acceptable but also delicious. Herbs, spices, stocks, reductions of stock, wine, vinegar, juice, whole grains, and purées of vegetables, fruit, or legumes are all delicious. Using them sensibly and artistically can result in tasty fare that customers love. An effective frame of mind is to think of healthy cooking as simply good cooking with good ingredients rather than as an unwelcome adaptation of classical cooking.

THINK ABOUT IT . . .

What recipes do you prepare in a foodservice operation, or at home, that could be made healthier by the changes suggested in this chapter? How could these changes be made without sacrificing taste?

Examples of Recipe Modification

Once food preparers understand the purposes of ingredients, they can begin to modify recipes to be lower in fat, sugar, and salt. This section provides some specific examples.

MODIFICATIONS IN BAKING

The fat in many recipes can be lowered by using a fruit purée, such as applesauce, in place of butter or oil (*Exhibit 8.8*). A purée is a finely mashed food, usually a fruit or vegetable, which is smooth and uniform in texture. The addition of a purée results in a moist, dense cake, and the crumb will still be tender.

Exhibit 8.8

To lower cholesterol, an egg substitute can be used in place of an egg. The rule of thumb is that one-quarter cup of egg substitute equals one egg. Egg substitutes consist of egg whites with a small amount of vegetable oil added to replace the egg yolk. Yellow food coloring is usually added for color.

To lower sugar, replace it with a sugar substitute by following the manufacturer's directions. Some artificial sweeteners are heat tolerant and may be more suitable for baked products.

MODIFICATIONS IN SOUPS, SAUCES, AND GRAVIES

Soups, sauces, and gravies lend themselves to culinary creativity and experimentation. Classic sauces are flavorful but tend to be loaded with fat. Many are thickened with roux, a cooked mixture of fat and flour. Others are emulsion sauces, such as hollandaise and mayonnaise. Emulsion sauces are made of two or more ingredients that do not combine easily. These sauces are usually stabilized with egg yolk and butter or oil. The result is a sauce made predominantly of fat. Here are some ways to reduce the fat content of soups, sauces, and gravies:

- Use a reduction of stock to produce a reduction sauce. A reduction sauce is formed when a liquid is boiled until the water evaporates and the remaining juice is thickened. Start with a stock made from vegetables, meat, poultry, or fish, and simmer until the contents are about one-third of their original volume. Stock and broth have the potential to be nearly fat free because the fat rises to the top and can be skimmed off. In the process of reduction, the stock develops body and its flavors intensify. As a result, less thickener is needed.

- Use a slurry in place of a traditional flour-and-fat roux. A slurry is a thin paste made from water or stock mixed with starch, such as cornstarch. It can be a thickening alternative. To use a slurry, dissolve starch in cold water and incorporate it into the hot sauce.

- Use skimmed stock. Rather than using a premade mother sauce—a classic sauce from which other sauces are made—make a sauce of pan drippings, wine, broth, or stock from which the fat has been skimmed.

- Use less oil in salad dressings by replacing bland salad oils with intensely flavored nut oils, olive oils, or infused oils.

- Dilute cream-based sauces, dips, and dressings with broth, juice, or skim milk.

- To mimic a creamy sauce for macaroni and cheese, blend cottage cheese and strained yogurt. Use cornstarch as a thickener when heating.

- In place of heavy cream, use canned evaporated skim milk.

- In a braise or soup, puréeing the vegetables in the cooking liquid will thicken the sauce while retaining all the nutrients.

- In place of gravy, use a coulis, a thick, puréed sauce made from either vegetables or fruit. You could also serve a salsa or chutney, as shown in *Exhibit 8.9*. These are relishes that can also be made from vegetables or fruit.

- In béchamel sauce, use low-fat milk and soft margarine.

- Two teaspoons of sour cream or plain yogurt can be added as a garnish on low-fat cream soup to give it the mouthfeel of full-fat cream soup.

- Vegetable *jus*, the French term for juice, and consommé make great sauces.

Exhibit 8.9

MODIFICATIONS FOR MEAT

Exhibit 8.10

- Choose low-fat meat such as beef or pork tenderloin, beef eye of round, beef flank steak, beef sirloin steak, pork loin chops (shown in *Exhibit 8.10*), turkey breast, ostrich, buffalo, venison, or rabbit.

- Trim visible fat.

- Cook the meat using a low-fat cooking technique such as dry-sautéing, stir-frying, grilling, broiling, pan-smoking, or roasting.

- For poultry, select white-meat chicken instead of legs and thighs, which have a higher fat content.

- When cooking chicken, leave the skin on and remove it just before serving.

- If using a marinade, boneless, skinless chicken breast will work fine.

MODIFICATIONS FOR SEAFOOD

Exhibit 8.11

- Do not overcook fish and seafood, so as not to ruin their delicate flavors.

- Dry-sautéing, grilling, and poaching are the best cooking methods for healthful seafood.

- Swordfish, mackerel, salmon, and tuna (see *Exhibit 8.11*) provide customers with omega-3 fatty acids.

- Shellfish, such as shrimp, lobster, and crawfish, have high cholesterol content but no saturated fat, so they are relatively nutritious choices.

MODIFICATIONS FOR VEGETABLES

Exhibit 8.12

- Instead of sautéing vegetables in oil, sweat them in a little stock, as shown in *Exhibit 8.12*. This extracts flavor from the vegetables and is a good foundation for the rest of the dish.

- To finish a vegetable, add a small amount of butter or nut oil.

- If you use fat, use it at the end of cooking, so its flavor still can be perceived.

MODIFICATIONS FOR DESSERTS

It is important to know the functions of a dessert's ingredients. If a substitute ingredient will change the integrity of the dessert, as with pie crust, then the substitution should not be made. Here are some specific suggestions:

- Use low-fat or fat-free cottage cheese, ricotta cheese, yogurt, or cream cheese. If fat-free items are used, it is important to use some type of starch to protect the proteins from heat when baking, or else they will curdle.

Exhibit 8.13

- The fat in a pie crust is there to make it flaky. If the fat is reduced or changed, it would be necessary to change the nature of the dessert from a pie to a strudel (*Exhibit 8.13*) or a cobbler. When making a strudel, phyllo dough can be used as the pastry to reduce the fat significantly. Note: *Spray the dough with atomized oil before baking*. For a cobbler, little or no fat is needed.

MODIFICATIONS FOR GARNISHES

Instead of using small pieces of fried items such as shallots or potatoes, use thinly sliced pieces of vegetables.

MODIFICATIONS FOR REDUCING SALT

- To decrease salt while adding flavor, increase the use of herbs and spices. Use citrus and vinegars to season before adding salt.

- To add more flavor, use small amounts of prosciutto, olives, capers, anchovies, Parmesan cheese, or light soy sauce in place of salt.

When making modifications to reduce or avoid an ingredient, remember to keep flavor in mind. Be creative, and use modifications as an opportunity to make food memorable.

ORGANIZING AND DISSEMINATING STANDARDIZED RECIPES

Using standardized recipes has many advantages, as it controls many components of a restaurant or foodservice operation. As discussed in chapter 6, if an operation standardizes all its recipes, it can control factors such as costs, waste, portion size, nutritional composition, equipment usage, and staff-training requirements. When a recipe is made according to the same standard every time, recipe modifications will become automatic very quickly. This ensures that changes made with health in mind will endure as long as the standardized recipe is used.

It is important to stress that recipes must be in a written format that everyone in the operation can follow. This is an important step in adopting a nutrition program. Once recipes have been standardized, they should be entered into a computer system or kept in a location where all staff can access them easily. Managers should remember that staff will also need access to the recipes for special requests.

For operations with highly computerized setups to which all staff has access, managers should consider printing the recipes and keeping a backup copy, in addition to an electronic backup, in case of a computer malfunction. Computer systems are convenient because they allow for permanent recipe files. This also allows recipes to be stored outside the premises. This can help prevent the loss of data that is required for the business to operate.

For kitchen staff, a portable set of easily printable recipes is ideal. Chefs and cooks can take a copy to their stations to check ingredients and measurements. The recipes should be assembled in an easily written format with large enough print for all staff to see. Back-of-the-house staff should not be guessing about the measurements, ingredients, or yield of any recipe. The location of the recipe binders, books, or computer files, as well as any access information such as password hints, should be posted for all staff. There are many suggested standardized formats for recipes, and each operation should adapt a format based on its preferences and requirements.

ENSURING THAT RECIPES ARE USED

After new or adapted recipes have been developed for a nutrition program, the operation will need to prepare the recipes to see how well they work with the facility and the staff. Employees should locate and gather all of the following: the recipes that will be prepared, the necessary measuring tools, all ingredients, all appropriate dishes, and appropriate cooking wares.

Managers must review the importance of adhering to the standardized recipe with employees. Training might include a chef's demonstration of various cooking techniques to help other cooking staff incorporate the techniques into their skill set. Stress accuracy in preparation, accuracy in cooking, and accuracy in serving and plating the recipes.

TEACHING PORTION-CONTROL PRINCIPLES

Controlling portion size is one aspect of maintaining a healthy diet. *Any* type of food, nutritious or not, becomes a problem when eaten in excessive amounts. For the sake of health as well as standardization, restaurant and foodservice managers should train their employees in portion-control principles and methods.

Taking Measure

Measuring devices and tools are used for both food preparation and front-of-the-house tasks. Getting measurements correct is critical for the sake of successful recipes. However, ensuring that food is cooked correctly is only one part of the equation. How much of that food is portioned makes a large difference to an operation's bottom line and impacts the accuracy of menu labeling. This section of the guide is designed to help managers understand the importance of establishing and using accurate measures in their operations.

Manager's Memo

Food portions have grown during the past 20 years, increasing the total number of calories individuals consume daily. This is just one of the many issues challenging registered dietitians as they try to help Americans control their expanding waistlines. Experts have named this concept portion distortion. Young people who have grown up during this period are accustomed to the larger portions. They have no standard with which to compare and therefore must learn new standards to maintain their weight.

Establishments have an opportunity to adopt new portion sizes when the menu is restructured. Operators may decide to offer half portions to those customers who want less food. Some operations may develop a separate section of the menu to offer lower-calorie meals, including special portion sizes. Some operations have already made selecting steaks and chops easier by offering customers different options by weight or size. Portions should be adjusted to cater to the establishment's clientele.

Manager's Memo

An emphasis on accurate measurement is included in this chapter to assist managers in adopting standardized recipes. Accurate measures can affect an operation's bottom line by preventing overproduction of food and by eliminating waste.

In addition, recipe conversions can also be challenging. To assist employees with recipe conversions, place conversion charts on laminated cards in production areas. Plan training sessions with assignments that test employee comprehension in an interesting and fun way. Ensure that employees can use available technology. For example, an operation may have a computer program that automatically converts recipes for yield. Also, consider rotating employees with math skills and an interest in math to positions that require these skills. Your bottom line may improve as well.

Exhibit 8.14

VOLUME MEASURES

Measure	Equivalent
1 gallon	4 quarts
1 quart	2 pints
1 pint	2 cups
1 cup	16 tablespoons
1 tablespoon	3 teaspoons
1 pound	16 ounces
2 tablespoons	1 fluid ounce
1 tablespoon	½ fluid ounce

Scales

Restaurants and foodservice operations use many types of scales. Some operations use large floor scales, usually found near the dock, to weigh in orders that are delivered in bulky containers or bags. In the bakeshop, there may be table scales or bench scales to weigh flour, butter, and other ingredients for baking. These same scales can be used in the preparation area to weigh meat and other ingredients for cooking large-batch recipes. Smaller scales may be employed in the foodservice line for checking portioning of a dish that is being prepared for service.

All scales are central to getting accurate results with standardized recipes. Weight measurement is a more accurate choice than volume measurement for large operations or large-batch cooking. Volume measures are taken using a tool that determines how much space an item takes up. Examples of tools used to measure volume are graduated pitchers, measuring cups, and spoons. Due to settling of ingredients and the densities of some products, weights are often more accurate than volumes.

Scales have different modes of operation depending on their size and their function. All scales must have accurate calibration and a readable screen or face. Employees will not be able to stop and read each scale manual, so managers and chefs must read the manual and get operational help from the manufacturer if needed. A brief set of easy-use directions should be developed and stored near the scale. Many smaller scales are digital, and it is easy to "zero" the scale so that a serving dish can be weighed. This allows for accurate weight of the food in its container. Many operations use a smaller digital scale to check the weight of items on the service line or at the back of the house in a restaurant. As portions are served, some will be measured by volume and some will be weighed to ensure that the correct portion is served or provided.

Volumetric Measures

As noted above, weighing is more accurate for dry ingredients like flour or solid ingredients like butter. However, volume measures are often used for liquids and for small amounts of ingredients such as baking soda and baking powder (see *Exhibit 8.14* for most common measures). During food preparation, volume measures may be used when adding milk or vinegar to a recipe. In smaller recipes where a teaspoon or tablespoon is used, the employee must know the difference between the sizes and must understand how to overfill the measure and then level it at the top. In foodservice operations, there are often aluminum volume measures for liquid amounts greater than a cup that are marked with lines along the side. Employees must understand what the lines represent and add liquids to the correct line. Clear measures are helpful because people can see that the liquids have reached a certain line by viewing it at eye level.

If employees are having trouble measuring, they should practice with flour, which is very inexpensive. For liquid measures, they may practice with colored water, which provides a contrast and may help employees to visualize the lines on the sides of volume measures. Practice does make perfect. Staff should be given time to practice after the demonstration and before they begin working in the kitchen.

A variety of tools are used to serve food, such as spoons, spoon ladles (spoodles), scoops, dippers, and ladles (see *Exhibit 8.15*). These are all volumetric measures. One excellent way to become educated on portions and portion sizes is to make a deliberate effort to observe the different portions dictated by the standardized recipes each time they are prepared in the kitchen.

Exhibit 8.15

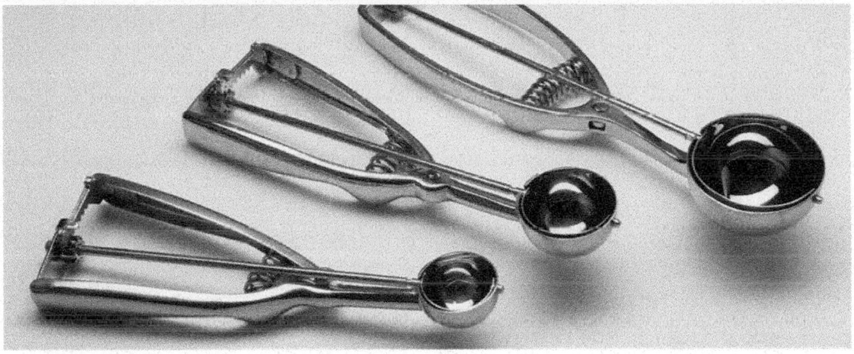

Number 16 is one-fourth cup.

Number 12 is one-third cup.

Number 8 is one-half cup.

Standardized recipes should include the scoop or spoon size to ensure a proper portion. A manager would be smart to observe these measures in order to teach them to new employees and to become more likely to detect portion mistakes by eye. Training employees on volumetric measures can be fun because the content is hands-on, and staff members tend to remember what they have worked with in the kitchen.

Temperature Tools

While pathogens (disease-causing microorganisms such as viruses, bacteria, and parasites) are always a concern, temperature measures are also used to ensure that food is cooked to a perfect doneness and to achieve the proper yield. Overcooking dries out food and reduces the yield. In addition, it results in low-quality food because some of the vitamins will be destroyed by the increased time at higher temperatures. This goes for food from all five food groups.

Employees who are preparing food need to be taught where to place the thermometer when measuring for accurate cooking temperatures. They also need to know how to calibrate thermometers. All restaurants and foodservice operations must abide by the correct temperatures to ensure that pathogens do not grow to unsafe levels in the food.

The *ServSafe® Coursebook* provides information about accurate temperatures for use by restaurants and foodservice operations. This information is essential to avoiding pathogens in the kitchen. Pathogens grow in the temperature danger zone of 41°F to 135°F (5°C to 57°C). In each professional kitchen, someone must have a certificate in food sanitation and safety. This person is trained to ensure proper and safe foodhandling in the kitchen.

OBSERVING AND EVALUATING EMPLOYEE PERFORMANCE

All employees should have a chance to be trained on all procedures regarding the menu items they will be preparing. Then the chef or manager should make observations of employees' ability to implement the menu. Many operations provide photos with the exact menu items on the plate so that staff can use a visual aid to check their food preparation for accuracy. The manager should note which employees are performing confidently and correctly and which are not.

Managers should provide positive feedback to employees who are implementing the nutrition program correctly. Those employees who do not seem confident and who make errors should be scheduled for retraining. They may need more practice or clarification. Reinforcement of accurate measuring and good plate presentation should be done to ensure that the staff understands the importance of these skills. In order for employees to follow the portioning that is taught to them, they need to know that they will be corrected if the plate served is wrong. Managing the measuring process in the kitchen will result in accurate recipes and correct, consistent portion sizes. It will also ensure that healthy ingredients are used in the correct amounts and unhealthy ingredients are either eliminated or kept to a minimum.

> **THINK ABOUT IT . . .**
>
> Some employees may resist the use of standardized recipes and measurement procedures. What can you as a manager do to help employees understand the importance of these issues?

SUMMARY

1. **Explain how cooking and cooking methods affect nutrition.**

   Light, heat, acidity, and alkalinity can change, diminish, or destroy the nutrients in food. Water-soluble vitamins and minerals can be lost due to leaching if they have been soaked in water. Therefore, fruit and vegetables should be washed and rinsed quickly and carefully to help retain their vitamins and minerals.

   In addition to careful preparation, minimal cooking time helps preserve vitamins and minerals, especially water-soluble vitamins. Steaming, microwaving, and stir-frying are good methods. Healthy cooking techniques are summarized in *Exhibit 8.4*.

2. **Explain the difference between the center-of-plate concept and the MyPlate model.**

   The traditional center-of-plate concept emphasizes a large, featured protein food item surrounded by smaller, less-important side dishes. The MyPlate model, which is more in line with current dietary recommendations, calls for a balanced plate of more equally sized portions of food items that offer a variety of nutrients.

3. **Describe how to modify and adapt recipes according to the latest dietary recommendations, and explain the importance of adopting standardized recipes.**

   Recipes should contain less solid fat, including saturated fat, trans fat, and cholesterol. Recipes can be adapted for these changes by using little or no butter, sour cream, shortening, or cream. Healthy fats such as olive oils, canola oils, and nut oils can be used in place of solid fats. The use of trans-fatty acids should be avoided.

   Recipes should contain fewer eggs and high-fat meat to reduce saturated fat and cholesterol. Turkey, chicken, and fish can be used along with lean cuts of beef in appropriate portions. Vegetable proteins such as beans and peas can be used to increase plant protein.

   Recipes can be adapted to increase flavor through cooking techniques and the use of spices and herbs to lower salt, and therefore sodium. Recipes should feature more whole-grain products and less refined grains. Added sugars should be reduced in recipes and in desserts.

   Standardizing all recipes in an operation can control many factors, including costs, waste, portion size, nutritional composition, equipment usage, and staff requirements. All staff must have access to the standardized recipes to ensure proper implementation.

4. **Identify effective ways to organize and store recipes and to make recipes accessible to staff.**

   Recipes should be assembled in a written format with large enough print for all staff to see. Employees should be trained on the location, organization, and use of the recipes. Use a consistent format that works for the operation. Computer systems are convenient because they allow for permanent files for recipes, and they allow copies of recipes to be stored off the premises.

5. **Explain how to train staff to use scales and measuring tools.**

   Use the appropriate scales and measures for each part of the operation. In addition to making the tools available to the staff, provide adequate training so that the equipment is used consistently and accurately. Some equipment, such as thermometers, also plays a role in food-preparation safety because some types of undercooked meat may present a health hazard to customers.

6. **Describe the importance of evaluating the effectiveness of employee training on measurement tools and procedures as well as providing feedback to employees.**

   During training, managers should provide immediate feedback to employees. Positive feedback is just as important as corrective feedback when it comes to live training. Set aside time for practice using measurement equipment. In order for employees to follow the portioning that they have been taught, they need to know that they will be corrected if the plate is served is incorrectly.

APPLICATION EXERCISES

Exercise 1

Shown below are menu items that are high in fat. Using the principles in this chapter, suggest five modifications to improve this meal's nutritional value.

Menu Items: Butter-roasted half-chicken with pan gravy, cheddar mashed potatoes, and a fried shallot garnish

Exercise 2

Gather up a selection of different measuring devices, including ladles and measuring cups.

Using an unmarked ladle and your best judgment, try to measure out a two-ounce serving of sauce onto a

plate. Set the plate aside. Using an unmarked ladle, try to measure out a 10-ounce serving of soup into a bowl. Set the bowl aside.

Next, using a measuring device, measure exactly two ounces of sauce onto a plate. Do the same to measure exactly 10 ounces of soup into a bowl. Compare the measured amounts with your estimated amounts.

How close were you? Did you serve too little, too much, or just the right amount? If you were working in a restaurant or foodservice operation, how would this impact food cost and calorie counts for the items served?

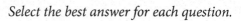

REVIEW YOUR LEARNING

Select the best answer for each question.

1. **Which technique is appropriate for building flavor while reducing the fat content of a sauce?**
   A. Using a reduction sauce
   B. Using an emulsion sauce
   C. Using a roux-based sauce
   D. Using olive oil in the sauce

2. **A moist-heat cooking technique used to prepare less-tender cuts of meat is**
   A. baking.
   B. grilling.
   C. braising.
   D. stir-frying.

3. **In which types of food are trans-fatty acids found naturally?**
   A. Grains and vegetables
   B. Fruit and juices
   C. Milk and meat
   D. Eggs and nuts

4. **Trans-fatty acids affect blood-cholesterol levels by**
   A. raising good-cholesterol levels and lowering total cholesterol.
   B. lowering bad-cholesterol levels and raising total cholesterol.
   C. raising bad-cholesterol levels and lowering good cholesterol.
   D. lowering both good- and bad-cholesterol levels.

5. **What is one potential benefit of using a standardized recipe in a restaurant or foodservice operation?**
   A. Simplifies service
   B. Increases waitstaff
   C. Controls food costs
   D. Encourages buying locally

6. **Which ingredient is frequently used to lower fat in baked goods?**
   A. Fruit purées
   B. Reductions
   C. Olive oil
   D. Slurries

7. How many quarts are in a gallon?

   A. 2

   B. 4

   C. 6

   D. 8

8. In addition to ensuring food safety, restaurants and foodservice operations should monitor the temperature of meat during cooking in order to

   A. lower the fat content.

   B. increase the saltiness.

   C. change the seasonings.

   D. keep moisture in the product.

9. Which preparation technique for vegetables retains the greatest amount of nutrients?

   A. Deep-frying

   B. Pan-frying

   C. Steaming

   D. Boiling

10. In order to help customers feel they are getting good value in their portions, restaurants and foodservice operations can

   A. use bigger plates.

   B. use smaller plates.

   C. serve refined grains.

   D. decrease fruit and vegetables.

9

Food Allergens and Special Dietary Requests

INSIDE THIS CHAPTER

- What Are Food Allergies, Food Intolerances, and Celiac Disease?
- Developing a Food-Allergen Program
- Identifying Allergens in the Operation
- Developing Policies and Procedures for Communicating about Allergies
- Training Staff on Standard Operating Procedures for Allergens
- Identifying Suppliers for Specialty Items
- Diets for Religious, Cultural, Social, or Health Needs

CHAPTER LEARNING OBJECTIVES

After completing this chapter, you should be able to:

- Describe the causes and symptoms of allergic reactions, and list the eight main food allergens.

- Describe the cause and symptoms of celiac disease and other food intolerances.

- Describe the steps for establishing a food-allergen program.

- Explain how to handle requests from customers with food allergies, sensitivities, and intolerances.

- Describe how to train staff to deal with allergens in a restaurant or foodservice operation.

- Describe how to acquire new and alternative ingredients.

- Recognize the most common religious diets and other dietary restrictions.

KEY TERMS

allergic reaction, p. 188

anaphylaxis, p. 188

celiac disease, p. 189

cross-contact, p. 195

epinephrine, p. 187

food-allergen program, p. 192

food allergy, p. 188

gluten, p. 189

halal, p. 202

kosher, p. 201

lactase, p. 190

lactose intolerance, p. 190

malabsorption, p. 190

meat analog, p. 200

pareve, p. 201

vegetarian, p. 199

CASE STUDY

While having dinner with friends at a restaurant, a customer explains to his server that he has a shellfish allergy. The waitress acknowledges that she is aware of the allergy and highlights some menu items that do not contain shellfish. The customer orders his food.

The customer notices that a different person delivers the food to the table—not the server who took his order. Within minutes of eating the first bite, he has an itching sensation around his mouth. He calls the original server to the table, and she realizes that a mistake has been made. Knowing that time is now an issue, she asks her manager what to do next. By the time the manager arrives at the table, the customer's friends have helped him use an epi-pen containing epinephrine, a hormone used to treat serious allergic reactions. In addition, they have called 911. The customer is unable to speak and is lying on the floor. Several other guests surround the table. The manager meets the ambulance at the door. Everyone hopes the customer gets to the hospital in time.

1. What might have happened to the customer's order?

2. Who is responsible for this mishap?

3. Did the server and the manager respond appropriately? Explain.

4. What are the possible outcomes of this mistake?

WHAT ARE FOOD ALLERGIES, FOOD INTOLERANCES, AND CELIAC DISEASE?

In the United States, approximately 12 million people have a food allergy, which is a negative reaction to a food protein. This number currently represents about 4 percent of the population, but the incidence of food allergies is on the rise. It is very important for restaurants and foodservice professionals to pay attention to customers who report food allergies. The goal is to protect customers from the offending food or ingredient and to earn their trust. This could translate into both new business and repeat business for establishments, since most people who have allergies want to participate in a lifestyle that includes dining out.[1] Following strict rules and procedures for dealing with food allergies also reduces the operation's exposure to liability stemming from food allergy–related incidents.

Causes and Symptoms of Food Allergies

A person develops a food allergy when the immune system, which is designed to protect the body from foreign invaders, reacts abnormally to a particular food by creating antibodies against it. The food or food ingredient that causes this reaction or response to occur is called the allergen. The next time the person eats the allergen, the immune system launches a defense against it, causing an adverse reaction or allergic reaction. From then on, each time the person eats the allergen, the same reaction occurs. In some cases, just coming into contact with the food is enough to cause the reaction. For some individuals, even tiny amounts of the allergen can be dangerous, and the reaction can get worse with repeated exposure.

Allergic reactions are associated with mild or severe symptoms such as itching around the mouth, swelling of the tongue, hives, metallic taste, and rashes. Although people can develop allergies to many types of food or food ingredients, about 90 percent of life-threatening allergic reactions are caused by just eight allergens: eggs, wheat, tree nuts, peanuts, soy, cow's milk and milk products, fish, and shellfish, as shown in *Exhibit 9.1*. These eight allergens can cause anaphylaxis, a severe reaction with rapid onset that is usually accompanied by a drop in blood pressure, closing of the throat, and the loss of consciousness. At this time, there is no cure for food allergies. People must simply avoid the allergens to prevent reactions. Although some people outgrow food allergies, allergies to peanuts, tree nuts, and shellfish are usually lifelong.

THINK ABOUT IT . . .

Even though eight food allergens cause about 90 percent of life-threatening allergic reactions, people can be allergic or sensitive to *any* food or ingredient. What might staff need to know to help customers avoid allergens?

[1] *"Welcoming Guests with Allergies," The Food Allergy and Anaphylaxis Network*, www.foodallergy.org

Exhibit 9.1

EIGHT RECOGNIZED ALLERGENS

Milk and dairy products

Eggs and egg products

Fish

Shellfish (e.g., crab, lobster, shrimp)

Tree nuts (e.g., almonds, Brazil nuts, cashews, chestnuts, hazelnuts, hickory nuts, macadamia nuts, pecans, pine nuts, pistachios, and walnuts)

Peanuts

Wheat

Soy and soy products

Celiac Disease

Celiac disease is an autoimmune condition that affects approximately two million people in the United States, or one out of every 133 Americans. The offending substance is gluten, a protein found in wheat, rye, and barley. A person with celiac disease also may avoid oats if they are milled at the same facility as wheat, rye, or barley.

When people with celiac disease eat these grains or anything containing them, their immune systems react by destroying their intestinal villi. People may suffer symptoms such as serious skin rashes, fatigue, abdominal bloating and pain, and seemingly unrelated conditions like osteoporosis and

Exhibit 9.2

HEALTHY SMALL INTESTINE AND SMALL INTESTINE AFFECTED BY CELIAC DISEASE

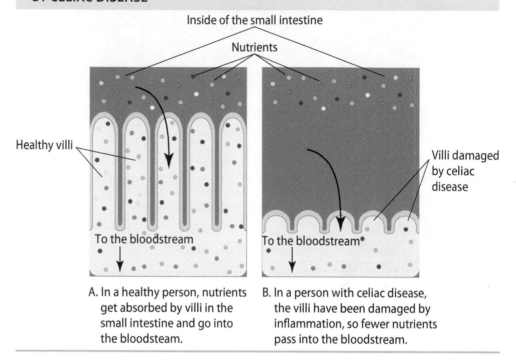

A. In a healthy person, nutrients get absorbed by villi in the small intestine and go into the bloodsteam.

B. In a person with celiac disease, the villi have been damaged by inflammation, so fewer nutrients pass into the bloodstream.

rheumatoid arthritis. For these individuals, avoiding gluten is imperative to decreasing symptoms and maintaining health (see *Exhibit 9.2*).

As discussed in chapter 2, the villi play an important role in the absorption of all nutrients. Eventually people with celiac disease can experience malabsorption, which is a difficulty absorbing nutrients from food. They may suffer from nutrient deficiencies if they do not follow a gluten-free diet.

As with food allergies, there is no cure for celiac disease. The treatment is to remove all potential sources of gluten from the diet. This is a difficult task, since gluten is found in many food items (see *Exhibit 9.3*). People with celiac disease must learn to examine everything they want to consume.

Lactose Intolerance

Lactose is the sugar found in milk and other dairy products. Lactose intolerance, which is the inability to digest this substance, is caused by a deficiency of the enzyme lactase. African American, Asian, and Native American populations have a decreased tolerance for lactose. In addition, aging is associated with a loss of enzyme activity, resulting in increased lactose intolerance. Common symptoms of lactose intolerance are diarrhea and intestinal discomfort due to gas and bloating.

THINK ABOUT IT . . .

Do you, a family member, or friend have a food allergy? Have you had to communicate a specific dietary restriction to restaurant staff? Was the wait staff able to understand your request and fill your order to your expectations?

Exhibit 9.3

GLUTEN-FREE DIET

Individuals following a gluten-free diet should avoid all forms of wheat, including einkorn, emmer, spelt, kamut, wheat starches, wheat germ, bran, bulgur wheat, cracked wheat, and hydrolyzed wheat protein as in thickeners and processed food.

In addition, avoidance of barley, rye, and triticale is necessary since they contain gluten. Oats may be avoided by some individuals. If oats are included in the diet, they should be obtained from sources that can ensure the oats have not been milled with other grains.

Avoid flour from wheat, rye, and barley. Common forms of flour include bromated, durum, enriched (including bread, cake, or pastry flours), farina, graham, phosphated, self-rising, and semolina.

Processed food items that could contain gluten are bouillon cubes, candy, cold cuts, French fries (with coatings), rice syrup, rice mixes, soy sauce, soups, sauces, malt vinegar, and gravies. Check all processed food labels for forms of wheat, rye, and barley.

Most beer is made with malt from barley; however, gluten-free beer can be purchased.

An adequate dietary intake can be achieved with a gluten-free diet, as alternate grains can be selected. Fruit, vegetables, dairy, and meat are all gluten-free when prepared with no food items from the list above. Tolerance of dairy products is dependent on the individual.

Some popular food items that are gluten-free are amaranth, arrowroot, buckwheat, corn or cornmeal, flax, legumes, nuts, quinoa, rice, seeds, soy, tapioca, and wild rice.

Lactose intolerance is usually a very manageable condition. People usually retain some tolerance for small amounts of lactose, usually less than the amount in a cup of milk. They can purchase lactase over the counter and take it when they eat dairy products containing lactose. In addition, low-lactose milk and products like low-lactose cottage cheese are available in the market. Many lactose-intolerant individuals can also enjoy yogurt and dairy drinks because these products contain bacterial cultures. Aged cheeses usually contain the least lactose because the bacteria cultures have consumed it.

Other Food Intolerances

One of the main differences between food intolerances and food allergies is that intolerances do not involve the immune system. However, people who are intolerant or sensitive to certain ingredients have some physical reaction that is undesirable or unpleasant. Some people may be sensitive to food additives like sulfites or monosodium glutamate, and they will ask questions regarding the content of menu items to avoid these substances. Waitstaff who are well informed regarding the ingredients found in menu items can help customers with selections and ensure that the customer gets the correct food (*Exhibit 9.4*).

Exhibit 9.4

DEVELOPING A FOOD-ALLERGEN PROGRAM

Restaurant and foodservice operations must be prepared to safely serve people with food allergies, food intolerances (such as gluten or lactose), and other special dietary needs. Although allergies and intolerances are caused by different medical conditions, in a practical sense they are about avoiding certain food items and ingredients. This is accomplished by creating a program that alerts all restaurant staff to the specific needs of the customer to avoid these substances. It is imperative that each operation adopts a food-allergen program to ensure the safety of their customers and to alleviate potential liabilities. A food-allergen program is defined in this book as a set of goals and actions with the objective of ensuring that customers who have indicated that they have a food allergy or food intolerance are not exposed to the offending substance through food or beverages in the operation.

In addition to food sanitation and safety regulations, many operations have external requirements that would be fulfilled by a formal allergen program. These operations may be part of a larger corporation or business entity; they may be regulated by local laws that affect their business; or they may need to meet certain requirements in order to obtain or purchase insurance.

An operation must take the following steps in order to determine the details of its food-allergen program:

- Review marketing plans for the development of a food-allergen program. Some marketing plans may already address this issue. In addition, it may be worthwhile to research potential demand and customer requirements.

- Determine whether the plan satisfies external requirements affecting the organization or establishment. Local laws, customer base, and insurance requirements should all be considered.

- Determine the extent of the program. Available resources and the regulatory environment can guide this step.

- Designate which person on the staff will plan and implement the allergen program.

- Designate who will be responsible for accommodating customers who report food allergies or intolerances. This should include someone for each shift throughout the week and weekend.

The marketing plan for an establishment should explain how its staff will handle the development of the food-allergen program. It might include specific targeted dates or budgets that will be devoted to the program's adoption. It may list program goals, such as increased traffic in the establishment or a budget devoted to preventing allergic reactions on the premises. Implementing an allergen program that is formalized, stated in writing, and in line with standard operating procedures will help keep staff informed. Standard operating procedures often decrease both staff mistakes and insurance costs. They also promote consistency in training and retraining of staff.

Food-allergen programs vary in extent. For example, one operation's program might primarily address simple change requests involving a limited number of menu items. Another program might involve training selected staff to assist customers. Other operations may try to attract customers by broadening their menu items, adding products such as gluten-free pasta or gluten-free beer, or advertising their proficiency in assisting customers who have allergies.

One major decision to be made at the outset is who will be responsible for the new food-allergen program as a whole and who will be responsible for training the staff and implementing the program. For many organizations, the responsible person is the chef or the manager in charge. Some larger organizations might provide trainers or other outside personnel who can assist in implementing a program.

IDENTIFYING ALLERGENS IN THE OPERATION

Once a restaurant or foodservice operation has decided to adopt a food-allergen program, the next step is to determine which allergens are present in the establishment. Managers should review ingredients, recipes, and plating to see what allergens they contain. Sophisticated software programs can search through recipes for allergens and assist the chef and managers with this task.

All recipes containing one or more of the eight main allergens, plus gluten, need to be marked clearly. This includes garnishes, sauces, appetizers, breads, drinks, soups, sides, salads, and desserts. The allergens may be marked physically on the recipe or added to computer data for future reference. Every item must be reviewed because even small traces of the offending allergen can cause a reaction. Items that are used in preparation, such as rubs, marinades, and coatings, also need to be reviewed. For example, a spicy dipping sauce that contains peanut oil or meat coated with egg and wheat flour could cause an allergic reaction.

Once recipes that contain targeted allergens are identified, the chef and managers can then develop a list of menu items that can be used as substitutions. Both chefs and waitstaff will use this list when recipes have to be changed. Excluding known allergens may require the purchase of new ingredients or a change in preparation methods. The list of substitutions and modifications must be accurate and should be checked carefully for mistakes or omissions. The information should be transmitted to the back of the house for the purposes of menu planning and recipe development, as well as to the front of the house for the purpose of communicating potential substitutions to customers.

Manager's Memo

A foodservice operation that wants to adopt an allergen program may want to hire a registered dietitian (RD) as a consultant. An RD will assist the operation in identifying all sources of the eight main allergens and sources of gluten found in menu items.

An RD can encourage the adoption of standardized recipes to ensure that the same ingredients will be used by all who prepare a menu item. Computer systems can be implemented to mark and sort items that contain any of the allergens or gluten. Chefs and cooks can easily access this information, allowing them to serve the customer better. An RD can also assist an operation in identifying menu items that work well for special dietary requests, such as for heart disease or diabetes.

Here is a summary of steps for identifying allergens:

- Review each menu item for eggs, wheat, rye, barley, soy, milk and milk products, fish, shellfish, tree nuts, and peanuts.
- Review all recipes, ingredients, preparation methods, and plating for these allergens.
- Determine the needed modifications and substitutions for each ingredient.
- Review menu items that require substitutions or modifications.
- Develop a list of modifications and substitutions for the back of the house to allow for preparation of allergen-free dishes.
- After menu items have been decided, prepare lists to be shared with the front of the house as alternative suggestions.

DEVELOPING POLICIES AND PROCEDURES FOR COMMUNICATING ABOUT ALLERGIES

After the managers, chefs, or other foodservice professionals have determined which allergens are present in the operation, the next step is to examine the communication path for customers who have allergies and intolerances. It is important to develop policies about how this information will be communicated throughout the operation.

Listening to Customers

Customers tend to offer clues to their particular dietary needs. Information is often revealed before the customer even looks at the menu. When they sit at a table, customers are generally already thinking about what they will be able to eat. Here are some possible ways that customers might indicate potential food allergies or other dietary needs:

- Asking questions about the ingredients used to prepare items, such as "Do you use peanut oil to cook the food?" or "What cooking oil do you use to prepare the stir-fry?"
- Handing the server a card that reports an allergy to a certain food or ingredient.
- Asking the server if he or she knows about celiac disease, gluten-free diets, or other dietary needs.
- Eliminating several menu items as choices, with comments like "I can't have this item or that item." These comments may indicate a preference or a special dietary need.
- Asking if a recipe can be prepared without a certain ingredient. For example, a customer following a heart-healthy diet may ask, "Can this item be made without butter or salt?"
- Requesting to speak directly to the manager.

It is the responsibility of the customer to declare or disclose food allergies or other special dietary needs. However, a trained staff member listening carefully to the customer can ask further questions and help customers feel confident that they will receive their food correctly. For example, people who are avoiding peanut oil should be asked if it is a preference or if they have a peanut allergy. People who are eliminating choices on the menu may have dietary restrictions, so the wait staff should be ready to listen carefully and be prepared to make suggestions.

Waitstaff who have been trained to help customers with suggested substitutions can talk through the choices with customers and help them place their orders. At this point some operations have the manager or chef take the responsibility of ensuring the food is correct and that the allergen is not present in the customer's food.

Preparation and Delivery

Next, the responsible person communicates the order to the kitchen. In most establishments, the order will need to be marked or tagged in some way. Many operations use point-of-sale (POS) software programs that allow them to mark or tag a special order or allergy. In this way, the kitchen staff receives the needed information quickly.

The kitchen staff reads the customer's order carefully and double-checks the appropriate recipes to make sure they do not contain the allergen. Information may be gleaned from data in the computer or from the carefully marked recipes discussed earlier. The responsible person, usually a manager, will ensure that the chefs are aware of the allergy and that all recipes and food items have been checked for the allergen. Then, being sure to use fresh, clean, and sanitized dishes, pans, utensils, knives, cutting boards, and counters, the chefs will prepare the menu items. This will prevent accidental cross-contact with the allergen. Cross-contact occurs when one food item comes in contact with another. *Exhibit 9.5* shows an example of cross-contact; when using the same fryer for both shrimp and chicken, shrimp allergens could be transferred to the chicken. Preventing cross-contact is especially critical for customers with allergies. These precautions are discussed in the ServSafe® materials that are also a part of this certificate program.

Exhibit 9.5

Next, the responsible person delivers the completed dish to the customer, makes sure that he or she has identified the correct customer, and checks that the staff understood the allergy correctly. As with all good table service, the waitstaff should check back with the customer to make sure that everything is going well.

A restaurant or foodservice operation can attract potential customers who have food allergies or food intolerances by posting their menu and nutritional information online. This effort on the part of the establishment provides customers who have special dietary needs the opportunity to preview the menu. If the individual finds menu items that fit into their dietary pattern, they can plan to dine at your establishment knowing they will not be jeopardizing their health.

Also, a well-designed Web site can expand your menu and provide much more information to your customers through its aesthetic properties. For example, an emphasis on gluten-free items might also be linked on the Web to people who are searching for restaurants with more gluten-free menu items or expertise in this area.

Correcting Mistakes

If the allergen is included in a food on the plate and it is discovered as the plate is delivered to the customer, the entire plate of food must be replaced and a new meal must be prepared. Customers with allergies may want to keep the food that is in error at the table in order to prevent restaurant staff from the mistake of simply replacing an item on the plate and returning the same plate to the customer. This type of mistake would be serious, as some of the allergen has already touched the plate. Even trace amounts of the allergen could cause the customer to have a reaction.

Managers should take the following steps to ensure effective communication regarding an allergy or intolerance:

- Develop policies detailing how waitstaff will communicate with the customer. Policies also should include who will take the order and when the responsible person should be included in the order. Develop methods to communicate with the customer about the menu items. This includes detailed menu descriptions, signs in the establishment or statements on the menu about efforts to fulfill special requests, and statements that more information is available on request.

- Develop policies detailing how the order will be sent to the kitchen staff and how it will be marked or tagged if a POS system is not used.

- Develop guidelines for chefs, cooks, and other kitchen staff on how the meal should be prepared to avoid cross-contact.

- Develop policies for waitstaff to avoid adding extra items to the meal or plate or serving any other food or beverage item to the customer without the responsible person checking for the food allergen or intolerance.

TRAINING STAFF ON STANDARD OPERATING PROCEDURES FOR ALLERGENS

An operation should not implement a new food-allergen program until the staff is trained to anticipate and react correctly to situations that may occur with customers. All staff should be educated on what an allergy is, how a reaction occurs, and the likely symptoms a customer will display if he or she receives the allergen. Although the trainer can provide explanations and definitions in person, this type of information is best demonstrated by video content that vividly demonstrates the serious consequences that can accompany a mistake in foodservice. In addition, it is beneficial to invite someone who has a severe allergy to visit during a training session to share what it is like to live with the allergy.

It is particularly important to train staff on what to do if a customer has an allergic reaction on-site. Allergic reactions can happen within seconds of being exposed to the allergen. Waitstaff should visit the table after the food is served to make sure everything is all right. If the customer has come into contact with an allergen, he or she might have a limited time, perhaps only minutes, to call for medical attention. Therefore, getting immediate help is critical, as is having the proper emergency procedures in place. All staff should know these emergency procedures, as well as the address and phone number of the restaurant or foodservice operation. This information should be posted at every telephone and at each entrance and exit of the establishment.

Bar and Dining-Room Staff

During allergen training, the bar and dining-room staff might be divided into small groups to role-play customer-communication scenarios with the manager or responsible person. In this way the manager or chef can gauge staff members' comfort in conversing with customers about their allergies or intolerances. After initial training is completed, managers should post reminders throughout the operation. Taking the time to have staff answer questions on a one-to-one basis will help to identify remaining knowledge gaps.

Kitchen Staff

The kitchen staff should be trained on how to access information about every recipe. They should also be given access to lists of menu item or ingredient substitutions. All recipes must have potential allergens clearly marked, and revised recipes and substitutions should be located either on an accessible computer or in an organized notebook or file. Chefs should be trained on how and where to store gluten-free supplies.

The term *cross-contact* should be introduced and defined. Examples of how cross-contact occurs are necessary to help the kitchen staff avoid this situation. Some of the experienced staff should demonstrate how to handle a special-order dish through the kitchen.

Exhibit 9.6

Evaluating the Training

The chef or manager in charge will need to assess all staff with regard to their learning about the food-allergen program. It is important both to observe staff as they work and to make note of concepts and procedures that need reinforcement or follow-up training (*Exhibit 9.6*). A person who has a good rapport with the staff should review and practice these concepts and procedures during off-peak hours. Staff will need to be trained and retrained because complacency and turnover will occur at some point. Scheduling regular training and requiring attendance are the only ways to ensure that everyone has been trained.

Managers should develop training sessions that cover the following topics:

- Allergens and cross-contact
- Menu item ingredients, modifications, substitutions, and alternatives
- Emergency procedures for handling allergic reactions
- Procedures for protecting customers from allergens
- Evaluation of previous training
- Retraining

IDENTIFYING SUPPLIERS FOR SPECIALTY ITEMS

Once menu items have been added and revised per the food-allergen program, the establishment can focus on checking with vendors to determine what items can be ordered and at what cost. Many vendors are helpful in locating hard-to-find ingredients. They are interested in expanding their business and will assist you in procuring what you need. Many organizations have competitive policies for ordering items, and those policies will include a description of the exact ingredients and the specifications required by the operation.

It may be difficult at first to establish the quantities of some types of food or ingredients that an operation will require as it expands its menu. However, operations must develop exacting specifications on the ingredients themselves in order to ensure that they receive the products without the allergens. For example, many soy sauces include wheat in the production and processing. Since wheat is an allergen and is not permitted in a gluten-free diet, someone in the operation will need to specify why a certain product is required so that the special item will be obtained. See *Exhibit 9.7* for a sample of what a product specification for gluten-free flour might look like.

Manager's Memo

Finding credible resources in nutrition is an important task, as there are many Web sites that do not provide accurate information. For food allergies, there is an online source that managers and other foodservice personnel will find helpful.

The Food Allergy and Anaphylaxis Network, or FAAN, is a nonprofit organization that can be found on the Web at *www.foodallergy.org/.* The membership of this organization is 22,000 people worldwide, many of whom have allergies themselves or have children or relatives with allergies. In addition, doctors, nurses, and dietitians are members of this organization.

Exhibit 9.7

STANDARD PRODUCT SPECIFICATION FOR GLUTEN-FREE FLOUR

Description: Gluten-free flour that can be substituted in most recipes for all-purpose, enriched, unbleached wheat flour.

Quality: Gluten-free flour must meet federal guidelines for labeling and contain less than 20 parts per million of gluten.

Weight/Size: 20 ounces or more per box; 12 boxes per case. Each box or container must be individually labeled with contents.

Performance Requirements: Flour must be recipe-ready and can be substituted one for one.

Safety Requirements: Container must have closure or seal to prevent loss and accidental exposure to other sources with gluten. Must be delivered in dry, unopened cases.

Tolerances: Flour may have added ingredients, such as rice flour, cornstarch, tapioca dextrin, xanthan gum, or rice extract for better performance. Certified gluten-free a plus.

The operation might also specify a low-salt or trans fat–free product. When any of these products are received, the operation must check them on delivery and ensure it received the exact product ordered. Staff must label these products and store them so that they can be identified by anyone who will use them in assisting customers with special dietary requests. Please refer to ServSafe® guidelines on receiving and storing products.

Operations may have to use specialty vendors for ingredients that will be used in small quantities, such as gluten-free products. The final objective is to order the product from a reputable vendor that can assure consistency and high quality. The operation should ask for competitive bids and solicit delivery information to get the best price and the most convenient service. Some operations can also participate in taste testing to determine which product works best for the recipe and meets the operation's standards for quality.

DIETS FOR RELIGIOUS, CULTURAL, SOCIAL, OR HEALTH NEEDS

Some people adhere to special diets for philosophical, cultural, or religious reasons. Restaurant and foodservice professionals can accommodate these individuals and provide food that fits their needs.

Vegetarian Diets

A vegetarian is someone who does not eat meat, fish, or poultry. Within this broad definition, vegetarians vary widely in their eating patterns. For example, vegans follow a diet devoid of all animal food and animal products. People choose a vegetarian diet for many reasons, including personal health, the environment, animal welfare, economic and ethical considerations, world health, and religious beliefs. A recent poll indicated that about 3 percent of American adults aged 18 or older are vegetarian.[2] *Exhibit 9.8* lists the most commonly accepted classifications for vegetarians.

The potential number of vegetarian customers is too large for restaurant and foodservice operations to ignore. Every restaurant and foodservice professional

Exhibit 9.8

TYPES OF VEGETARIANS

Type	Will eat	Will not eat
Lacto-vegetarian	Grains, vegetables, fruit, soy and other legumes, beans, nuts, seeds, dairy	Meat, fish, poultry, eggs
Ovo-vegetarian	Grains, vegetables, fruit, soy and other legumes, beans, nuts, seeds, eggs	Meat, fish, poultry, dairy
Lacto-ovo-vegetarian	Grains, vegetables, fruit, soy and other legumes, beans, nuts, seeds, dairy, eggs	Meat, fish, poultry
Vegan	Grains, vegetables, fruit, soy and other legumes, beans, nuts, seeds	Meat, fish, poultry, and all other animal products, such as dairy and eggs

[2] *The Vegetarian Resource Group from May 1–5, 2009, via its QuickQuery[SM] online omnibus service, interviewing a nationwide sample of 2,397 U.S. adults aged 18 and older* (www.vrg.org).

Exhibit 9.9

Vegans do not consume animals or animal products. Instead, they get their protein from vegetable sources.

should attempt to understand vegetarians' dietary needs. In fact, the National Restaurant Association reports that 8 out of 10 U.S. restaurant and foodservice operations with table service offer vegetarian entrées.

In its position paper on vegetarian diets, the Academy of Nutrition and Dietetics states that "appropriately planned vegetarian diets, including total vegetarian or vegan diets, are healthful, nutritionally adequate, and may provide health benefits in the prevention and treatment of certain diseases."[3]

COMPLEMENTARY PROTEINS

In order to maintain their health and to get the correct amount of protein, vegetarians must eat a variety of grains, vegetables, fruit, legumes and beans, nuts, and seeds daily (see *Exhibit 9.9*). For vegans it is also important to receive all nine essential amino acids daily. They can achieve this by combining incomplete but complementary plant proteins to get all nine amino acids in sufficient quantities.

VEGETARIAN FOOD ITEMS

Vegetarian food items, widely available in today's markets, make it easy to follow a vegetarian diet and help restaurant and foodservice operations cater to vegetarians. Fortified food items such as soy milk, calcium-fortified juice, breakfast cereals, and meat analogs add variety as well as needed nutrients. Meat analogs are food items that are made of plant proteins, usually textured soy, but that are fabricated to look and taste like meat, fish, or poultry.

These meat-replacement products also help vegetarians obtain the needed amounts of protein and other nutrients that are found in meat, fish, and fowl. Examples of meat analogs include soy burgers, soy sausages, and soy chicken products. See *Exhibit 9.10* for a list of food items that provide nutrients normally obtained by eating animal flesh.

Exhibit 9.10

REPLACEMENT FOR ANIMAL SOURCES OF NUTRIENTS

Supplied nutrient	Source
Protein	Tofu and other soy-based products, legumes, seeds, nuts, grains, and vegetables
Zinc	Whole grains, whole-wheat bread, legumes, nuts, and tofu
Iron	Legumes, tofu, green leafy vegetables, dried fruit, whole grains, and iron-fortified cereals and breads
Calcium	Tofu processed with calcium, broccoli, seeds, nuts, kale, legumes, lime-processed tortillas, soy beverages, and calcium-enriched orange juice
Vitamin D	Fortified soy beverages and sunlight
Vitamin B$_{12}$	Fortified soy beverages and cereals

[3]Journal of the American Dietetic Association, *July 2009 (Vol. 109 | No. 7 | Pages 1266–1282)*

Religion-Influenced Diets

Religious restrictions on food choices vary widely and impact many people's food choices. These restrictions may discourage the consumption of certain types of food, or they may prohibit it altogether. Religion-influenced diets rarely result in health problems, but they may require changes in the menu, recipes, and practices of restaurant and foodservice operations.

KOSHER DIET

Orthodox and Conservative Judaism involve the observance of kosher food and dietary laws. These laws govern all meals, whether at home, at work, or eating out, and restaurant and foodservice professionals should understand them. For Jewish people who keep kosher, non-kosher food is considered to reduce spiritual sensitivity. The kosher diet is defined by religion; it is not a style of cooking. There is no such thing as "kosher-style" food.

Many kinds of meat, as well as all fruit, seeds, and vegetables, are allowed on a kosher diet. However, one may not eat any animal that eats other animals. Also, individuals may eat only animals that are killed by a kosher slaughterer in the most merciful way. Birds of prey are forbidden, as are pork, rabbit, and horse meat. Meat must be inspected for disease, and certain parts of the animal, such as the hindquarters and the fat below the abdomen, cannot be eaten. Meat must be free from blood out of respect for living creatures, and kosher diners may not eat swordfish, octopus, squid, monkfish, or any other sea creature lacking fins or removable scales. All shellfish is forbidden, including lobster, crab, mussels, and oysters, as is meat from animals with cloven hooves, such as pigs.

Additionally, certain food items must always be separated from other food items. For example, meat items and dairy items must never be mixed in one dish, eaten in the same meal, prepared together, cooked together, stored together, washed together, or eaten with the same utensils or off the same dishes. For example, beef Stroganoff or a cheeseburger (*Exhibit 9.11*) could never be kosher because they contain both milk and meat. Eggs, acceptable seafood, vegetables, and fruit may be eaten with either meat or milk. Such food items are called pareve because they are neither meat nor dairy items. For a restaurant or foodservice operation to be considered kosher, the above dietary rules must be followed under rabbinical supervision.

Exhibit 9.11

HINDU DIET

Hindus do not eat food items thought to retard spiritual or physical growth. Some meat is allowed, but pork, fowl, duck, snail, crab, and camel are avoided. Cows are considered sacred and may not be eaten or harmed. Although many Hindus are strict vegetarians, those who do eat meat are forbidden from eating beef. However, other products from the cow, such as milk, yogurt, and butter, are considered pure and may be eaten.

MUSLIM DIET

Muslims also have dietary restrictions that impact restaurant and foodservice operations. Muslims eat only meat that has been slaughtered in the prescribed way following halal rules, which means the food has been sanctioned by Islamic law. They cannot eat pork, ham, bacon, or any other part of a pig, such as lard. They do not eat gelatin from an animal source, birds of prey, or other carnivorous animals. Finally, they do not consume alcohol.

OTHER RELIGIOUS RESTRICTIONS

The following additional food-related religious restrictions affect restaurant and foodservice operations:

- Fasting is observed in many religious groups worldwide, usually as a form of discipline or to atone for sins. Fasting may last for a certain number of days or occur at a certain time of day. For example, Christians fast during Lent and followers of the Church of Jesus Christ of Latter-day Saints (commonly called Mormons) fast on the first Sunday of every month.

- Seventh-Day Adventists advocate a lacto-ovo-vegetarian diet and avoid meat, fish, fowl, coffee, tea, and alcoholic beverages.

- Caffeine-containing food items and beverages are either prohibited or restricted by many religions, since caffeine is considered a stimulant that may have unhealthy or addictive consequences.

- Mormons do not consume wine and other alcoholic drinks because these substances are believed to be stimulants.

- During the month of Ramadan, devout Muslims fast from sunup to sundown and eat only before or after these times. Ramadan is the ninth month of the Islamic calendar, which is a lunar calendar; because of this, it varies from mid-September to early December. The act of fasting is said to redirect the heart away from worldly activities. Its purpose is to cleanse the inner soul and to free it from harm. Fasting during Ramadan is not obligatory for people for whom it would cause problems: children, people with an illness or medical condition, the elderly, diabetics, nursing or pregnant women, and travelers who intend to spend fewer than five days away from home.

- Many Christians observe Lent for the 46-day period before Easter. Since Easter is based on a lunar calendar, Lent falls somewhere between mid-February and mid-April. During Lent, observant Christians restrict the quantity and types of food they eat. Fasting and abstinence were more severe in the past; today, the most noticeable practice is not to eat meat on Friday, which typically causes an increase in the consumption of fish on that day.

ACCOMMODATING RELIGIOUS DIETS

Most restaurant and foodservice operations can accommodate religious eating patterns or at least provide information that helps guests make informed decisions. Consider these points:

- Menu items cooked in wine might not be selected, even though alcohol evaporates during cooking.

- Non–meat eaters may select meat substitutes or vegetarian options.

- Prepared kosher items may be sourced from suppliers, which not only eases preparation and labor but also provides ingredient information on the product label for guests to see.

Accommodating Social and Health Needs

Many people follow a specific diet to mitigate a medical condition or to follow a certain health regimen recommended by their friends. Most restaurants and foodservice operations have a selection of menu items that is large enough to accommodate these diets. However, special diets may require changing the combinations on the plate or modifying cooking techniques, as described in chapter 8.

High-Protein, Low-Carbohydrate Diet

A high-protein, low-carbohydrate diet emphasizes consumption of food high in protein, such as meat, fish, fowl, beans, and eggs. It minimizes or prohibits consumption of cereals and starchy carbohydrates like potatoes, bread, and pasta. Eating fruit also is minimized or avoided because of the high sugar levels it usually contains. Whether other carbohydrate sources such as leafy green vegetables or yellow and green vegetables are included depends on the exact variation of this type of diet.

Obtaining most of one's calories from high-protein food items is not a balanced diet because it lacks nutrients such as vitamins, minerals, and fiber, which are provided by cereals, starches, and carbohydrates. Anyone following this diet must replace these essential nutrients through daily supplements. Another consideration is that meat, especially certain cuts of red meat, is high in fat and cholesterol, so individuals who follow this diet may be consuming too much of these substances.

High-protein, low-carbohydrate diets are often low in calories because they decrease appetite and limit food choices and quantities of food eaten. These are the primary reasons why they cause short-term weight loss.

THINK ABOUT IT . . .

Some operations differentiate themselves by catering to diners with specific dietary needs. What establishments can you think of where this is true? How do these operations market their menus?

Meals for People with Heart Disease and Diabetes

According to the Dietary Guidelines for Americans 2010, some 81.1 million Americans have heart disease and 24 million have diabetes. Two-thirds of the population is either overweight or obese, so many heart patients require low-calorie meals as well. It is beneficial for restaurants and foodservice operations to consider producing healthier meals for *all* of their customers.

When planning meals for people with heart disease, the emphasis is on reducing solid fats or saturated fats, reducing cholesterol and added sugars, and reducing salt. The chef can increase fiber in the meal by providing more fruit, vegetables, and whole grains. Chefs should include leaner cuts of meat, such as those from the tenderloin, sirloin, and round, in these meals. Because poultry and fish are lower in saturated fats and total fats, they are good choices for protein sources. In addition, chefs may need to salt food lightly or avoid salt entirely.

If dairy products are used, they should be low-fat dairy products, including low-fat cheeses. Dishes that are vegetarian or contain extra fruit and vegetables might be popular with people who have cardiovascular disease because of their lower amounts of saturated fat and higher vitamin and mineral content. Whole-grain breads should be served, and the use of whole grains in side dishes, soups, and salads is also advised.

In order to increase fiber, many chefs add beans to their soups. They may also plan main dishes and side dishes that contain beans. The chef should use high-quality cooking oil, such as canola, olive, walnut, soybean, or corn oil. Customers following a diet for heart disease usually use soft margarine. Because butter has high saturated-fat content, very little butter may be used.

Many people with diabetes have type 2, and they are often either overweight or obese. In order to serve customers with diabetes, there should be an emphasis on reducing calories and reducing added sugars. Since people with diabetes often have cardiovascular complications, it would be wise for them to follow the restrictions for heart disease as well.

SUMMARY

1. **Describe the causes and symptoms of allergic reactions, and list the eight main food allergens.**

   A food allergy occurs when the body reacts abnormally to a particular food by creating antibodies against it. The food or food ingredient is called the allergen. When the person eats the allergen again, the same reaction occurs. Even tiny amounts of the allergen can cause an allergic reaction in some individuals. There are no cures for allergies, and some of them, such as those to peanuts, tree nuts, and shellfish, are lifelong in most cases.

Eight food allergens cause about 90 percent of life-threatening allergic reactions. They are eggs, wheat, tree nuts, peanuts, soy, cow's milk and milk products, fish, and shellfish.

2. **Describe the cause and symptoms of celiac disease and other food intolerances.**

Celiac disease is an autoimmune condition that affects one out of every 133 Americans. A person with this condition cannot eat wheat, rye, or barley because they contain a protein called gluten. People with celiac disease avoid gluten because when they eat food containing it, their immune systems react by destroying their intestinal villi. There is no cure for celiac disease, and a gluten-free diet is required to maintain health.

Lactose intolerance is the inability to digest lactose, which is the sugar found in milk and other dairy products. It is caused by a deficiency of the enzyme lactase. Symptoms of lactose intolerance are diarrhea, gas, and bloating. Many people with lactose intolerance can enjoy some dairy. One of the main differences between food intolerances and food allergies is that intolerances do not involve the immune system. Some people may be sensitive to food additives like sulfites or monosodium glutamate.

3. **Describe the steps for establishing a food-allergen program.**

To establish a food-allergen program, an operation must review its marketing plan, company policies, legal requirements, and customer needs. Then it must set processes and procedures used to determine and reduce allergen risks in the operation.

Some specific actions that may be taken as part of a food-allergen program can include reviewing ingredients, recipes, and plating for selected allergens. Cross-contact can be a source of potential allergens. Managers may also choose to review menu items for possible modifications and substitutions. They must determine which menu items will be modified or substituted and then prepare detailed instructions for staff. Plans for communicating customer's allergen-related requests must also be developed.

4. **Explain how to handle requests from customers with food allergies, sensitivities, and intolerances.**

Restaurant and foodservice operators must design tools that can be used by front-of-the-house staff when discussing the menu with customers. Managers and chefs should work together to create policies and procedures on how to communicate with guests about their allergies and intolerances.

Staff should be trained on these policies and procedures, and managers need to be sure they are strictly enforced. Determine who will be assigned the responsibility of taking the order of a person with an allergy or intolerance. Identify how the special order will be communicated to the kitchen staff. Develop policies to ensure that all employees eliminate allergens from menu items and avoid cross-contact at all stages of food preparation and service.

5. **Describe how to train staff to deal with allergens in a restaurant or foodservice operation.**

    Determine emergency procedures for allergic reactions, including how to summon medical care and how to conduct follow-up communications. Deliver training on standard operating procedures for allergies and intolerances and evaluate the response of staff.

6. **Describe how to acquire new and alternative ingredients.**

    In order to receive the correct products for the food-allergen program or any special dietary requests, vendors must be given strict specifications for avoiding certain allergens or providing certain products for customers. The manager should ensure that the correct products are received. Products should be labeled and stored so they can be identified and used correctly by staff.

7. **Recognize the most common religious diets and other dietary restrictions.**

    Customers may request a variety of special diets, including kosher, halal, vegetarian, low fat, and others. Restaurants and other foodservice operators must determine which religious, cultural, medical, or social needs–based diets the operation is able to accommodate and which existing or new menu items are needed.

APPLICATION EXERCISE

Find a family member or friend who has a food allergy. Interview him or her about difficulties with avoiding the allergen. Solicit the answers to these questions:

1. Did you ever have a serious reaction from eating something that contained the allergen?

2. Which types of restaurants do you like to dine in?

3. How do you order food in restaurants? What do you tell the waitstaff when you order?

4. What steps have restaurants taken that have been especially helpful in accommodating your food allergy?

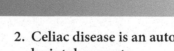

REVIEW YOUR LEARNING

Select the best answer for each question.

1. **What life-threatening allergic reaction can be caused by consuming peanuts?**

    A. Anaphylaxis
    B. Acidemia
    C. Antimony
    D. Achalasia

2. **Celiac disease is an autoimmune condition caused by intolerance to**

    A. gluten.
    B. sucrose.
    C. brown rice.
    D. ascorbic acid.

3. What is the sugar in milk that some people cannot digest properly?

   A. Fructose

   B. Maltose

   C. Glucose

   D. Lactose

4. What meat is not permitted in halal or kosher diets?

   A. Chicken

   B. Lamb

   C. Beef

   D. Pork

5. The most important thing for a server to do when encountering a customer who reports a food allergy is to

   A. talk about allergies in general terms.

   B. get the customer a drink from the bar.

   C. give the customer the regular menu.

   D. listen to the customer about the allergy.

6. According to the Dietary Guidelines for Americans 2010, how many people in the United States have diabetes?

   A. 2 million

   B. 6 million

   C. 10 million

   D. 24 million

7. The term used for vegetarians who consume milk but not eggs is

   A. lacto-ovo-vegetarians.

   B. lacto-vegetarians.

   C. fruitarians.

   D. vegans.

8. What should a server do if a mistake is made and a customer with an allergen receives it on his or her plate?

   A. Take the allergen off the plate at the table

   B. Call the manager to complain loudly

   C. Remove the allergen in the kitchen

   D. Order an entirely new plate of food

9. A chef uses a knife to chop walnuts for a dessert and then uses the same knife to slice a carrot for a customer with a nut allergy. This is an example of

   A. cross-connection.

   B. cross-allergens.

   C. cross-infected.

   D. cross-contact.

10. Which type of incomplete proteins can be consumed together to form complete protein with all essential amino acids?

    A. Complementary

    B. Supplementary

    C. Aminomentary

    D. Alimentary

10 Developing Staff and Defining Responsibilities

INSIDE THIS CHAPTER

- **Responsibilities of Front-of-the-House and Back-of-the-House Staff**
- **Training Staff to Meet Nutrition Goals**
- **Monitoring and Enforcing Nutrition Standards**

CHAPTER LEARNING OBJECTIVES

After completing this chapter, you should be able to:

- Describe the responsibilities of front-of-the-house and back-of-the-house staff in implementing a nutrition program.

- Explain the ADDIE model for developing training in support of a nutrition program.

KEY TERMS

ADDIE model, p. 212

education, p. 212

job aid, p. 216

performance standard, p. 213

skill gap, p. 212

training, p. 212

training tool, p. 216

George is the manager of a large, fine-dining restaurant owned by an investment group. The restaurant is located on the East Coast and is often visited by tourists, suburban commuters, foreign dignitaries, and foreign students attending universities nearby. It is a very busy place, with a crew of 35 staff on the day shift and 25 staff at night.

The restaurant's communication log reflects recent incidents concerning special dietary requests that were mishandled by staff. One was a nearly life-threatening situation involving a reported allergy. Another involved a religious request for special food that resulted in lost business. These incidents are always part of a report that is used to communicate potential problems to an establishment's investors.

George has been dreading the task of writing the report he will have to present to the investors. He decides that he needs to train all staff on the restaurant's new nutrition program to prevent more of these mishaps.

The nutrition program, which is being piloted to certain customers, emphasizes healthy menu options adaptable to low-calorie, low-sodium, vegetarian, and gluten-free diets. It also aims to create a safe environment for all people with food allergies. The program will be marketed to target audiences soon.

1. What must George know in order to train his staff?

2. When should the staff be trained? Explain.

RESPONSIBILITIES OF FRONT-OF-THE-HOUSE AND BACK-OF-THE-HOUSE STAFF

Once a manager has decided on the goals of a nutrition program and has determined the changes to the menu and preparation processes, an operation's staff must be trained to implement the program. All employees of a restaurant or foodservice operation are responsible for meeting the goals of the nutrition program in some way.

No matter how large or small the operation, each employee should be held accountable for the obligations of his or her position. For example, cooks are responsible for cooking the food items needed for their scheduled shifts. The waitstaff is responsible for taking customers' orders. Although the cooks and the waitstaff are performing different tasks, both groups play a role in accomplishing the shared goal of meeting customers' needs and expectations.

Clearly defined roles and responsibilities are essential to successful implemention of a nutrition program. Consider a nutrition program that designates the manager as the responsible person for overseeing the operation's overall implementation. Nutrition programs for both allergen control and healthy dining are likely to require staff to substitute ingredients or menu items and to perform modifications to menus and menu items. The manager must identify points of control for recipe modifications as well as cooking techniques used to make food tasty but also lower in fat or salt or free of specific allergens. The manager will work with other employees to ensure that the appropriate points of control are covered in order to meet the needs of the nutrition program. In this case, the assistant manager will train staff and enforce the nutrition program on each shift. Remaining staff from various parts of the establishment will also play specific roles in the plan's implementation.

Front-of-the-House Employees

Front-of-the-house employees play an essential role in a restaurant or foodservice operation by interfacing with the customers. A front-of-the house employee has a direct impact on the customer and the products being served. The primary role of front-of-the-house staff is to interact with the customer (*Exhibit 10.1*). Hosts and waitstaff are front-of-the-house employees in restaurants, while servers are front-of-the-house staff in an operation with tray-line service. At a quick-service restaurant, the employee who is taking orders serves this role. Each of these employees has a unique obligation and responsibility in regard to the successful delivery of a meal. When implementing a new nutrition program, it is the manager's responsibility to clearly define each employee's role within the operation.

Manager's Memo

In this chapter, the role of the manager is discussed in relation to the other roles in the restaurant or foodservice operation. Traditionally, areas of an operation considered the front of the house are areas that customers may enter. This would include parking areas, reception areas, lounges or bars, dining rooms, restrooms, and patios. The positions found in these areas include valets, parking attendants, receptionists, hosts or hostesses, bartenders, sommeliers, and food and beverage staff. Employees in these areas should be trained to interface with your customer.

The back of the house includes those areas to which the customer generally does not have access. The chefs and cooks are employed in this area, and it is here that food preparation takes place. The size of the kitchen staff and their roles will vary depending on the size of the operation. The positions found here include executive chef, sous chef, line cook, grill cook, fry cook, and pastry chef. The dish washers, cleaning crew, and auxiliary personnel such as expeditors are also found in the back of the house.

Front-of-the-house employees have a primary responsibility to maintain and observe the standards of service and food preparation assigned to their specific positions. Although not all special requests require the direct supervision of the manager, employees should inform their supervisors of all allergy disclosures from customers. A secondary responsibility of employees who directly impact or interface with the customer is to assist coworkers in achieving their obligations to the nutrition program. The front-of-the-house employee must be trained to communicate special requests that will require more than a simple substitution. The manager should monitor these changes and carry them through the operation to the back of the house.

There are many different types of special dietary requests. Someone who has a heart condition may request a leaner cut of meat or ask that a dish be baked or broiled rather than fried. A customer may need suggestions on what menu items are appropriate for vegetarians or vegans. Some customers may want low-calorie meals due to weight-loss goals or diabetes control. Waitstaff should be prepared to assist these customers with their selections and communicate them to the back of the house for correct preparation.

Exhibit 10.1

THINK ABOUT IT . . .

Imagine that a restaurant is rolling out a nutrition program catering to vegans and vegetarians. What roles might the front-of-the-house employees play in the implementation of such a program?

Back-of-the-House Employees

The primary responsibility of back-of-the-house employees is to prepare food to customers' expectations. When it comes to implementing nutrition programs, back-of-the-house employees are responsible for receiving communications regarding special dietary requests and ensuring that the food is cooked correctly (*Exhibit 10.2*). This means checking recipes and substitution lists. It includes making sure that food is measured and portioned correctly. Back-of-the-house employees ensure that there is no cross-contact with allergens for those who require allergen-free diets. In addition, they are responsible for ensuring that no other types of ingredient mistakes occur, such as adding butter to the food of someone who is attempting to lower his or her cholesterol and saturated-fat intake. Depending on the size of the operation, there may be a foodservice supervisor or food-production supervisor in the line of communication. Remember that communication is the key to handling customer requests involving special dietary needs. Training all employees on how to handle these disclosures is the responsibility of the manager.

Exhibit 10.2

THINK ABOUT IT . . .

A customer reports to the host that she has been on a low-cholesterol diet since her heart attack. What role does the host play in ensuring that the customer has an enjoyable and heart-healthy experience?

TRAINING STAFF TO MEET NUTRITION GOALS

It is essential that restaurant and foodservice managers train their employees to meet the needs of the customer when it comes to the nutrition program. **Training** is defined as activities that are designed to introduce new tasks and to assist employees in performing them. Managers use training as a tool to improve their employees' skills, knowledge, or attitudes. Along with training and employee development, education of employees should be a goal of the manager. **Education** differs from training in that education is a more formal process designed to transfer knowledge and skill to an employee or individual. Education is a long and ongoing process, whereas training is a set of brief activities focused on orienting employees to the daily tasks associated with their positions. While training tends to be more brief in duration, it is not a one-time event. All employees should receive ongoing refresher training throughout their careers.

When training existing employees on newly developed standards, it is important for the manager to identify the current skills of each employee. The manager also needs to identify the new skills that each employee will need. The difference between the current skills of an employee and the skills that he or she needs to develop is called a **skill gap**. Recognizing a skill gap is important in designing training activities. This recognition allows managers to focus their training and to make it effective. In addition, the trainer must know the capabilities of the operation and the feasibility of carrying out new tasks within that particular setting.

Training development can be a challenging undertaking, but the rewards far outweigh the time and cost of preparation. The manager should consider the staff's current capabilities and knowledge, as well as the tools needed for implementing the program. Managers can design their own training using the ADDIE model.

The **ADDIE model** is an instructional design model used for training development. *ADDIE* stands for analyze, design, develop, implement, and evaluate. Read the text below and trace the steps of the ADDIE model in *Exhibit 10.3* to see how these steps are utilized to develop a training program.

Exhibit 10.3

ADDIE MODEL

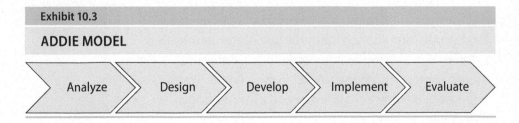

Analyze → Design → Develop → Implement → Evaluate

Analyze

The first step in the ADDIE model is to analyze the goals of the nutrition program. The manager can then translate these goals into performance standards. A **performance standard** defines what task must be done and how the task is to be completed to satisfaction. The performance standard will assist both the manager and the employee during the training and development process as well as during the day-to-day execution of tasks and responsibilities.

Then the manager determines the needs of the program, which define what must happen in order for the goals and performance standards to be met. For example: What does the operation want to achieve? What is the goal? What must be done to accomplish the new goal once it is set? Finally, the needs are compared with the current state of the restaurant or foodservice operation and its staff. *Exhibit 10.4* shows an example of the document a manager might create when completing the analysis step for a food-allergen program.

Exhibit 10.4

SAMPLE ANALYSIS STEP

Goal: To ensure that all food is prepared and served according to customer specifications.

Performance Standard: All employees are responsible for preparing and serving food according to the food-allergen program and maintaining safe foodhandling procedures with 100 percent accuracy.

Needs Assessment:
1. All foodservice staff must know the eight main food allergens.
2. All food-preparation employees must follow the standard operating procedure (SOP) to avoid cross-contact with food allergens.
3. All foodservice staff must communicate to the manager and food-preparation staff any customer disclosure of food allergies.

Current Capabilities:
1. A test of foodservice staff reveals that over 50 percent of employees cannot name all eight major food allergens.
2. There are newly developed standardized recipes that omit the eight main allergens.
3. Currently there is no SOP for reporting customer disclosure of food allergies.

Design

The design stage of the model focuses on the organization and layout of the training program. After analyzing what is needed, the next step is to outline a logical way to deliver the training. It is important to establish the order in which training activities must be completed, and then to determine who should be trained. The design of the training program should include the following:

- Prioritizing the training needs identified in the analysis phase
- Establishing which employees should be trained
- Developing a timeline for the training program
- Identifying which training tools and standard operating procedures (SOPs) will be used or developed
- Identifying the delivery methods that will be used during training activities

There are many different types of training that may be presented to employees. The type of training selected depends on the type of knowledge to be presented, the skill of the instructor, and time and budget constraints, among other considerations. When selecting a training delivery method, it is important to remember that most people learn better by doing rather than by simply being told what to do. *Exhibit 10.5* shows a few different options for delivering training.

Exhibit 10.5

TRAINING DELIVERY OPTIONS

On-the-Job Training: This training method pairs learners with experienced employees. The experienced employee trains the learner while performing the job.

Information Search: This training technique asks learners to find the information themselves. Employees are split into small groups to research a topic, and they then share the information they found with the other groups.

Games: Games can make difficult or boring information seem more exciting. Depending on the topic, managers may either develop their own games or purchase learning games from various trade associations and training organizations.

Role-Play: This training technique asks learners to read a script and perform roles. For example, one employee may take the role of a customer with a severe peanut allergy, while another employee performs the role of a server.

Demonstration: Managers may perform demonstrations to teach a specific task, such as how to clean a piece of equipment. Demonstrations work well if the instructor tells the learner how to do the task, shows the learner how to do the task, and finally allows the learner to practice the task.

Training Videos and DVDs: These instructional tools are a convenient way to share information and to allow staff to see and hear the information to be learned. It is important for instructors to perform follow-up activities with the learner to ensure that they understand the information.

Technology-Based Training: Training such as online learning offers a convenient way to deliver information. This type of training may be offered to individuals when it is inconvenient to bring employees together as a group. Learners using these tools can learn at their own pace.

Exhibit 10.6 shows part of a sample design outline completed by a manager. The manager starts by restating the performance objective. Next, she lists each of the program needs from the analysis phase. In this sample, only the first need is shown. However, a manager should undertake this design outline for all needs.

Exhibit 10.6

TRAINING DESIGN OUTLINE

Performance Standard:

All foodservice employees are responsible for preparing and serving food according to the food-allergen program and maintaining safe foodhandling procedures with 100 percent accuracy.

Training Design Outline:

I. All foodservice staff must know the eight main food allergens (egg, wheat, fish, shellfish, peanuts, tree nuts, milk, and soy).
   a. Training session is to educate staff on the eight main allergens.
   b. All front-of-the-house and back-of-the-house employees must complete this training.
   c. Delivery method of training is a lecture with supporting material.
   d. Manager is responsible for training, with assistance of chefs.
   e. Training duration is 35 minutes.
   f. Training frequency is once at time of hiring for new hires and annually for current employees.

Training Tools and SOPs Needed:

II. All foodservice staff must know the eight main food allergens.
   a. Develop a reference guide to common food allergies.
   b. Create a training acknowledgment statement letter for verification of training.
   c. Produce a large poster to place at all work stations.

For each need, the manager notes the following:

- The type of training
- Who must complete the training
- The specific delivery method of training
- Who is responsible for executing the training
- The duration and frequency of the training

Notice how the outline in *Exhibit 10.6* addresses the training tools that will be needed for training. The creation of these materials is addressed during the development stage of the training-plan process.

The design process is essential to ensure that all the training needs are identified and organized. The design of the training program acts as a road map. It is intended to ensure that important components are not overlooked and that future training will be as efficient and effective as possible.

With the design outline complete, the next step in the training process is to develop the materials needed to conduct training.

Exhibit 10.7

Develop

Training tools and SOPs are essential for training to be effective. Training tools are materials developed to effectively communicate training information to staff. These tools can include diagrams, summarized information, SOPs such as standardized recipes and step-by-step checklists, videos, and so on. When utilizing the ADDIE model, the development stage is the time to identify existing materials or to create new ones.

The development stage usually requires the investment of time and money. Many training tools and supporting materials can be purchased from the National Restaurant Association and other public and private organizations. Training activities might include educational videos, posters, and booklets on specific topics. The information covered by these materials is general in scope. Managers and trainers can supplement this material with training tools that are specific to their operations.

In addition, the trainer may want to develop job aids that employees can use once the training is complete. A job aid is any type of information or process that directs, guides, or enlightens performance on the job. Employees may keep their job aids, and managers may choose to post job aids in the establishment to remind employees of important concepts or tasks (*Exhibit 10.7*). Job aids for a food-allergen program might consist of lists of substitutions and modifications that accommodate people who have food allergies.

Implement

In the implementation phase, the manager must review the design of the training program and then determine the training sessions in anticipation of rolling out the program. Planning for a large staff involves multiple training sessions to incorporate different shifts and multiple groups, such as hosts and servers, food-production staff, and ordering and receiving staff. All employees who will impact the operation need to be involved.

The manager will need to communicate information about the training, such as where, when, and why, in advance so that employees can come to the training prepared and ready to learn. By this point written materials should be prepared and audiovisual materials developed. The instruction should be delivered according to the preparation and planning (see *Exhibit 10.8*). The trainer and manager should maintain a list of employees who attended each session.

Manager's Memo

A manager can benefit from government and professional associations when developing training tools. Here is a list of Web sites devoted to food safety and nutrition information.

Food and Nutrition Information Center
fnic.nal.usda.gov

Allergies and Food Safety
www.fsis.usda.gov/PDF/Allergies_and_Food_Safety.pdf

Gateway to Federal Food Safety Information
www.foodsafety.gov/

National Restaurant Association Tools & Solutions
www.restaurant.org/tools/

Evaluate

During the last step of the ADDIE model, the manager should check that employees have learned the information that was taught in the training. This can consist of either a formal or an informal process. For the example given in this chapter, an informal way to evaluate an employee is to quiz him or her on the eight main allergens. A more formal evaluation tool, such as a written quiz or test, might also be helpful. Some operations assess mastery of certain aspects of training by using written tests. As employees continue to help implement the nutrition program on-site, they can be further evaluated on the job. The trainer should also keep in each employee's personnel file a standard form confirming that he or she attended training. This will include a running list of all the training sessions that the employee has attended.

Exhibit 10.8

A training checklist is beneficial to the manager and helps to ensure that all training has been completed. The completed checklist should be kept in the employee's file. *Exhibit 10.9* provides an example of what might be included on the training checklist.

Exhibit 10.9

TRAINING CHECKLIST

Training Topic	Date Completed	Renewal
Instructor-led training on eight main food allergens	_____	_____
Hands-on demonstration training for food allergens	_____	_____
Instruction on communication of customer food allergies	_____	_____
Manager's signature	Date	

The training session will be further developed based on feedback to the trainer. Feedback is information received in response to an inquiry. In this case the feedback would be information received by the trainer about the quality and effectiveness of the training and how much was learned. The trainer will revise the materials and train the next group of employees until everyone has completed the training.

Manager's Memo

When you are announcing a training session, remember to include the what, why, who, when, where, and how. A typical approach might look something like this:

What: Training for new nutrition program

Why: Rollout of nutrition program beginning September 30

Who: All employees

When: September 10, 4:00–4:30 p.m.

Where: Main dining room

How: Demonstrations and a movie

All service staff, hosts and hostesses, chefs, assistant managers, and ordering and receiving staff must attend. Please mark your calendars. We will be reviewing the new program. Employees who do not work that day can attend another session on September 12.

Clay's Country Kitchen: Developing a Training Program

Remember the example from Clay's Country Kitchen? The manager, Elias, is implementing a nutrition program with several major components:

- A vegan entrée section
- Additional gluten-free items
- Additional whole-grain breads and buns
- More fresh fruit and vegetable ingredients
- Healthful improvements to the children's menu section

Elias determined the menu items that needed to be replaced and worked with select members of his team to revise recipes, create new ones, and revise his preparation processes. Now he is ready to roll this program out to the entire restaurant.

To do so, Elias must train both the front-of-the-house and back-of-the-house staff. He uses the ADDIE model to guide his training efforts. In his analysis phase, he determines that all front-of-the-house staff should be able to highlight the healthier options on the menu, as well as to be able to respond to questions from guests related to vegan and gluten-free options. He also determines that his back-of-the-house staff needs to know how to cook using these new ingredients and modified recipes, and that they must be able to do so in a way that avoids cross-contact for vegan and gluten-free items.

In polling his front-of-the-house staff, Elias determines that much of the staff is unaware of the issues associated with gluten-free diets and that only a small percentage of that group understands what items vegans seek to avoid. He also realizes that his front-of-the-house staff is unaware of many of the other menu changes and the reasoning behind these changes. In observing the back-of-the-house staff, he realizes that while his chef seems to understand cross-contact issues and is aware of the menu changes, much of the chef's staff does not share the same understanding.

During the design stage, Elias creates a training design outline to note what training steps need to happen, who needs to attend each session, and along what timeline the training will take place. He knows that some of his training could be addressed to the staff as a whole, but other portions are specific to job tasks.

During the development stage, Elias creates several overall training sessions for all staff related to healthy food and the needs of customers with food allergies. Elias learns that one of his hosts follows a vegan diet and that one of the prep cooks is very familiar with celiac disease. He works with each of these employees to create overview lessons, using presentation software and handouts, to cover the concerns that diners choosing vegan or gluten-free meals might have.

Additionally, he works with his chef to create specialized training on the new standardized recipes. Each recipe is printed and laminated and added to the binder of recipes. In addition, he and the chef create a list of "dos and don'ts" regarding cross-contact. They hang copies of this list at each work station in the kitchen.

Finally, Elias works with the dining-room manager to create handouts about each of the new items so that the front-of-the-house staff can familiarize themselves with the changes. The dining-room manager also creates small cards with the SOP for the allergen program as a reference for all waitstaff. Larger versions of this SOP are laminated and hung near the front-of-the-house prep stations.

Elias' changes are implemented over the course of two weeks. The group sessions are held before shifts on Mondays, which is the operation's slowest day. The smaller sessions are also held before shifts on Wednesdays and Sundays. Elias creates a list of the sessions and the required attendees for each lesson, and he distributes it to all employees two weeks in advance.

To ensure that the training program is a success, Elias has written quizzes for each employee to complete after each session. The quizzes are not long, but they cover the basics of each session. The results of the quizzes can help Elias determine if any employees require additional training.

Elias tracks each employee's progress using a training checklist, which he keeps in his office. He also observes employee performance during each shift to ensure that the new plan is being carried out.

MONITORING AND ENFORCING NUTRITION STANDARDS

Once a nutrition program has been implemented and each employee has been trained, the program should be maintained. Managers maintain a nutrition program by monitoring and enforcing its implementation. Employee job descriptions should be reviewed and updated to include the new performance standards expected from them (*Exhibit 10.10*). Anyone who is designated as a responsible person for a specific nutrition program should be tested carefully to see if he or she has the ability to supervise this important task.

Exhibit 10.10

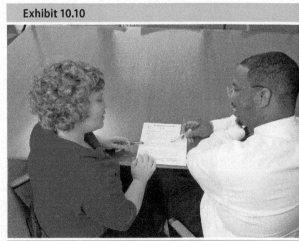

Enforcement of the program is dependent on the policies of the organization. Anyone can make a mistake, but if employees follow SOPs, mistakes are less likely to occur. Employees who do not pass a basic training session should be retrained individually to see if they can master the information. Training issues are often related to other issues, such as language differences or varying speeds of learning a task. Job aids will help people who have difficulty remembering information they seldom use.

SUMMARY

1. **Describe the responsibilities of front-of-the-house and back-of-the-house staff in implementing a nutrition program.**

   All employees have responsibilities in implementing a nutrition program. Managers often oversee the program. Front-of-the-house employees, such as hosts and servers, interact with customers and maintain the standards of service and any food preparation assigned to their positions. As part of that role, these employees must inform their supervisors of customers' special dietary or nutritional needs. Back-of-the-house employees, such as cooks and chefs, are responsible for preparing food according to customers' expectations and following all SOPs. These employees are also responsible for providing customers with substitutions or modifications.

2. **Explain the ADDIE model for developing training in support of a nutrition program.**

   Managers can develop their own training sessions in support of their nutrition program by following the ADDIE model. Managers first analyze the needs of the program. Analysis includes stating the goals of the program, developing performance standards to measure the program's implementation, determining the needs of the program, and evaluating the operation's current capacity for delivering against the performance standards. Managers then use the performance standards and needs assessment to design a training program. At the design stage, managers consider variables such as the type of training, the employees to be trained, and the materials to be used in the training. During the development step, managers create the materials to be used in the training. The implementation step involves the actual employee training, using the materials previously developed. Finally, the evaluation stage allows managers to assess employees' mastery of the new training. The evaluation phase also provides feedback that helps managers to adjust future trainings.

APPLICATION EXERCISES

Exercise 1. Creating a Training Module Using ADDIE

Using the five-step ADDIE model, create a training module for the staff in your work environment or in your favorite restaurant. Address one of the following topics:

- How to avoid cross-contact with allergens in the kitchen

- How to properly buy, receive, store, cook, hold, and serve vegetables to maintain nutrients

- How to identify hidden sources of salt in the preparation of food

Create any materials, such as posters or job aids, that your module may require. Your instructor may ask you to break into small groups and deliver your training to each other.

Exercise 2. Training Issues and Solutions

Interview a supervisor or trainer in a restaurant or foodservice operation. Ask the following questions:

- What are common training issues they have encountered in the work environment?

- What equipment or training materials are available on site for their use?

- What methods have they found that work in training employees? What methods have been less effective?

- What incentives can be used to increase interest and motivate employees to attend training and learn essential information?

Exercise 3. Job Aids

When you are on the job, think of a task that is difficult to do or to remember. Create a job aid to help you accomplish this task in the future.

REVIEW YOUR LEARNING

Select the best answer for each question.

1. **Which training delivery method allows learners to learn at their own pace?**
   A. Lecture
   B. Demonstration
   C. On-the-job training
   D. Technology-based training

2. **Which training technique asks learners to perform research and report to the group?**
   A. Demonstration
   B. Information search
   C. On-the-job training
   D. Technology-based training

3. **The most likely person to be responsible for a food-allergy program in a restaurant or foodservice operation is the**
   A. cook.
   B. server.
   C. host.
   D. manager.

4. **The primary role of the front-of-the-house staff is to**
   A. order and receive products.
   B. interact with the customer.
   C. do a thorough cleaning job.
   D. be the best cook or chef.

5. **Who is responsible for customers with an allergy or a special dietary request in a restaurant or foodservice establishment?**
   A. All staff
   B. Waitstaff
   C. Host or hostess
   D. Food-production staff

6. **The person who has the primary responsibility to disclose a food allergy is the**
   A. customer.
   B. waitstaff
   C. manager.
   D. greeter.

7. **In the ADDIE model of instructional design, what does the second *D* represent?**
   A. Decipher
   B. Develop
   C. Determine
   D. Design

8. **A tool that is developed to help an employee remember seldom-used information is a**
   A. job aid.
   B. marketing plan.
   C. training checklist.
   D. performance standard.

9. **What part of the training-development analysis defines the task that must be done and the way in which it should be completed?**
   A. Personal goal
   B. Needs assessment
   C. Current capacities
   D. Performance standard

10. **The difference between the current skills of an employee and the skills that the employee needs is called the**
    A. skill gap.
    B. worker limit.
    C. deficit point.
    D. training mark.

11

Marketing and Evaluating Nutrition Programs

CHAPTER LEARNING OBJECTIVES

After completing this chapter, you should be able to:

- Identify the features of a marketing plan.

- Describe the steps involved in designing a marketing plan based on nutrition goals.

- Identify the components of the promotional mix.

- Explain the key points in executing a marketing plan.

- List the key phases in the life cycle of a new program.

- Explain how to evaluate the success of a nutrition program and adjust the program accordingly.

KEY TERMS

CASE STUDY

Chef Kayla is the food production manager for the cafeteria at a local children's hospital. The hospital requested that she develop a nutrition program outlining policies on allergens, celiac disease, and special dietary needs. Kayla has created a marketing plan that includes the following components: menu planning and ingredients, promotion of the nutrition program's new menu, and new pricing. She is now designing menu boards and preparing promotions for the program. Kayla finds it easy to calculate food costs and pricing, but she struggles with ideas for effective promotions.

1. What are the target markets for a children's hospital foodservice operation?

2. What types of promotions might be most effective in this setting?

3. What factors affect the short- and long-term success of this nutrition program?

DEVELOPING A MARKETING PLAN

Each chapter of this book includes information that restaurant and foodservice professionals can utilize to design and implement nutrition programs. Beginning chapters introduce nutrition principles, nutrition analysis, and food and menu labeling. Later chapters present information about assessing an establishment's market, developing nutrition goals as part of a marketing plan, purchasing quality food, cooking with health in mind, meeting the special dietary requests of guests, and training the staff. This chapter will walk through marketing a nutrition program and assessing the effectiveness and profitability of the new plan. The chapter will illustrate the development and implementation of the marketing program using the Clay's Country Kitchen example first introduced in chapter 6.

The Basics of a Marketing Plan

The management team of any restaurant or foodservice operation should devise a marketing plan, which is a document that guides staff in increasing the operation's visibility to its target audience in order to increase business. Recall that a successful nutrition program is tied to specific revenue goals. A marketing plan is a detailed listing of specific activities designed to reach the revenue goals of an operation. A marketing plan is like a road map for an operation's marketing efforts. It tells what marketing activities will be used to achieve revenue goals and when these activities will be employed.

Developing a marketing plan is a formal process that involves answering the following questions:

- What marketing activity should be undertaken?
- Who will do it?
- When will it be done?
- How much money will be needed to implement the plan?
- How will the results of the plan be measured?

When managers plan, they want to affect the future. When creating a marketing plan, managers want to influence the way their current and future customers feel about their nutrition program, how often customers will come to their operations, and what these guests will buy when they visit.

A variety of approaches can be used to develop a marketing plan, but all effective marketing plans should include the following five features:

- Documentation
- Target goals
- Timeliness
- Marketing plan cost estimates
- Customer-focused goals

DOCUMENTATION

It is important to recognize that a marketing plan should be a formal, written document. It is simply not possible for restaurant and foodservice managers and owners to do a good job planning what should be done, when it should be done, and who should do it without carefully recording the decisions made in response to these important questions.

Restaurant and foodservice managers and owners are very busy. They have to attend to many details. Unless marketing plans are committed to paper, and reviewed regularly, it would be easy for a manager to forget when an important marketing activity should be done, or even who should do it.

TARGET GOALS

It is also important to understand that a marketing plan may have several parts, each of which addresses a strategic business segment. A strategic business segment is a specific revenue-generating source.

For example, an establishment that contains a dining room, a banquet room, and a lounge may consider each of those three areas to be a unique strategic business segment. So special marketing activities may be undertaken to promote the banquet room only. Similarly, special marketing activities may be targeted at the establishment's lounge or dining-room customers.

One important job of restaurant and foodservice managers is to know their operations' individual strategic business segments and whether those segments can benefit from specific and targeted marketing activities. If they can, then the marketing plan should directly address those specific activities.

TIMELINESS

An effective marketing plan addresses a specific time period, such as a year or a month. If managers are to carefully monitor what activities should be undertaken, and when they are best done, then it is essential that specific time periods for completion are identified. In some cases, the time period identified for completing an activity will be critically important to its effectiveness.

For example, assume that a restaurant is creating a nutrition program to compete with a new organic supermarket with café that is opening in the same target market. The supermarket broke ground on a new building in January and is set to open in August. The restaurant manager wants to establish her nutrition program three months before the supermarket opens.

Clearly, June is too late to start planning. Instead, the restaurant manager should start planning as soon as possible. In this case, preliminary planning should begin in January.

MARKETING PLAN COST ESTIMATES

Any dollars committed to marketing activities are dollars that cannot be spent on other operational needs, such as equipment, supplies, or staff. For that reason, it is essential that the estimated costs of undertaking each marketing activity be thoroughly considered.

Some forms of marketing may be expensive, while others are not. In all cases, however, the costs of undertaking a marketing activity must be well known to restaurant and foodservice managers before they are undertaken. In some instances the costs of a specific marketing activity will not be known. Then it is important to secure a cost estimate before undertaking the activity.

To illustrate, assume that a manager decides that it would be good to place an advertisement in a local newspaper that is widely read by the establishment's target market. In this case it will be important for the manager to know the cost of placing an ad in the paper prior to including that activity in a marketing plan.

The size of an establishment's marketing budget will often vary based on the revenue it currently achieves, its revenue goals, and a variety of other factors. In all cases, however, the costs of the individual activities to be included in the marketing plan must be known in advance if the manager is to stay within the operation's established marketing budget.

CUSTOMER-FOCUSED GOALS

Recall that marketing is a means of communicating with customers. For that reason it is essential that an establishment's customers are continually kept foremost in the mind of a marketing manager. The best managers know that each marketing activity undertaken should be chosen carefully and only after considering a number of factors:

- What message is to be communicated?
- How can the message best be sent?
- What is the customers' desired response?
- How can customer responses be evaluated?

Developing the Marketing Plan

The development of a marketing plan is a complex process. It cannot be completed in an hour or two. The best restaurant and foodservice managers will set aside some time each week or month to work on their marketing plan.

It can be difficult for managers to find the uninterrupted time required to develop a marketing plan during regular operating hours. Many managers set aside specific times to work on their marketing plans. These can be times when their operations are closed, or when other managers can prevent interruptions to the planning process.

A manager may write the marketing plan alone or with help from others in the business who can provide valuable information or insight (*Exhibit 11.1*). Involving others in the process can be beneficial because it can result in greater commitment to the plan.

Exhibit 11.1

A well-developed marketing plan should do the following:

- Review the operation's target market
- Assess the operation's competitors
- Identify the operation's revenue and financial goals
- Use a SWOT analysis to assess the operation and its current marketing environment
- Identify marketing objectives
- Identify marketing strategies and supporting tactics
- Establish a marketing budget
- Create a marketing-activities schedule that conforms to the budget

It should be easy to understand the marketing plan by examining each of the sections within it.

REVIEW THE OPERATION'S TARGET MARKET

In the first section of the marketing plan, managers identify the guests that the establishment seeks to attract. As noted in chapter 6, managers can use customer demographics and psychographics to describe existing customers and others that the operation seeks to serve.

Remember that few operations can be successful if they try to be all things to all people. The needs and wants of customers in different market segments vary greatly. Instead, successful managers must carefully identify those segments that they can serve best. Experienced restaurant and foodservice managers know that a thorough understanding of whom they want to attract will help them make many marketing-related decisions.

When preparing this section of the marketing plan, managers must consider possible changes in their target customers. Recall the trends addressed in chapter 6 related to food labeling and healthier eating. Any of these trends, as well as others like them, can create changes in a target market that must be addressed by managers.

ASSESS THE OPERATION'S COMPETITORS

The competitive assessment used to determine the nutrition program's goals, as mentioned in chapter 6, can be included in the marketing plan. Documenting the findings as part of the plan will help to keep the plan focused on the original factors that helped drive the nutrition program itself.

REAL MANAGER

PROJECT MANAGEMENT

If you think leading a project is a simple task, think again. Even a small project can run into snags caused by people's behaviors and attitudes, unforeseen obstacles, and scope creep. At the initiation of a project, you should create a project scope sheet and get everyone to sign off on the document. This will be priceless as the project progresses.

Next Steps?

1. Develop your assumptions and create a detailed project timeline.

2. Determine team membership. It is easiest to select individuals who tend to get along, but some may say that does not lead to the best product or result.

3. Decide how to track and document the project. The need for documentation should never be underestimated. Whether it be a construction or renovation project, a departmental reorganization, or something a bit smaller in scope, keep your eye on the initial goals of the project.

Remember: Project management is not simple, but you should not forget to have a few laughs throughout the process. Your team will appreciate a sense of humor every now and then.

IDENTIFY THE OPERATION'S REVENUE AND FINANCIAL GOALS

The establishment of revenue and financial goals provides direction for the entire marketing plan. These goals should be identifiable and measurable, and they should be the same goals stated at the start of the nutrition program.

INCLUDE SWOT ANALYSIS RESULTS

As with the competitive assessment, managers should include the SWOT analysis results in the marketing plan. These results, like those of the competitive assessment, will help keep the marketing plan focused on the goals of the nutrition program.

IDENTIFY MARKETING OBJECTIVES

Some managers have difficulty clearly identifying their marketing objectives. In some cases that is because they state their objectives in terms of vague phrases or slogans, such as "We will be the number one establishment in our market" or "We will be the leader in customer service." These phrases or sentiments, good as they may be, are not objectives. Just as financial objectives must be quantifiable, a marketing objective should meet these criteria:

1. Expressed in monetary terms; for example:

    a. Vegan menu items will comprise at least 5 percent of total sales.

    b. Serve two hundred dinners per night.

    c. Increase customer check average by $5.

2. Indicate an appropriate time frame; for example:

    a. Within three months

    b. By the end of the year

    c. By July 1

IDENTIFY MARKETING STRATEGIES AND SUPPORTING TACTICS

Marketing activities can be classified as either strategic or tactical. Strategic activities address an operation's basic business objectives. These strategic activities include identifying target markets, determining which products and services will be offered for sale, and determining the direction of the business. The goal setting at the start of the nutrition plan development, for instance, is a strategic activity.

Tactical marketing activities are used to implement marketing strategies. For example, if one marketing strategy is to increase sales of products made with whole grains, one tactic would be to advertise in health-related publications in the local market. Remember that for each marketing strategy designed to achieve an operation's marketing objectives, one or more accompanying tactics should be clearly specified.

ESTABLISH A MARKETING BUDGET

If financial resources were unlimited, carefully identifying how much should be spent on marketing would not be important. Unfortunately, marketing funds are not unlimited. In all cases, the marketing budget must be large enough to fund all of the identified strategic and tactic efforts. Managers develop marketing budgets using one of four methods:

- Estimate of what the business can afford after other costs are paid

- Percentage of actual or forecasted revenue

- Amount spent on promotions by competitors of the business

- Marketing plan objectives and the actions needed to achieve them

The first two methods—what the business can afford and the percentage of revenue—are the simplest methods used to determine a marketing budget. In the first instance, a manager might develop the marketing budget by looking at revenue and costs from the previous year and projected revenue and costs for the year in question. This can help the manager to gain a sense of what additional monies might be available for this year's marketing budget. In the second instance, a manager would forecast monthly sales, determine the monthly percentage for marketing, and sum the 12-month marketing amounts to arrive at the annual marketing budget.

Basing a marketing budget on the amount competitors spend on their promotions is relatively simple, although obtaining the accurate information needed to do so may be difficult. The final method, basing the marketing budget on the marketing plan's objectives, helps to keep marketing efforts focused on goals. This method is the ideal one to use; however, it can also be the most complex method because it entails accurately forecasting cost information for potential marketing suppliers such as media outlets, advertising agencies, and vendors selling promotional products and services.

CREATE A MARKETING-ACTIVITIES SCHEDULE THAT CONFORMS TO THE BUDGET

Once the marketing tactics have been identified and the amount of money available has been established, managers create a marketing-activities schedule that identifies what will be done, when it will be done, and who will do it. This schedule is used to guide marketing efforts.

Designing the Promotional Mix

The communication that an operation establishes with the public is a critical link in its short-term and long-term success. A promotional mix is defined as the various ways in which a given business chooses to reach or communicate with its customers or its target market (see *Exhibit 11.2*). The various pieces of a promotional mix address the tactical marketing items outlined in the marketing plan and support the strategic ones. To cover the multiple areas of

Exhibit 11.2

THE PROMOTIONAL MIX

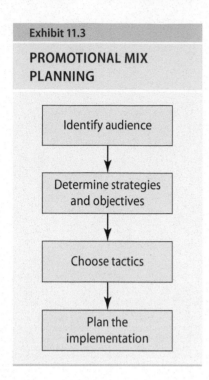

Exhibit 11.3

PROMOTIONAL MIX PLANNING

Identify audience

↓

Determine strategies and objectives

↓

Choose tactics

↓

Plan the implementation

communication, a manager needs to pay particular attention to each aspect of an operation's promotional mix: sales promotions, advertising, public relations, and personal selling.

The first step in designing the promotional mix for a nutrition program is to identify the target audience (see *Exhibit 11.3*). The promotional mix must include activities that will reach this group of people. The overall target audience will mirror the target market that was established at the start of the nutrition program development and was outlined in the marketing plan.

Next, managers develop their communication strategies and objectives. This part of the process involves many aspects, such as assessing what customers already know about an operation or its menu items, determining when to implement the communication activities, setting promotion objectives and measurements, and determining at a high level the message and image to be communicated. Once the manager has determined the promotion strategies and objectives, he or she can establish the proportion of the components in the promotional mix. Then, the manager can choose the tactics that will best support his or her strategy:

- For advertising and public relations, managers choose the types of media for their communication.

- For sales promotions, managers choose the types of sales promotions.

- For sales promotions and personal selling, managers choose whom to sell to.

After identifying tactics, managers can begin planning the details for implementing their promotion.

As with marketing plans, it is important to document the promotion plan. Having a written plan helps to focus marketing communications efforts and helps to avoid wasted time and money pursuing irrelevant or even counterproductive activities. A written plan also provides an essential foundation for tracking the results of the marketing efforts.

SALES PROMOTION

Sales promotions are special incentives to get customers to visit an establishment or to purchase new items. There are many types of sales promotions and different tools or materials that can be used in a sales promotion. Coupons are an example of a sales promotion. Coupons entice people who have not eaten at the operation but will do so if the financial risk is smaller, or if there are incentives they perceive as valuable, such as a free appetizer. The operation's management team must decide what coupons will be given, how much they will be worth, how many people will receive them and how often, and when the coupons will expire. Operations should be prepared to handle increased traffic when a coupon has been distributed to the target audience.

Another example of a promotion is when an establishment provides something free or at a reduced price with the purchase of a full-priced item (see *Exhibit 11.4*). Combo meals are an example of this type of promotion, as are promotions that provide free kids meals with the purchase of an adult meal.

PUBLICITY AND PUBLIC RELATIONS

Restaurant and foodservice managers should learn how to integrate their marketing efforts into the community they serve through positive publicity. Publicity is information about an establishment that is distributed for free but is not produced by the operation. A newspaper article that focuses on a restaurant's new dairy-free menu is one example of free publicity. The main benefit of publicity is that people often find it more believable than advertising. Forms of publicity include newspapers, newsletters, Web sites, billboards, placards, and radio and television time. Word of mouth is also an extremely effective form of publicity.

Publicity can be either positive or negative. Because establishments do not control publicity, managers must recognize that while positive publicity is a great advantage, negative publicity can damage the credibility of an operation. If an operation receives negative publicity, such as a bad food review or a report of a food allergy incident, managers may need to use other tools in the marketing mix, such as advertising or public relations, to overcome it.

Public relations (PR) is the part of an establishment's communication activities that addresses the operation's image in its community. The goal of a restaurant or foodservice operation's PR effort is to position the establishment in a positive light. If the community perceives the operation as adding value beyond the scope of its business, the operation will likely attract more customers.

Because they are sometimes (but not always) related, some people may think that publicity and PR are synonymous terms. They are not. Many PR activities may lead directly to positive publicity. In other cases, however, PR activities are undertaken simply because businesses want to be contributing members of their communities. In fact, one challenge facing managers is knowing whether or not to engage in a PR activity when there is no expectation of significant publicity resulting from the activity.

ADVERTISING

Advertising is any form of marketing message that managers pay for and deliver in an identifiable but non-personal way. Examples of advertisements include newspaper ads, commercials played on the radio or television, and the placement of ads on a Web site. This paid form of communication uses mass media to deliver the operation's message to large audiences. Mass media can

Exhibit 11.4

Manager's Memo

What is in a name? The health
trend continues to grow as more
people realize their health is
being affected by large amounts
of solid fats, added sugar, and
excess sodium in their food.

However, the name of a menu
item matters. Research shows that
labeling a menu item *healthy* will
likely make it unpopular. Customers
may want a healthy dish, but they
expect it to be as satisfying as
other menu items. Selecting
descriptors such as *fresh, flavorful,
tasty,* and *straight from the garden*
will increase interest in a healthy
menu item. Waitstaff should be
aware of these terms when they
conduct suggestive selling.

Exhibit 11.5

reach a large audience, but it has to be repeated in order to be effective.
Advertising is generally the most expensive activity in the promotional mix,
as the operation has to fine-tune the message for its target market.

Recall that managers use customer demographics and psychographics to
identify target markets and that these managers create marketing campaigns
to reach these markets. Advertising is often the most visible part of a
company's marketing efforts. Advertising is often used to create awareness of
sales promotions and PR events. A well-planned advertising campaign is a
coordinated series of advertisements and promotions used in the same time
frame to meet certain objectives. An effective advertising campaign can
achieve many operational goals:

- Communicating a message to a large audience, often using a variety
  of media
- Generating awareness of and interest in a product or service
- Persuading the audience to take action, such as purchasing a product
- Strengthening existing customer preferences and loyalty
- Creating or reinforcing an image of a product or organization
- Differentiating an operation's products and services from its competitors

PERSONAL SELLING

The final portion of the promotional mix, **personal selling**, involves a
meeting or interaction of two or more people for the purpose of exchanging
information and making and closing a sale. Sometimes just called selling or
sales, personal selling creates a relationship between the customer and the
operation's staff. This enables the staff to tailor the marketing message to the
customer's individual needs.

Personal selling on the part of service staff takes the form of suggestive selling
and upselling. Suggestive selling involves making recommendations or
suggestions to guests about items the guests might be interested in
buying. A related concept is upselling, where the server provides guests
opportunities to purchase related or higher-priced products that the
guest will enjoy. This can result in a larger sale. A common example of
upselling happens when a quick-service restaurant employee asks a
guest who has just purchased a hamburger, "Would you like fries with
that?" Suggestive selling and upselling can be powerful personal-selling
strategies that significantly impact an operation's total sales. In a
restaurant or foodservice operation, suggestive selling should maximize
guest satisfaction and increase the average check, resulting in increased
profitability. The success of suggestive selling depends on having the
right people with product knowledge, effective communication skills,
and appropriate sales training (see *Exhibit 11.5*).

EXECUTING THE MARKETING PLAN

When the marketing plan and budget are in place, managers are ready to execute their plans. At the start of the implementation phase, managers break the plan into discrete tasks, assigning resources to each one. They also schedule the tasks on a calendar to determine when each task will start and end.

Marketing-Task Assignments

A typical marketing plan will include a variety of marketing tasks and activities. Consider, for example, the marketing plan that calls for advertising a special organic brunch timed with Earth Day in the local newspaper. If this task is to be completed in a timely manner, someone must be responsible for it. Contacting the newspaper to determine specific steps needed for ad placement, assisting in the creation of the ad, and approving the final invoice for the advertisement are all tasks that must be accomplished if this marketing activity is to be successful.

In many cases, the manager will undertake the marketing tasks. In all cases, it is the manager's job to identify who is responsible for each activity included in the marketing plan.

MARKETING-ACTIVITIES SCHEDULES

A marketing-activities schedule contains three key listings:

- What is to be done?
- When will it be done?
- Who will do it?

This part of the marketing plan need not be complicated. *Exhibit 11.6* is an example of a form that can be used to build an operation's marketing-activities schedule.

Exhibit 11.6

SAMPLE MARKETING-ACTIVITIES SCHEDULE

Marketing objective	Supporting marketing activity	Date to be initiated	Date to be completed	Assigned to

Exhibit 11.7

A marketing-activities schedule can be thought of as a "to-do" list for marketing. The advantage of the schedule is that it not only states what is to be done, and when, but it also shows who is responsible for doing it. Such a schedule provides accountability to ensure that all tasks are completed by the assigned resource. It is important to note that managers may delegate to others the responsibility for completing one or more marketing activities, but managers must still follow up to ensure the activities have been completed.

Once the marketing budget and activities schedule are in place, managers should validate their draft plan with others prior to implementing it. Owners, other experienced managers, and supervisors may all have input that will help improve the plan (see *Exhibit 11.7*). In addition, providing these key individuals a chance to shape the plan may be helpful when it comes to getting their support for implementing it. Finally, once the plan has been reviewed and is finalized, it should be distributed to all those who have a stake in its successful implementation.

Developing and Implementing a Marketing Plan: Clay's Country Kitchen

Recall the example of Elias, the manager of Clay's Country Kitchen, first introduced in chapter 6. Elias decided to develop a nutrition plan with the following goals:

- To improve nutritional aspects of the entire menu so that low-calorie, low-sodium options comprise at least 25 percent of the menu
- To eliminate incidents of food allergies
- To raise customer satisfaction to 93 percent
- To increase overall sales for the establishment by 10 percent over three months

To support these goals, Elias updated the menu to include the following:

- A vegan entrée section
- Additional gluten-free items
- Additional whole-grain breads and buns
- More fresh fruit and vegetable ingredients
- Healthful improvements to the children's menu section
- Nutrition information printed on the menu

Elias works through the steps of creating a marketing plan. His strategic goals are those listed above. He has made tactical operational changes, first by conducting his nutritional analysis and then by adjusting the types of food and the preparation methods. He has also outlined his tactical marketing steps. His staff has been trained, and now he is ready to promote the new menu.

Recall that one of the opportunities Elias identified was the construction of a new 30-family condominium unit across the street. Elias decides to advertise directly to the new tenants. He pays for an ad in a local directory that the developers of the condo are providing to the tenants. The ad includes a coupon for 10 percent off the purchase of any vegan, gluten-free, or low-calorie item.

In addition, Elias runs an ad on a local radio station. This ad highlights the new healthier children's menu. The ad directs parents to mention having heard the ad in order to receive a free children's meal with each adult meal purchase for the next 30 days.

Next, Elias works with the publisher of a local paper. The publisher is running a story on food allergies, which is an opportunity for publicity. The article will focus on establishments that are making menu changes to accommodate food allergies. Clay's Country Kitchen will be heavily featured, with quotes from both Elias and his chef.

Finally, as part of the training process discussed in chapter 10, Elias has educated his waitstaff on the new, healthier options. He has devised an incentive program to reward staff members who effectively perform suggestive selling or upselling on the new menu items.

LIFE CYCLE OF A NEW PROGRAM

Products and programs go through phases of development called the product life cycle. In the example of Clay's Country Kitchen, the restaurant manager promotes his new menu with advertising, sales promotions, publicity, and personal selling. In terms of the product life cycle, Clay's new menu is in the introductory phase. In the introductory phase of a menu, the restaurant rolls out the program to the public and builds awareness. In the second phase, or growth phase, the restaurant will try to build customer recognition. During this phase the program will differentiate the restaurant from other restaurants in the minds of the public. In this stage, the establishment aims to increase its customer base and build loyalty and return customers.

At some point during or after these phases, the menu will be familiar to regular customers. They will expect to order various menu items when they return to the establishment and will ask for certain dishes. Many will be disappointed if their favorite items are unavailable. The public will know that the town has a restaurant whose menu is designed to be nutritious, or they will recognize the outstanding and healthy children's menu. This phase in the product life cycle is called the maturity phase. At this point the establishment is reinforcing its customers' preferences and building customer loyalty. Most of the menu has been carefully adjusted to attract customers, and procedures are running well for both the front of the house and the back of the house. In the final phase of the product life cycle, called the decline phase, minimum advertisements or reminders are needed to support both the program and the operation.

MEASURING PROGRAM SUCCESS

Recipes have been updated, staff is trained, and the marketing plans are under way. Yet the manager is not finished with the implementation of the nutrition program. The next step is to assess how well the program meets its goals.

Restaurants and foodservice operations should have a plan in effect to collect sales data. Today, much of this collection is computerized via a point-of-sale (POS) system. This system enables managers to track orders and receipts in order to determine sales totals and sales per item. Looking at the sales each week, month, and quarter is essential to monitoring progress during the implementation of a new menu. It is also important to track this data in order to determine which menu items are *not* selling well. Some items need more promotion than others.

The manager should look at each detail of the marketing plan to determine if its objectives have been reached. Sales are only one way to measure success. Other types of data should be collected as appropriate to the marketing plan, as well as the nutrition program as a whole.

Evaluating Sales Promotions

Many managers use coupons to aid in sales promotions. The following strategies can provide data about the customers who used coupons:

- Attach or code the coupons to the receipt to determine the number of new menu items sold on a particular date and the price of the meal.
- Separate the redeemed coupons by type. If the coupons have different codes, this information will provide additional insight about the target audience that redeemed them.
- Compare pre-promotion and post-promotion sales of certain menu items that were added or changed to accommodate target audiences.
- Determine if the staff was able to accommodate the extra business generated by the promotion.

In addition, managers can also track sales of promotional items. For instance, in the Clay's Country Kitchen example, Elias should track the number of children's meals that were free because an adult meal was purchased.

Tracking Publicity

There are some direct measures of the success of a public relations effort. For example, the number of articles written about a special event or the number of times an event is aired on television gives the management an idea of an operation's exposure to the public. A restaurant or foodservice manager should carefully monitor customer traffic and sales after a publicity piece is released or aired on television or on the radio. This is a time to gauge the reaction of the target audience and to measure any increase or decrease. When customers book a party or event at the establishment, staff should ask where they heard about the operation or its services. The operation could conduct a survey of its target market to see if it is being reached effectively. Social media Web sites allow the public to post comments and endorsements, which are another effective avenue for collecting information about the operation.

Assessing Advertising

Advertisements can usually reach a broader audience than other forms of promotion can. Advertising has the advantage of utilizing multiple forms of media but requires repeated exposure to achieve results. As a result, advertising is usually the most expensive component in the promotional mix. The results from advertisements can be difficult to track, but managers can use some of the same approaches they do with sales promotions. In fact, tracking sales related to a specific promotion advertised during a specific time span is an indirect way to measure the effectiveness of an ad.

Monitoring Personal Selling

Managers have a variety of options in tracking personal selling efforts. Most POS systems can correlate menu items sold to the waitstaff that sells them, allowing managers to see which employees are effectively and continuously upselling. Managers can also track check averages before and after a personal selling campaign to determine which staff members are most adept at personal-selling techniques.

Observing Staff Performance

Managers must do more than just track promotional mix items, however, if their nutrition programs are to be successful. They must also track staff comprehension and performance, especially related to back-of-the-house staff and the use of standardized recipes.

OPEN FOR BUSINESS
MANAGER'S MATH

Natalie is the manager of the Gray Derby Lounge. She is considering buying advertising spots on a popular local TV station. The station manager is offering Natalie two different packages. The first package includes 15 spots of 30 seconds each. The second package includes 25 spots of 30 seconds each. The first package sells for $800. The second package sells for $1,250. In each case, the ads will run during the same time periods and on the same days.

1. How much will Natalie spend per spot if she purchases the first package?

2. How much will Natalie spend per spot if she purchases the second package?

(Answers: 1. $53.33 each; 2. $50 each)

Exhibit 11.8

THINK ABOUT IT . . .

Recall a time when your favorite restaurant changed its menu. What factors do you think drove the change?

After the nutrition program launch, managers should evaluate the staff's understanding of the content of the training and their ability to apply the concepts while on the job. As discussed in chapter 10, training should be followed by an evaluation. Feedback from employees and managers can be helpful in deciding whether further training is necessary. In addition, ongoing observation of employees can uncover training gaps. For example, a chef can be observed taking internal temperatures in the kitchen or measuring ingredients (*Exhibit 11.8*). A manager can evaluate communication of special dietary requests between front-of-the-house and back-of-the-house staff and observe how orders are marked or entered into computerized ordering systems. Cooks can be evaluated by comparing dishes against their standardized recipes.

Managing the Menu

A menu represents a restaurant or foodservice operation. It is the foundation from which the establishment develops its business. Therefore, an excellent menu can inspire the staff that prepares it and fulfill, or exceed, the expectations of customers. **Menu management**, also called menu merchandising, is the ongoing evaluation, adjustment, and promotion of a menu by an operation to achieve profitability. Operations should evaluate their menus often to ensure they are attracting their target audience and building their business as effectively as possible. Managers review the menu to determine which items to change at the start of a nutrition program, but they should also review the menu after the program is launched. Doing so allows managers to assess the popularity of the new menu items.

One of the basic components of menu management is menu-item analysis. This is a method of deciding whether to keep or eliminate menu items based on their popularity and profitability. Sales data that reflect how many and which menu items have been sold are important when adjusting the menu.

A manager might run reports from his or her POS system at various intervals after the nutrition program launches. The manager would evaluate the sales not only for the new items but also for the existing items that were popular. He or she would compare the costs of producing each item with the sales price to determine not only which items sell well but also which items contribute the most to the operation's profitability. Items with low sales may need to be further promoted or replaced. Items with relatively high costs may need to have their recipes further adjusted to bring profitability in line with the rest of the menu. Menu analysis is an ongoing process.

Measuring Success: Clay's Country Kitchen

The manager at Clay's Country Kitchen, Elias, has launched his nutrition program and the associated marketing efforts. Six weeks have passed, and Elias is working to determine how effective his changes have been. Recall his goals:

- To improve nutritional aspects of the entire menu so that low-calorie, low-sodium options comprise at least 25 percent of the menu
- To eliminate incidents of food allergies
- To raise customer satisfaction to 93 percent
- To increase overall sales for the establishment by 10 percent over three months

Elias' first goal appeared to be met when he launched the program. In fact, more than 30 percent of the menu items met the low-calorie, low-sodium criteria. However, in tracking sales data, Elias was disappointed to discover that some of his new items were not selling well. In examining the data, he found that the children's menu items were very popular. The items made with more fresh fruit and vegetables were selling moderately well, although there was some room for improvement. The whole-grain breads and buns, however, were a complete flop.

Elias talked to his waitstaff. Feedback from customers related to the fresh fruit and vegetables was very positive, so Elias determined that those items likely just needed some additional promotion. He also added a refresher training course for his waitstaff regarding personal selling and reminded the team of the sales incentives for suggestive selling of these new items.

However, customers complained that the whole-grain breads, while healthy, did not taste as good as the other breads. Elias determined that the problem was twofold. First, perhaps there were too many whole-grain items on the menu. Second, the vendor who was supplying the breads often delivered product that was not up to the restaurant's quality standards. Elias evaluated the menu and realized that he could replace one of the items that contained whole grains with a gluten-free entrée that contained more fruit and vegetables. He would still meet his goal regarding 25 percent of the menu items. In addition, he replaced the bread vendor with another local vendor that could meet the restaurant's quality standards.

Elias also tracked incidents of food allergies. The publicity he received from the newspaper article resulted in increased sales. However, despite the increased volume, there had been no food-allergy incidents. Elias attributed this fact to the diligence of both the front-of-the-house staff and the back-of-the-house staff. Several times he observed servers discussing potential allergens and alternatives with customers. He also noticed that his cooks were being very mindful about cross-contact, and they would often remind each other of the procedures learned during training.

To track customer satisfaction, Elias took two approaches. First, he ensured that his restaurant was listed in several local social media sites that rated food establishments. He monitored comments on these sites, and he addressed negative feedback directly with the customer in a respectful way. Second, Elias established a survey that customers could take using their smart phones. Both the menu and the customer receipts included a Web address and a code that customers could use to provide feedback via a five-question survey. After six weeks, it appeared that Elias was meeting this goal.

Finally, Elias evaluated his overall sales goals. His target was a 10 percent increase in sales over three months. At six weeks, he was at the halfway point. His sales had seen a noticeable increase, but at 9 percent, he was slightly short of the goal.

In tracking his sales promotions and advertisements, Elias realized that the children's menu promotion had been highly successful, but that when the promotion ended, sales dropped off slightly. He resolved to revamp the program to draw in more parents. He extended the program indefinitely and used advertising to convey this message. The cost of children's menu items was offset enough by the increase in adult meal sales that profitability was bumped up to Elias' target.

At the six-week mark, Elias realized that he still had some challenges to address, but that overall, his nutrition program was working. He was close to hitting most of his goals, and he knew the steps he needed to take to ensure that all goals were met.

Gabriel, the restaurant's owner, was happy with Elias' efforts, as were the restaurant's employees. While Elias would have to continue to monitor the program and make incremental adjustments as needed, he was proud of his accomplishments in providing a healthier menu to his customers.

SUMMARY

1. **Identify the features of a marketing plan.**

   A marketing plan should contain the goals of the operation's nutrition program. A goal should be specific to the operation, measurable, achievable, relevant, and timely. The goals of the program should be used to determine the work that needs to be completed and when. While marketing plans may vary by the operation, each plan should include the following features: documentation, target goals, timeliness, marketing plan cost estimates, and customer-focused goals.

2. **Describe the steps involved in designing a marketing plan based on nutrition goals.**

   A well-developed marketing plan should review the operation's target market and include information from the competitive analysis and the SWOT analysis. It should also identify the company's revenue and financial goals associated with the nutrition program. Within the document, the marketing objectives, as well as the strategies and supporting tactics for achieving those objectives, should be identified. Finally, a marketing plan should include a marketing budget and a marketing-activities schedule that conforms to that budget.

3. **Identify the components of the promotional mix.**

   The promotional mix consists of sales promotions, publicity, advertising, and personal selling. Sales promotions are incentives to attract new customers or to highlight new menu items. Publicity is information about an establishment distributed via a third party. Advertisements are paid messages about an operation. Personal selling involves upselling and suggestive selling.

4. **Explain the key points in executing a marketing plan.**

   Tasks must be assigned so that each task has a clear owner accountable for the task's completion. Tasks should be tracked on an activities schedule so that managers know what needs to be done, when it will be done, and who is doing it.

5. **List the key phases in the life cycle of a new program.**

   Products go through several phases over their life cycle. In the introductory phase of a menu, the restaurant rolls out the program to the public and builds awareness. In the growth phase, the restaurant tries to build customer recognition. During the maturity phase, the establishment reinforces its customers' preferences and builds customer loyalty. During the decline phase, minimum advertisements or reminders are needed to support both the program and the operation.

6. **Explain how to evaluate the success of a nutrition program and adjust the program accordingly.**

   There are several ways that managers can assess a nutrition program. All methods are designed to tell the manager how well he or she has met the goals established at the beginning of the program. First, managers will review sales data. Next, they will track data related to each of the items in the promotional mix. Finally, they will observe staff behavior to ensure that staff members are properly implementing the program.

APPLICATION EXERCISE

Promoting a Menu

You are the owner of a local sandwich shop. You have recently decided to introduce a line of vegan and vegetarian sandwiches. You are hoping to attract customers who frequent a natural-food store in the neighborhood.

Establish some goals for the program. Then design a promotional mix that uses at least one of each type of promotion. Explain how you will track the success of the promotional mix against your overall goals.

REVIEW YOUR LEARNING

Select the best answer for each question.

1. The four aspects of the promotional mix are sales promotions, advertising, public relations, and
   A. rebates.
   B. marketing.
   C. banner ads.
   D. personal selling.

2. Which of the following best represents a measurable nutrition program goal?
   A. Increase sales of low-calorie items by 5 percent this month
   B. Provide healthier food to more customers this year
   C. Lower the number of food-allergy issues
   D. Decrease sodium in most menu items

3. What is the most expensive promotion method for a restaurant or foodservice operation?
   A. Promotions
   B. Advertising
   C. Publicity
   D. Sales

4. The manager of a seafood restaurant donates a large sum of money to a local organization working to fight obesity in school children. The attention that the restaurant gets is a result of what type of promotional mix item?
   A. Upselling
   B. Publicity
   C. Advertising
   D. Sales promotion

5. In what stage of the product life cycle is an establishment likely to gain customer recognition and differentiate itself from the others in the market?
   A. Introductory phase
   B. Growth phase
   C. Maturity phase
   D. Decline phase

6. A manager would use which tool to track what promotional items need to happen, when they need to happen, and who is responsible for doing them?
   A. Marketing plan
   B. Promotional mix
   C. Marketing budget
   D. Marketing-activities schedule

7. The waitstaff at a fine-dining restaurant has been trained to pair wines and beers with dinner menu entrées. This is an example of what type of marketing activity?

   A. Advertising

   B. Sales promotion

   C. Suggestive selling

   D. Public relations

8. What type of communication is free to restaurants and foodservice operations?

   A. Publicity

   B. Promotions

   C. Advertisements

   D. Personal selling

9. Which activity involves recommending a related or higher-priced product?

   A. Upselling

   B. Publicity

   C. Promotions

   D. Advertising

10. The process of ranking menu items according to their popularity and profitability is called

   A. menu-item generation.

   B. menu-item churning.

   C. menu-item analysis.

   D. menu-item velocity.

12 Menu Labeling

INSIDE THIS CHAPTER

- Legislation Impacting Restaurants and Foodservice Establishments
- Proposed Menu-Labeling Regulations
- Truth-in-Menu Practices and Disclaimers
- Monitoring the Operation for Compliance

CHAPTER LEARNING OBJECTIVES

After completing this chapter, you should be able to:

- Describe the federal legislation that governs menu labeling in restaurants and foodservice establishments.

- Summarize the menu-labeling requirements for covered establishments.

- Explain nutrient-content claims and health claims as they relate to restaurants and foodservice operations.

- Identify acceptable truth-in-menu practices and appropriate menu disclaimers, and explain their placement in marketing materials.

- Describe systems to monitor the operation for compliance with applicable labeling regulations.

KEY TERMS

combination meal, p. 248

covered establishment, p. 247

food on display, p. 249

health claim, p. 246

menu disclaimer, p. 253

nutrient-content claim, p. 246

Section 4205 of the Patient Protection and Affordable Care Act, p. 247

self-service item, p. 249

standard menu item, p. 248

truth-in-menu law, p. 253

variable menu item, p. 249

vending machine, p. 252

CASE STUDY

Nancy is a manager for a quick-service restaurant that is part of a national chain with over 180 units throughout the United States. While searching through the mail from the main office, she found a letter reminding managers to order new menu boards for their units. A nutrition analysis had been done on new menu items, and the menu boards were scheduled to be updated to reflect the changes.

Nancy thought these directives from the main office increased expenses for the unit without a very good reason. She thought customers paid no attention to calories anyway. "What was all the fuss about anyhow?" Nancy put the reminder at the back of her "to-do" pile thinking she would just skip the new boards and save the unit money.

1. What did Nancy not consider in her decision to postpone changing menu boards?

2. What are the potential issues she may have created with her decision?

LEGISLATION IMPACTING RESTAURANTS AND FOODSERVICE ESTABLISHMENTS

The business environment for restaurants and foodservice operations changes regularly. It is subject to competition, economic realities, food trends, and agricultural issues. It is also subject to federal, state, and local laws and regulations. It is critical for foodservice professionals to evaluate their operations in relation to all of these factors. They should also educate themselves on these vital aspects of business. The following section describes one important regulatory change regarding the labeling of menus.

Background on Menu Labeling

The Nutrition Labeling and Education Act of 1990, or NLEA, modified the Food, Drug, and Cosmetic Act. It also set the framework for a food label for canned and packaged goods. At the time it was enacted, this legislation exempted menu labeling in restaurants and foodservice establishments. A later provision of NLEA now requires menu labeling for restaurants and other foodservice establishments that make either a nutrient-content claim or a health claim on their menus.

A nutrient-content claim is one that characterizes the level of a nutrient on the food label or restaurant menu. An example of a nutrient-content claim is stating that an item is low in sodium. If a restaurant or foodservice operation wants to claim that a menu item is low in sodium, the item can contain no more than 140 milligrams of sodium per serving to meet the legal definition.

A health claim is an expressed or implied statement on the menu characterizing the relationship of a substance to disease or health. An example of a health claim is a statement that an item is heart healthy. These types of claims require the restaurant or foodservice operation to meet the definitions provided by the Food and Drug Administration (FDA).

Restaurants and foodservice operations that make claims are required to indicate what basis was used to determine the claim on request. The law requires a reasonable basis. A reasonable basis may come from a nutrient analysis of the menu item or a cookbook with a recipe analysis to meet the provision. See chapter 3 for review of NLEA and examples of the FDA definitions.

Consumer demand for more nutrition information increased. At the same time, concern by public health professionals over the nation's poor health continued. As a result, state and local governments began to write and enact additional menu-labeling laws. By the late 2000s, several states and municipalities had passed legislation requiring the labeling of menus. This made it difficult for businesses operating in multiple states and municipalities to comply with a patchwork of different labeling requirements.

To address this concern, industry groups, consumer advocates, and health professionals worked with Congress. Together, they crafted federal legislation that provided consistent, nationwide menu-labeling regulations. In March 2010, Section 4205 of the Patient Protection and Affordable Care Act was signed into law. The FDA was given the responsibility of enforcing the provisions of this national menu-labeling legislation. The FDA has developed proposed regulations, and the agency is reviewing feedback collected from interested parties to clarify regulations.

PROPOSED MENU-LABELING REGULATIONS

The following is a brief summary of the main points included in the proposed FDA regulations for Section 4205 of the Patient Protection and Affordable Care Act. Current and future restaurant and foodservice managers are encouraged to check the actual version of the regulations at the FDA's Web site, *www.fda.gov*.

Businesses Affected by the Menu-Labeling Law

This law applies to chain restaurants and similar retail food establishments having 20 or more locations. Those operations can either be operating under the same name or slight variations in the name, or selling substantially the same menu items. These businesses are required to provide the following on the menu or menu board: calorie information for standard menu items, a succinct statement about recommended daily calorie intakes for adults, and a clear and conspicuous statement notifying customers of the availability of additional nutritional information. In addition, they are required to have additional nutritional information available on-site and available to consumers on request.[1]

Under the regulations, businesses that meet the definition are referred to as "covered retail food establishments" or covered establishments. See *Exhibit 12.1* for a listing of the types of businesses that are included in this definition.

Section 4205 preempts state and local laws and regulations. It prohibits the states from enforcing other nutrition-labeling laws for covered establishments unless the laws are identical to the federal requirements.

Exhibit 12.1
COVERED AND NON-COVERED ESTABLISHMENTS
Covered establishments
Table-service establishments
Quick-service establishments
Cafeterias
Pastry and retail confectionary stores
Coffee shops
Snack bars and ice cream parlors
Multipurpose establishments presenting themselves publicly as restaurants
Establishments within larger establishments (such as a coffee shop in a bookstore)
Grocery stores
Convenience stores
Vending machines
Operations not considered covered establishments
Movie theaters
Amusement parks
General merchandise stores
Hotels
Trains and planes

[1]http://www.fda.gov/food/labelingnutrition/ucm217762.htm

THINK ABOUT IT . . .

Why might an operation choose to voluntarily register with the FDA to provide menu labeling?

Businesses that are not covered under the federal legislation are still subject to state and local mandates. These establishments can volunteer to be included under the federal law. To do so, they must register with the FDA every other year.

The legislation also includes provisions for those that operate 20 or more vending machines. Vending-machine operators are required under these provisions to provide nutrition information to their customers. Vending-machine regulations will be summarized later in this chapter.

Restaurant or Similar Retail Food Establishment Defined

These regulations cover restaurants with 20 or more locations and similar retail food establishments. The type of ownership does not exempt businesses that qualify "as a covered establishment." At this time, the FDA has proposed three possible definitions for a "similar retail food establishment."

An establishment is covered under the law if it represents itself as a restaurant to the public, its primary business is to sell food, and one of the following conditions applies:

- More than 50 percent of its floor area is used for preparing, purchasing, serving, consuming, or storing food.
- More than 50 percent of its gross revenues are generated by the sale of food.

These two definitions for a "retail food establishment" include grocery stores and convenience stores, and both would be subject to labeling rules.

A third definition would define "similar retail food establishment" as a business selling restaurant food or restaurant-type food to consumers. Under this definition, grocery stores and convenience stores would not be considered covered establishments.

Identifying Food Requiring a Label

Covered establishments are required to label their standard menu items. A standard menu item includes the following categories: combination meals, variable menu items, self-service items, and food on display.

- **Standard menu items** are defined as those appearing routinely on the menu. For example a hamburger on a bun or multi-serving items such as a whole baked meatloaf.
- **Combination meals** include multiple items such as a hamburger on a bun, potato chips, coleslaw, and a beverage (*Exhibit 12.2*). It may be represented on the menu or menu board pictorially, numerically, or in narrative form.

Exhibit 12.2

- **Variable menu items** are standard menu items that include a flavoring option such as in milk shake flavors (chocolate, vanilla, or strawberry) or as in a pizza that might have multiple toppings but is listed as a single menu item.

- **Self service items** are food items that are offered at salad bars, buffet lines, cafeteria lines, or similar self-service facilities. This covers food items that the customer serves himself or herself, such as those at hot and cold food bars and from beverage dispensers.

- **Food on display** is food that is visible to the customer before their purchase, such as a piece of pie or a piece of pizza. Food on display would not include meat and cheeses sold at the grocery or a delicatessen where the customer is taking the food home for further preparation.

Beverages will require labeling and include those that are dispensed from fountain machines, such as soda, lemonade, tea, and milk.

Food Not Requiring a Label

Types of food that would not need to be labeled under the law are custom orders, daily specials, items being test marketed that appear on the menu board for less than 90 days, and temporary items that appear for less than 60 days.

A custom order is a food order prepared in a specific manner according to a customer request. In fulfilling a customer's request, the restaurant or foodservice operation deviates from the usual preparation or cooking practices. Therefore, the item will not contain the same number of calories as the standard menu item.

A daily special is being defined as a menu item that is prepared and offered for sale on a particular day, but it is not listed on the menu of the covered establishment.

Items not required to be listed on the menu or menu board include condiments and other items placed on the table or counter for general use, such as salt and pepper, ketchup, and mayonnaise (*Exhibit 12.3*). At this time alcoholic beverages are not required to be labeled.

Menus and Menu Boards

The menu or menu board must contain the calorie declaration for each covered establishment. The menu or menu board is the primary writing that a customer uses to make an order selection. The definition of menu is being interpreted from the customer's vantage point. A covered establishment may have multiple menus.

THINK ABOUT IT . . .

Do you think that restaurants and other food service establishments will decrease calories and sodium in response to menu-labeling provisions? Why or why not?

Exhibit 12.3

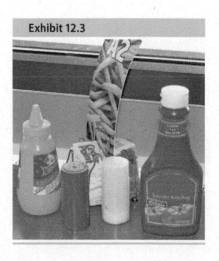

The definition of menus includes examples such as a carryout menu, an Internet menu, an overhead or drive-through menu board, or a traditional menu provided at the table. Although the primary menu of indoor dining might be a printed menu, a flyer that is used to order carryout might also serve as the menu. While a flyer may be counted as a menu, advertisements are not considered a form of menu.

The regulations mention a variety of menu types as examples:

- Breakfast menus
- Lunch and dinner menus
- Dessert menus
- Beverage menus
- Children's menus
- Other specialty menus

Exhibit 12.4

EXAMPLES OF CALORIE PLACEMENT

Example 1

Sandwiches	Cal
Grilled-cheese sandwich	440

Example 2

Sandwiches	
Grilled-cheese sandwich	440 Calories

Posting Calorie Declarations

The law requires covered establishments to post the number of calories found in each menu item on menus or menu boards where the item is listed for sale. The number of calories must be provided next to the menu item. This is done to clearly link the item to the number of calories so there is no confusion. There are two ways that calories may be shown. The word *Calories* may be written out or abbreviated in either example. *Exhibit 12.4* shows calorie declaration variances for a grilled-cheese sandwich.

Calorie declarations must follow font, size, and prominence rules. Calories must be presented in the same color and font size as the menu item and in a contrasting background similar to the menu item. This font size cannot be smaller than the price of the menu item or smaller than the smallest type used for the menu item. If food items are listed on a drive-through menu board, the calories must be listed there as well. No stanchions may be used to provide calorie information for drive-through menu boards.

Exhibit 12.5

As noted above, variable menu items are standard menu items that come in different flavors, varieties, or combinations. The FDA is proposing that these types of food be presented in a range of calories from lowest to highest. Self-service food or food on display items may be presented per serving or per item. Establishments may use the serving size of the serving utensil, such as a ladle, to determine portions (*Exhibit 12.5*). They may use a common household measurement when determining calories. Examples might be 300 calories per scoop or 400 calories per cup of potato salad.

Self-serve beverages are being considered as a variable menu item. When they are listed as various flavors, such as cola, root beer, and orange soda, they must be labeled for the exact flavor and size on the menu or menu board. If they are offered under the general classification of soda, a calorie range may be offered on the menu or menu board. In either case, calorie declarations must appear in both locations, at the fountain machine and on the menu or menu board.

Daily Calorie Recommendations and Additional Information

Two statements are required on menus or menu boards that are intended to help the public with their food selections. The first statement provides more information on daily calorie recommendations. The proposed wording is "A 2,000 calorie daily diet is used as the basis for general nutrition advice; however, individual calorie needs may vary."

The second statement refers to additional nutrition information a covered establishment must have on its premises. It reads, "Additional nutrition information available upon request." Both of these statements must adhere to the color and font-size restrictions. Information to fulfill this provision could appear on a separate sign near food items for food on display.

In addition, the covered establishment would have to maintain written information on the following nutrients in their standard menu items and make it available to the diner on request:

- Calories
- Calories from fat
- Total fat
- Saturated fat
- Trans fat
- Cholesterol
- Sodium
- Total carbohydrates
- Dietary fiber
- Sugars
- Protein

At this time, the regulations provide no required medium for the additional information. It could be provided on cards, signs, pamphlets, or the Internet.

Manager's Memo

When new regulations are written for restaurants and other food-service operations, it is a good idea for managers and other foodservice professionals to visit the Web site of the National Restaurant Association. The National Restaurant Association often provides information regarding new laws and regulations so that its members can clarify how government regulations may affect their businesses.

In addition, the National Restaurant Association reports the important trends in the foodservice business. When a manager knows the trends, he or she can incorporate them into the marketing plan and hopefully increase business and profits.

Basis of Information and Accuracy of Nutritional Information

The nutritional information that is required may be developed or originated by "reasonable basis." A reasonable basis means it originates through such sources as software nutrient databases or programs, cookbooks, laboratory analysis, or labels from products already packaged and labeled. Covered establishments are required to demonstrate a reasonable basis for this additional information available to consumers on demand. Under the proposed law, the FDA could examine the basis of the additional information and the documentation.

The amount of calories, sugars, total fat, saturated fat, trans fat, cholesterol, and sodium contained in a sample of a standard menu item must not exceed more than 20 percent of the declared value.

In addition, the amount of protein, total carbohydrates, and dietary fiber contained in an appropriate sample of the menu item would not be less than 80 percent of the declared value. Covered establishments should maintain records on how they arrived at the calorie values they are declaring.

In order for covered establishments to comply with the regulations above, they will have to be consistent in their purchasing, recipe standardization, and preparation. Operations must also adhere to designated serving sizes for their standard menu items. Additionally, they will need to organize and store the required additional nutritional information and train staff on its retrieval and usage.

Vending-Machine Regulations

The menu labeling regulations also include those businesses operating 20 or more vending machines. Regulations define a vending machine as a "self-service device that upon insertion of a coin, paper currency, token, key, or by optional manual operation, dispenses servings of food in bulk, in packages, or prepared by the machine, without the necessity of replenishing the device between each vending operation." The types of vending machines listed by the FDA as examples of vending machines dispensing food included those for the following: candy, gum, soda, sandwich, milk, coffee, and popcorn.

Vending-machine operators would have to provide nutritional information for the products they sell to consumers. This law would preempt or replace state and local laws for the covered vending-machine owners and operators. Vending-machine operators who want to register with the FDA may do so voluntarily and be covered under the law.

CALORIE INFORMATION FOR VENDING MACHINES

If vending-machine food does not have calorie descriptions, it is the responsibility of the manufacturer or supplier to provide the nutritional information. Covered vending-machine operators must ensure that nutrition labeling is truthful and not misleading to the customer or consumer.

Covered vending-machines operators essentially have three choices for declaring the nutritional information required by the law. They can provide calorie disclosures, allow customers the opportunity to view the nutritional information on the packages of food, or present the nutrition information at the point of purchase. Calorie declarations must be clear and conspicuous and must be in a readable font and print size. Vending-machine operators may also use the word *Calories* or the abbreviation *CAL*.

Nutritional information must be presented by labeling the entire package as vended rather than by the individual serving. If a package contains three portions or servings, the calories listed will be for all three portions together. If the item has a condiment or additional item in the package, the calorie declarations are labeled together as one calorie value. When an item has a food label, calorie declarations must be for the same value of the item as labeled. For example, a cookie must contain the same number of calories as listed on the package.

Calories could be posted next to each item in the vending machine or the calories could be combined and placed on a sign in close proximity to the machines. The sign has to be clear and conspicuous to the person viewing the food, or it must be on the selection button.

A separate disclosure of calories is not needed for items if the nutrition-facts panel can be seen from outside the machine before the customer makes the purchase. The regulations require that the viewing panel be fully visible without any obstruction. Smaller or abbreviated nutrition-facts panels may not be used because they may not be seen in a vending machine.

TRUTH-IN-MENU PRACTICES AND DISCLAIMERS

The menu is the tool that allows an establishment to communicate its products and advertise its business. It provides crucial information to customers about the food being prepared and served. The laws that govern the menu are known as truth-in-menu laws. A restaurant or foodservice operation must represent its food correctly to its customers. For example, it must serve what is described on the menu, being careful to describe its preparation methods and its ingredients accurately. It should ensure that the origin and the size of menu items are correctly described and agree with what is ordered and served. In addition, the operation or establishment is responsible for the accuracy of any nutrient-content or health claims that are made. Those covered establishments are now also responsible for the nutrient values and formatting required by the national menu legislation.

A menu disclaimer is a statement informing the customer that there is no legal warranty or guarantee of satisfaction implied or responsibility accepted. Some disclaimers are necessary for restaurants and foodservice operations to

BY THE CUSTOMER/ FOR THE CUSTOMER

Each restaurant or foodservice manager needs to understand how to respond to questions regarding the number of calories and other information on the menu. Customers will see this information and may have further questions.

The effects of the national law are hard to know until it is fully implemented, but restaurants may consider adjusting calories and sodium levels downward to keep them reasonable in comparison to the calorie goals of the succinct statement on the menu. Many dishes can be adapted to lower calories and sodium and still be delicious. Customers will be making comparisons among menu items.

include on their menus due to state and local laws. An example is the disclaimer that warns a customer about eating undercooked meat and eggs. Another disclaimer might be necessary when working with customers that have food allergies, even though every precaution will be taken to protect a customer.

As noted earlier in this chapter, it is important to remember that all nutrient calculations are estimates. This is true even when reliable means such as laboratory analyses and nutrient-database calculations are performed correctly. With calorie counts now required for some operations on the menu and additional nutrient content available upon request, operations will want to carefully review the accuracy of their data.

Operations may also choose to include a disclaimer regarding their nutrient calculations. The disclaimer may indicate that calculations are completed by reliable methods, such as nutrient-database calculations and vendor data, but they represent an estimate of nutrient content. There may be variations in nutrient content across serving sizes and varying ingredients.

Since menu disclaimers contain language that may protect the operation, managers will want to review federal, state, and local laws and consult with professionals before adding disclaimers to their menu.

MONITORING THE OPERATION FOR COMPLIANCE

Adjusting to new regulations requires a concerted effort and in most cases a financial commitment as well. It will be no different when implementing the menu-labeling laws. The following are suggestions to help with the compliance needed for menu labeling. Each covered establishment should begin the process by adding compliance to menu regulations to its marketing plan. Since menu changes occur regularly in restaurants and foodservice operations, obtaining a nutritional analysis on new menu items should become part of the menu-planning process. Each time new menu items are added, covered establishments will need to complete a nutrient analysis for that item.

Exhibit 12.6

Managers should develop an initial training program for their staff regarding menu-labeling laws and regulations (*Exhibit 12.6*). The training should inform staff where nutritional information needed for the public will be kept and how to retrieve it easily. For covered establishments, menus and menu boards need to be changed to reflect calorie counts. If the operation has developed new menu items, a menu-item analysis may be desirable. The analysis will help managers to gauge the popularity of new menu items designed for lower calories, saturated fat, cholesterol, sugar, or sodium. If the operation is fully computerized, consider how nutrition information will be integrated. A software program may allow for easy information retrieval.

Restaurants and foodservice operations could capture relevant comments regarding either nutrition information or the menu on the communication log. Ask staff to report any issues regarding nutrition information being shared with customers. Managers should capture customer reactions to the nutrient values on the menu. Add language to position descriptions requiring staff to adhere to menu-labeling regulations, such as posting information or changing menu boards when needed.

Develop measures to capture menu-labeling costs, and compare these costs to increases or decreases in profits. If the operation is a covered establishment, try to determine what effect menu-labeling regulations may have on your business. If the operation is not a covered establishment, decide whether or not the voluntary program would be beneficial to your organization.

SUMMARY

1. **Describe the federal legislation that governs menu labeling in restaurants and foodservice establishments.**

    Two federal laws govern menu labeling in restaurants and foodservice operations: the Nutrition Labeling and Education Act and Section 4205 of the Patient Protection and Affordable Care Act of 2010. NLEA applies to operations that make health or nutrient-content claims on their menus. Section 4205 applies generally to chain restaurants and requires nutrition information to be made more available to the consumer.

2. **Summarize the menu-labeling requirements for covered establishments.**

    This law applies to chain restaurants or other foodservice establishments with 20 or more units having the same name or variations of that name, or preparing the same menu items. Under this law, menus are required to have calorie counts on standard menu items, a declaration of usual daily calorie needs, and a statement regarding the availability of additional information. In addition, operations must actually keep this information on-site.

    Vending-machine operators with 20 or more machines are required to label food sold to their customers. Non-covered businesses and vending operators may volunteer to be under the federal law by registering with the government.

3. **Explain nutrient-content claims and health claims as they relate to restaurants and foodservice operations.**

   Nutrient-content claims tell the consumer how much of a nutrient is contained in the food. A health claim is an expressed or implied statement connecting a nutrient to disease or health, such as calling an item heart healthy. Restaurants and foodservice operations that make either claim are required to specify the basis used to establish the claim.

4. **Identify acceptable truth-in-menu practices and appropriate menu disclaimers, and explain their placement in marketing materials.**

   Each restaurant or foodservice operation must follow the truth-in-menu laws. These cover such things as the size, the origin, or the preparation of the food. Operations are responsible for the accuracy of nutrient-content claims or any health claims that are made. Covered establishments must also ensure that their nutrient data is accurate.

5. **Describe systems to monitor the operation for compliance with applicable labeling regulations.**

   In order to be compliant with labeling laws, managers and other foodservice professionals should identify the need for menu labeling in the marketing plan. Operations need to plan for training, implementation, and evaluation of this environmental change.

   Activities that are important include revision of menus and menu boards, a menu-item analysis, and communication about how nutritional information will be handled. Managers should decide how nutrition information will be integrated into the operation, including adding this task to job and task descriptions.

APPLICATION EXERCISE

Visit the Web sites for two chain restaurants which provide nutrition information for their menu items. Select two menu items that you would order for yourself. Then, answer the questions below:

- How do the operations provide the nutrition information?

- Did the nutrition information match the new federal menu nutrition labeling requirements?

- Did you learn anything new about the nutritional content of the menu items you have ordered for yourself?

REVIEW YOUR LEARNING

Select the best answer for each question.

1. **What body is responsible for developing the regulations for Section 4205 of the Patient Protection and Affordable Care Act?**
   A. Food and Drug Administration
   B. National Restaurant Association
   C. Academy of Nutrition and Dietetics
   D. United States Department of Agriculture

2. **How many individual units must a restaurant or foodservice operation have to be considered a "covered establishment"?**
   A. 5
   B. 10
   C. 15
   D. 20

3. **What is the best example of a "standard menu item"?**
   A. Skim milk on a regular breakfast menu
   B. Milk shake added for a holiday
   C. Omelet for the daily special
   D. Salad being test marketed

4. **What is the recommended daily calorie level for adults provided in the menu labeling regulations?**
   A. 1,200
   B. 1,500
   C. 2,000
   D. 2,500

5. **What is the best reason that a custom order is exempted from menu labeling?**
   A. It is similar food just cooked with different techniques.
   B. It is identical to the standard menu items and values.
   C. Its calorie value is averaged with other menu items.
   D. It is different than standard menu items and values.

6. **Which menu item requires a calorie label?**
   A. Alcoholic beverages at the bar
   B. Bottles of ketchup at the table
   C. Salt packet with a drive-through order
   D. Ketchup with a food item in a vending machine

7. **What is an example of a truth-in-advertising statement?**
   A. Not responsible for lost or stolen property.
   B. Uncooked eggs may contain harmful bacteria.
   C. Beef filets purchased from a nearby organic farm.
   D. Calorie values are estimates based on nutrient-database calculations.

8. **What best describes the font size and color of ink for calorie counts declared on a menu?**
   A. Font size and color do not matter if calories appear near the menu item.
   B. The size of font for calories must be larger than the menu item's price.
   C. The size and color of font must each be different from the menu item's price.
   D. Font size must be at least the size of the menu item's price and in the same color.

9. **The purpose of menu disclaimers is to**
   A. ensure that customers get a tasty meal.
   B. assure customers that managers are up to date on trends.
   C. specify that the operation is not guaranteeing satisfaction.
   D. state that customers are getting good value for their dollar.

10. **Calories, sugars, and total fats could exceed the declared calorie value on the menu by only what percentage?**
    A. 20
    B. 30
    C. 40
    D. 50

FIELD PROJECT

Real-World Analysis

This field practicum project will reinforce the concepts of this book by showing how nutrition is used in the restaurant and foodservice industry to provide healthier food. It will help you to develop the analytical skills you need to be successful.

Assignment

One effective way to exercise your nutritional knowledge is to apply it to a real-case scenario at an actual restaurant, and the activities below provide you with an opportunity to learn from practitioners in the restaurant and foodservice industry. By understanding the constraints and requirements of an actual operation, you will enhance and sharpen your applicable knowledge of nutrition, and you will sharpen your recipe-refining and healthy-cooking skills.

1. Select a restaurant that has a full menu and has not adopted menu labeling.

2. Get permission from the manager and the chef to review some of their menu items:

   - Explain that you are doing a research project to review menu items for healthy options and that you would like to provide feedback about some of their recipes to show how they could be made healthier by using low-fat cooking methods and reducing amounts of fat and salt.

3. Select five menu items to review—two appetizers, two entrées, and one dessert. Choose menu items that fit one or more of the following:

   - High in fat
   - Could be prepared using whole grains or whole-grain flour
   - Could include more vegetables or fruit
   - Could benefit from reduced sodium levels

4. Calculate the nutritional content of each menu item:

   - Look for the amount of carbohydrate, protein, fat, sodium, cholesterol, and vitamins and minerals.
   - Look at all the ingredients; you may have to review food labels to determine nutritional content for the ingredients.
   - Look at the types of fats used—polyunsaturated, monounsaturated, saturated, or trans fat—and document that information.
   - You may use nutritional-analysis software if you have it available.

5. Assume that the five items you chose make up one person's diet for one day:

   - Determine whether the nutritional content of the day's food falls within the recommendations of the Dietary Guidelines for Americans 2010. Determine whether the nutritional content of the day's food falls within the USDA dietary guidelines and percentages.
   - Identify the dietary categories that are within and outside the guidelines.

6. Review and document the preparation and cooking methods used for each menu item:

   - Can you improve the methods used to prepare the item in a way that makes it lower in fat by lowering solid fat and calories?

   - Provide a cooking technique for preparing the item in an alternative manner that retains the integrity of the dish.

7. Rewrite the recipe to improve the nutritional balance of the menu items:

   - Look for opportunities to decrease solid fat and sodium by using alternative ingredients and cooking methods. Use whole grains and increase the amounts of vegetables or fruit.

   - Is there a way to decrease trans fat and saturated fat in the recipe?

   - Give suggestions to decrease salt and yet increase flavor.

   - Keep in mind that the recipe must retain its tastiness and flavor.

8. Recalculate the nutritional content of each revised menu item. Show how your changes improved the recipe by lowering solid fat, calories, or sodium. You may have added vegetables, fruit, or whole grains and improved the nutritional balance. The recipe needs to taste good and look good.

9. Discuss your results with the chef and determine if your changes are acceptable and reasonable.

10. Discuss with the chef ways that he or she might train staff members to deploy the new recipes. Document at least three suggestions.

11. Identify at least four ways you might promote this new menu. Be sure to use at least one instance of each component of the promotional mix.

12. Write an in-depth report explaining all of your actions and discoveries from start to finish:

    - Provide the chef and your instructor with a copy of your report.

GLOSSARY

Acceptable Macronutrient Distribution Range (AMDR) The range of intakes for a particular energy source, such as carbohydrates (45 to 65 percent), lipids (20 to 35 percent), and protein (10 to 35 percent), that reduces risk of disease while providing enough essential nutrients.

ACF-certified chef A chef who satisfies American Culinary Federation–established requirements that include points earned from education, experience, and awards, as well as passing a national certification exam and a proctored practical exam. ACF-certified chefs select and prepare nutritional ingredients to make healthy menus of different cuisines.

ADDIE model An instructional design model used for training development. *ADDIE* stands for analyze, design, develop, implement, and evaluate.

Adequate Intake (AI) The daily dietary intake level assumed to be adequate for good health when there is insufficient evidence to set a Recommended Dietary Allowance (RDA).

Adipose tissue Body fat.

Advertising Any form of marketing message that managers pay for and deliver in an identifiable but non-personal way.

Agricultural biotechnology Changing living organisms in order to produce something of use, such as plants or animals, microorganisms, or products. This includes genetic modification as well as the use of biological organisms in the production of food.

Allergen A food or food ingredient, such as milk, eggs, peanuts, tree nuts, fish, shellfish, soy, and wheat, that can cause an allergic reaction or response for some people.

Allergic reaction A condition that occurs when the immune system launches a defense against an allergen, causing an adverse reaction.

Alpha-linolenic acid An essential fatty acid that is found in canola, soybean, walnut, peanut, pecan, almond, wheat germ, and flaxseed oils.

Amino acid A chemical compound that has special functions in the body, including building and repairing muscles; supplying nitrogen for tissue growth and maintenance; maintaining fluids; keeping the body from getting too acidic or basic; and acting as a transporter of lipids, vitamins, minerals, and oxygen as part of the blood.

Anaphylaxis A severe allergic reaction with rapid onset that is usually accompanied by a drop in blood pressure, closing of the throat, and the loss of consciousness.

Antioxidant A chemical that fights the excessive oxidation of molecules in the human body.

Basal metabolism Bodily functions such as respiration, muscle contraction, nervous system and hormonal functions, production of body heat, and circulation.

Beta-carotene An inactive form of vitamin A that is activated by the body.

Bioavailability The degree to which the nutrients people consume can be absorbed and become available for use by the body.

Body mass index (BMI) A numerical calculation that reflects the relationship between a person's height and weight that is used to determine if the person's weight is in a healthy range.

Calorie An energy unit that is one-thousandth of a kilocalorie. In the United States, another term for **kilocalorie**.

Carbohydrate A basic class of nutrients containing the elements carbon, hydrogen, and oxygen; it includes starch, sugar, and dietary fiber.

Celiac disease A chronic, hereditary, intestinal disorder in which an inability to absorb gluten results in an immune response that damages the intestinal mucosa.

Center-of-plate concept The concept that a meal should be focused on an expensive centerpiece item, usually a protein-rich food such as meat, poultry, or fish, with the rest of the meal's components treated as accompaniments.

Certified organic A plan that specifies practices and substances used in the production of organic food.

Chemical loss The reduction of nutrients due to destruction or transformation of the chemical composition of food.

Cholesterol A sterol that is a component of cellular membranes and is found only in animal food such as meat, fish, poultry, and cheese.

Coenzyme An activator of other enzymes—body chemicals that catalyze, or speed up, a specific chemical reaction.

Combination meals Meals that include multiple items, such as a hamburger on a bun, potato chips, coleslaw, and a beverage.

Competitive analysis A formal or informal process of assessing competitors in a specified geographic area or industry segment that examines the products and services offered by these establishments and their relationship to the target market.

Complete protein A food that contains all nine essential amino acids.

Complex carbohydrate A carbohydrate that contains numerous combinations of saccharides, including oligosaccharides and polysaccharides.

Conventional food Food products grown using approved agricultural methods. In the United States, such methods are studied and regulated by the U.S. Department of Agriculture (USDA).

Coulis A thick, pureed sauce made from either vegetables or fruit.

Covered establishment A business that is covered by Section 4205 of the Patient Protection and Affordable Care Act; this law applies to chain restaurants and similar retail food establishments having 20 or more locations.

Crossbreeding The breeding of different varieties of plants or animals exhibiting favorable characteristics to produce offspring with the best qualities of each variety.

Cross-contact A situation in which one food item comes in contact with another, as when the same cooking vessel is used for both items.

Cruciferous vegetable A vegetable rich in phytochemicals, such as broccoli, cauliflower, and cabbage.

Daily Reference Value (DRV) The nutrient-intake value for protein, carbohydrate, fat, and other components, such as cholesterol, set by the Food and Drug Administration (FDA) to formulate the Daily Value.

Daily Value (DV) A food-label reference value determined from the FDA's Reference Daily Intakes (RDIs) and Daily Reference Values (DRVs).

Decline phase The stage in the product life cycle in which minimum advertisements or reminders are needed to support both the program and the operation.

Dehydrating Reducing the water available to the body by chemically causing fluid excretion.

Diabetes mellitus A disease characterized by hyperglycemia, or high blood-sugar levels. It is caused by genetic, metabolic, and other conditions, such as pregnancy.

Dietary Approaches to Stop Hypertension (DASH) eating plan A diet that is low in sodium but high in other minerals to help normalize blood pressure.

Dietary fiber A type of carbohydrate that contains long strands of bonded glucose molecules and cannot be broken down by human digestive enzymes.

Dietary Guidelines for Americans 2010 A document that provides information and advice on food choices, healthy weight, and disease prevention for people aged two years and older.

Dietary Reference Intakes (DRIs) Recommended daily nutrient- and energy-intake amounts for healthy people of a particular age range and gender, based on current scientific evidence.

Digestion The process of breaking food down to its simplest or most elemental parts, which the body can then absorb and use.

Digestive tract The part of the body composed of the oral cavity, pharynx, esophagus, stomach, small intestine, large intestine, rectum, and anus.

Disaccharide Two monosaccharides bonded together to form a two-unit sugar.

Education A more formal process than training, designed to transfer knowledge and skill to an employee or individual.

Empty-calorie food Food that contains higher proportions of calories and relatively few, if any, nutrients.

Emulsion sauce A sauce made from two or more ingredients that do not combine easily.

Energy balance Eating the same number of calories as the number of calories utilized or expended daily, assuming that the level of physical activity remains consistent.

Enrichment Restoring nutrients that are removed when food is processed.

Enzyme A protein substance that speeds up metabolic reactions.

Epinephrine A hormone used to treat serious allergic reactions.

Essential amino acid One of the nine amino acids that people must obtain from food.

Essential fatty acid A fatty acid that is necessary for normal growth and development; it cannot be manufactured by the body and must be obtained from food.

Essential nutrient A nutrient that is required by the body and has to be obtained through the diet on a daily or near-daily basis.

Estimated Average Requirement (EAR) The estimated average daily dietary intake level that meets the nutritional requirements of half the healthy people of a particular age range and gender.

Estimated Energy Requirement (EER) The dietary energy intake believed to maintain energy balance in a healthy adult of a certain age, gender, weight, height, and level of activity.

Fat-soluble vitamin A vitamin that is soluble in fat but not in water; it can be stored in the body's adipose (fat) tissue.

Fatty acid An organic molecule found in animal and vegetable fats; it consists of a carbon and hydrogen chain with an acid at one end.

Fiber A complex carbohydrate that cannot be digested by the human body but which goes through the digestive tract and provides bulk for regularity.

Food additive An ingredient other than the ingredients of the original food that is put into food to perform specific functions, such as improving flavor, color, and texture; retaining nutritional value; preventing spoilage; and extending shelf life.

Food-allergen program A set of goals and actions with the objective of ensuring that customers who have indicated that they have a food allergy or food intolerance are not exposed to the offending substance through food or beverages in the operation.

Food allergy A negative reaction to a food protein.

Food irradiation The process of treating food with ionizing radiation, which can reduce or eliminate bacteria and parasites that cause foodborne illness.

Food label A label that lists the nutrients included in a product, along with their amounts.

Food on display Food that is visible to the customer before its purchase, such as a piece of pie or a piece of pizza.

Fortification Adding nutrients to a food that it did not have originally.

Free radical An unpaired electron that is formed during the metabolic activity of the body. Free radicals can harm the cellular membranes and cause damage that leads to inflammation and cancers.

Freeze-drying A process that removes all the moisture from food to prevent spoilage.

Genetically modified organism A plant or animal whose genetic makeup has been altered using recombinant DNA technology.

Glucagon A hormone that has the opposite effect of insulin; it promotes the release and production of glucose by the liver and brings up low blood sugar.

Glucose Blood sugar.

Gluten A protein found in wheat, rye, and barley.

Glycogen The form in which the body stores carbohydrates in both the liver and the muscle tissue.

Growth phase The stage in the product life cycle in which the establishment aims to increase its customer base and build loyalty and return customers.

Halal Food that has been sanctioned by Islamic law.

Hard water Water that contains large amounts of minerals such as calcium or iron.

Health claim An expressed or implied statement on the menu characterizing the relationship of a substance to disease or health, such as a statement that an item is heart healthy.

Healthy diet A diet that contains nutrient-dense food choices from the five food groups; it contains all essential vitamins and minerals, as well as enough fiber, fluid, and phytochemicals to maintain good health.

Heme iron Iron from animal sources, which is more readily absorbed by the body than iron from other sources.

Hemoglobin The active molecule in red blood cells; it is a protein in the body that carries oxygen through the blood.

Herbicide A chemical formulated to kill weeds.

High-density lipoprotein (HDL) A complex of lipids and proteins in approximately equal amounts that functions as a transporter of cholesterol in the blood; also referred to as *good cholesterol* because it lowers blood-cholesterol levels.

Home-meal replacement Food that has been prepared, cooked, chilled, and made ready for simple reheating.

Hybrid plant A common example of crossbreeding, with half the genes coming from one plant and half the genes coming from another plant.

Hydrogenated Oils made to react chemically with hydrogen in order to make them more solid and to increase their shelf life.

Hyperglycemia High blood-sugar levels.

Incomplete protein A food that is missing one or more of the essential amino acids.

Infused oil An oil that has been heated with seasonings to enhance flavor.

Insulin A hormone that is secreted by the pancreas and circulates in the blood; its role is to help glucose enter the cell, thus reducing blood-sugar levels.

Introductory phase The stage in the product life cycle in which the restaurant rolls out the program to the public and builds awareness.

Iron-deficiency anemia A condition that occurs when there is a lack of iron in the diet or a problem with absorption of iron in the body, resulting in low levels of hemoglobin.

Job aid Any type of information or process that directs, guides, or enlightens performance on the job.

Jus The French term for juice.

Ketosis A condition caused when glucose is insufficient and the liver cannot fully break down the lipids being metabolized.

Kilocalorie The amount of energy needed to heat one kilogram of water (about 2.2 pounds) by approximately two degrees Fahrenheit (one degree Celsius).

Kosher Food and dietary laws prescribed by Orthodox and Conservative Judaism.

Laboratory analysis An analysis done on carefully prepared samples of a standardized recipe or typical food that would be served to the customer.

Lactase The enzyme that allows the digestion of lactose.

Lactose intolerance The inability to digest lactose, the sugar found in milk and other dairy products, caused by a deficiency of lactase.

Lecithin A phospholipid found both in the body and in some food, such as egg yolks.

Linoleic acid An essential fatty acid found in corn, safflower, soybean, cottonseed, and canola oils.

Lipid A fatty substance that is present in blood and body tissues; lipids include cholesterol, triglycerides, and phospholipids.

Lipoprotein A compound composed of proteins and various blood lipids from the diet or generated in the liver; it is a transport mechanism for fat in the body.

Low-density lipoprotein (LDL) A complex of lipids and proteins with greater amounts of lipids than protein, which functions as a transporter of cholesterol in the blood; also referred to as *bad cholesterol* because it can increase the risk of cardiovascular disease.

Maillard reaction The interaction between an amino acid and a sugar to form browning and a variety of flavors.

Major mineral A mineral that the body needs in quantities of one hundred milligrams or more per day.

Malabsorption A difficulty absorbing nutrients from food.

Marbling Fat that lies intramuscularly in meat and adds to tenderness and flavor when cooked.

Marketing-activities schedule A schedule used to guide marketing efforts; it identifies what will be done, when it will be done, and who will do it.

Marketing plan A document that guides staff in increasing the operation's visibility to its target audience in order to increase business.

Maturity phase The stage in the product life cycle in which the establishment is reinforcing its customers' preferences and maintaining customer loyalty.

Meat analog A food item that is made of plant proteins, usually textured soy, but fabricated to look and taste like meat, fish, or poultry.

Menu disclaimer A statement informing the customer that there is no legal warranty or guarantee of satisfaction implied or responsibility accepted; for example, the disclaimer that warns a customer about eating undercooked meat and eggs.

Menu labeling Prominent labeling of menus with calorie counts for standard menu items, mandated for restaurants and vendors with 20 or more locations.

Menu management The ongoing evaluation, adjustment, and promotion of a menu by an operation to achieve profitability, also called *menu merchandising*.

Metabolism The process by which living organisms and cells break down complex chemicals into their components and reassemble the components into larger molecules needed by the body.

Micronutrient A vitamin that the body needs in very small amounts.

Mineral An inorganic essential nutrient that provides no calories but is needed for regulatory activities of the body.

Monosaccharide A single-unit sugar.

Monounsaturated A fatty-acid molecule that contains one double bond.

Mother sauce A classic sauce from which other sauces are made.

Nitrogen balance The state in which a person's nitrogen intake and nitrogen usage are equal; it is used to measure protein balance because nitrogen is a part of protein.

Nonheme iron Iron from vegetarian sources, which is not absorbed by the body as well as heme iron.

Nutrient A chemical compound that is essential to the body because it helps maintain, generate, and repair tissues.

Nutrient-content claim A claim that characterizes the level of a nutrient on the food label or restaurant menu; for example, a statement that an item is low in sodium.

Nutrient density The number of nutrients per calorie of a particular food.

Nutrition The science of how the nutrients in food affect health.

Nutrition analysis The process of determining the nutritional content or composition of a food.

Nutrition facts label The part of the food label that contains the nutrition information required by the FDA.

Nutrition program A set of goals and actions with the objective of achieving a nutritional standard.

Obesity A condition of people with a body mass index (BMI) of 30 or greater.

Obesogenic Providing conditions that lead to obesity.

Omega-3 fatty acid A fatty acid that can help to reduce inflammation, thin the blood, and prevent stroke.

Omega-6 fatty acid A fatty acid that constricts blood vessels, promotes blood clotting, and increases inflammation.

Organic food Food that has been produced without synthetic fertilizers, sewage sludge, irradiation, or genetic engineering.

Overweight A condition of people with a body mass index (BMI) of 25 to 29.9.

Packaged processed food Food such as frozen food, canned food, and jar baby food, as well as products that consumers themselves process further, such as biscuit and pancake mixes.

Pareve Food items defined by kosher laws that are neither meat nor dairy items.

Pathogen One of a group of disease-causing microorganisms, such as viruses, bacteria, or parasites.

Performance standard A standard that defines what task must be done and how the task is to be completed to satisfaction.

Personal selling A meeting or interaction of two or more people for the purpose of exchanging information and making and closing a sale.

Pesticide A chemical formulated to kill insects.

Phospholipid A part of the cell membrane that is able to link with both water and fat; its arrangement in the membrane allows the cell membrane to be semi-permeable.

Physical loss Peeling, trimming, cutting, and other physical actions that can cause nutrient loss.

Phytochemical A plant chemical that may assist the body in preventing or fighting diseases; also known as a *phytonutrient*.

Plaque A fatty deposit on the wall of a blood vessel.

Polysaccharide A molecule composed of long chains of glucose molecules, such as starch or fiber, that takes much longer to digest than sugar.

Polyunsaturated A fatty-acid molecule that contains more than one double bond.

Precursor An inactive form of a vitamin that is activated by the body.

Processed food Food that has undergone any type of planned or deliberate change before being delivered for consumption.

Promotional mix The various ways in which a given business chooses to reach or communicate with its customers or its target market.

Protein A large, complex molecule that provides amino acids as its primary role.

Publicity Information about an establishment that is distributed for free but is not produced by the operation.

Public relations (PR) The part of an establishment's communication activities that addresses the operation's image in its community.

Puree A finely mashed food, usually a fruit or vegetable, that is smooth and uniform in texture.

Recombinant DNA technology Technology that allows the DNA, or genetic code, of two organisms to be combined; this results in a permanent change to the genetic code of the receiving plant or animal, as well as its offspring.

Recommended Dietary Allowance (RDA) The average daily dietary nutrient intake sufficient to meet the nutrient requirement of nearly all (97 to 98 percent) healthy individuals of a particular age and gender group.

Reduction sauce A sauce formed when a liquid is boiled until the water evaporates and the remaining juice is thickened.

Reference Daily Intake (RDI) A nutrient value for vitamins and minerals set by the FDA to formulate the Daily Value.

Registered dietetic technician (DTR) A person who has completed a two-year, Academy of Nutrition and Dietetics–approved undergraduate program and 450 hours of supervised practice. A DTR is qualified to analyze recipes and menus and suggest modifications to address health concerns and special needs of customers and clients.

Registered dietitian (RD) A person who has completed a four-year, Academy of Nutrition and Dietetics–approved undergraduate program, has advanced training through an internship or master's degree, and has passed a national exam. An RD is qualified to analyze recipes and menus and to suggest modifications that address health concerns and special needs of customers and clients.

Retinol The active form of vitamin A.

Roux A cooked mixture of fat and flour.

Sales promotions Special incentives to get customers to visit an establishment or to purchase new items.

Saturated fatty acid A fatty acid that has no double bond present between the carbon atoms in its carbon chain.

Section 4205 of the Patient Protection and Affordable Care Act Legislation that provides consistent, nationwide menu-labeling regulations; this law applies to chain restaurants and similar retail food establishments having 20 or more locations.

Selective breeding The process of reproducing the best plants of the harvest or the best animals of the herd.

Self-service items Food items that are offered at salad bars, buffet lines, cafeteria lines, or similar self-service facilities.

Simple carbohydrate A sugar that consists of monosaccharides and disaccharides.

Skill gap The difference between the current skills of an employee and the skills that he or she needs to develop.

Slurry A thin paste made from water or stock mixed with starch, such as cornstarch.

Soft water Water that contains minerals in smaller amounts than hard water.

Sous vide A food-preparation method that utilizes vacuum packaging; its name comes from the French term for "under vacuum."

Soy A legume that is native to eastern Asia but now is grown throughout the world, also called *soybean*, *soya*, or *soya bean*.

Standardized recipe A recipe that gives a known quality and quantity at a known cost.

Standard menu items Items that appear routinely on a menu.

Sterol A hydrocarbon consisting of a steroid and an alcohol as well as carbon bonded to carbon in a closed ring.

Strategic business segment A specific revenue-generating source, such as a banquet room or a lounge.

Sucrose Table sugar, also known as *plain sugar, brown sugar*, and *confectioner's sugar*.

Sustainability Practices that meet current resource needs without compromising the ability to meet future needs, including innovative approaches to growing quality products and to increasing the food supply without damaging the environment and consuming valuable resources.

SWOT analysis An analysis of an operation's strengths, weaknesses, opportunities, and threats.

Target market The specific groups of customers an operation seeks to serve.

Tolerable Upper Intake Level (UL) The highest level of daily nutrient intake that poses no risk of adverse health effects to almost all individuals of a certain age range.

Trace mineral A mineral that the body needs in very small amounts.

Training Activities that are designed to introduce new tasks and to assist employees in performing them.

Training tool Material developed to effectively communicate training information to staff, including diagrams, summarized information, standardized recipes, or videos.

Trans fat A fat that is formed when oils have been partially hydrogenated, allowing some of the double bonds to be broken and rebonded with hydrogen atoms.

Transgenic organism An organism in which the DNA of one species is implanted in another.

Triglyceride A molecule formed by one glycerol molecule and three fatty acids, which is a form of fat stored in the body.

Truth-in-menu laws Laws that require a restaurant or foodservice operation to represent its food correctly to its customers; the establishment must serve what is described on the menu and describe its preparation methods and ingredients accurately.

Unsaturated fatty acid A fatty acid that contains one or more double bonds in the carbon chain.

USDA Organic A designation by the USDA stating that food labeled with this seal must be at least 95 percent organic and must meet USDA organic standards, which include the use of renewable resources and the conservation of soil and water in growing food.

Variable menu items Standard menu items that include a flavoring option, such as milk shake flavors.

Vegan A person who eliminates all animal products from his or her diet.

Vegetarian A person who does not eat meat, fish, or poultry.

Vending machine A self-service device that dispenses servings of food after insertion of money or tokens, without the necessity of replenishing the device between each vending operation.

Vitamin An organic essential nutrient that provides no calories but is needed for regulatory activities of the body.

Volume measure A measurement taken using a tool that determines how much space an item takes up.

Water-soluble vitamin A vitamin that is soluble in water but not in fat; it is generally not stored in the body.

INDEX

A

absorption, 25–29, 32–33
Academy of Nutrition and Dietetics, 11, 200
Acceptable Macronutrient Distribution Range (AMDR)
  for carbohydrates, 39, 60, 66, 94
  with DRIs, 39
  for lipids, 39, 60, 88, 94
  for protein, 39, 60, 76, 94
ACF-certified chef, 12
acids
  alpha-linolenic, 85–86, 87
  amino, 19, 47, 76, 78, 79, 95, 119
  EPA, 92
  essential amino, 19, 78, 79, 95
  essential fatty, 86–87
  fatty, 20–21, 53, 86–87, 91–92, 94, 95
  folic, 45, 47, 59
  hydrochloric, 78
  linoleic, 85–86, 87, 94
  linolenic, 87
  omega-3 fatty, 91–92, 95
  omega-6 fatty, 91–92, 95
  pantothenic, 54
  saturated fatty, 21, 43, 84, 173
  unsaturated fatty, 43, 84
ADA (see American Diabetes Association)
ADDIE model, 212–213, 216–217, 220
additives, food, 55, 154–156, 159
Adequate Intake (AI), 39–40, 60, 87, 119
adipose tissue, 73, 86, 94
adult breakfast skippers, 8
advertising, 231–232, 237
African Americans
  with diabetes, 60, 74
  lactose intolerance and, 190
  sodium intake reduced for, 43, 60, 119, 167

age
  calories needed per day by, 46, 60
  demographics, 128–129
agricultural biotechnology, 151, 158
AHA (see American Heart Association)
AI (see Adequate Intake)
alcohol
  daily consumption rates of, 43
  with dietary sugar, 59
  digestion of, 28, 32
  metabolic effects of, 93
  Muslims and, 202
  as non-nutrient source of calories, 22–23
allergens, 4, 59, 176, 206
  big eight, 61, 82, 95, 188–189, 204–205
  employees trained on, 196–198
  identifying, 193–194
  ingredient labeling and, 55–56
  programs for food, 192–193, 205
allergic reaction, 188
allergies
  celiac disease and, 188–191, 205
  customers and policies and procedures for, 194–196, 205
  customers with food, 61, 82, 126
  food, 61, 82, 95, 126, 186, 188–189, 190–191, 205
  nuts, 176
  protein and food, 82, 95
Allergies and Food Safety, 216
alpha-linolenic acid, 85–86, 87
AMDR (see Acceptable Macronutrient Distribution Range)
American Diabetes Association (ADA), 11
American Heart Association (AHA), 11, 89, 90

amino acids, 47, 76, 119
  essential, 19, 78, 79, 95
  nonessential, 19, 78, 79
  proteins and, 19, 76, 78, 79
anaphylaxis, 11, 188, 198
anemia, 5, 30, 113, 115, 118
animal sources, of nutrients, 200
antioxidant, 108, 155
Asian Americans
  with diabetes, 74
  lactose intolerance and, 190

B

back-of-the-house employees, 211, 220
balancing
  calorie, 42–46, 60
  energy, 30
  nitrogen and protein, 78–79
  weight managed with calorie, 43–44, 60
basal metabolism, 18
beta-carotene, 108
beverages, 44, 45, 55 (see also alcohol; water)
bioavailability, 103
biotechnology, agricultural, 151, 158
blood, minerals in, 113
blood-pressure regulation, minerals and, 111–112
BMI (see body mass index)
body
  lipids in, 86
  water weight of human, 39
body mass index (BMI), 13, 29–31, 33
body weight (see weight)
bone health, 112–113
breastfeeding, 43, 115
breeding, 150–151
business, menu-labeling laws and, 247–248
butter, 89, 172–174, 204

freeze-drying, 156, 159
front-of-the-house employees,
    210–211, 220
fruit, 44
    cancer and, 58–59
    MyPlate Food Group 4, 48–49
FSIS (*see* Food Safety and Inspection
    Service)

G

GAP (*see* good agricultural practices)
Gateway to Federal Food Safety
    Information, 216
genetically modified food, 149,
    150–152
genetically modified organism, 149,
    150, 158
gestational diabetes, 75, 94
glucagon, 72
glucose, 28, 68, 72, 94
gluten, 4, 189
gluten-free, 134, 136
    diets and celiac disease, 191
    flour, 191, 198
glycogen, 72
GMP (*see* good manufacturing
    practices)
good agricultural practices (GAP),
    150
good manufacturing practices (GMP),
    150
government resources, for nutrition
    information, 11
grains
    cancer and, 58
    MyPlate Food Group 1, 47, 49
    whole, 44, 47, 49, 71–72, 92
growth phase, 235

H

HACCP plan (*see* hazard analysis
    and critical control points plan)
halal, 202, 206
hard water, 118
hazard analysis and critical control
    points (HACCP) plan, 150

HDL (*see* high-density lipoprotein)
health
    carbohydrates and effects on,
        73–76
    claim, 246
    claims with labeling, 58–59
    cooking for, 164–167
    diets with social needs and, 203
    fats for heart, 91–92
    HHS, 11–12, 42
    lipoproteins and, 89–91
    minerals and bone, 112–113
    NIH, 11
    with vitamins and minerals,
        100–107
healthy
    diet, 38
    eating patterns, 44
    fats for heart, 91–92
    food labeled as, 57
    menu options, 4–5
    plates, 49–50
    weight, 29–31, 33
Healthy Dining program, 42
heart
    AHA, 11, 89, 90
    disease, 4, 13, 30, 58, 80, 204
    fats for healthy, 91–92
heart disease, diets for, 204
heme iron, 45, 113
hemoglobin, 113
herbicide, 149, 152
heritage plants, 157
HHS (*see* United States Department
    of Health and Human Services)
high-density lipoprotein (HDL), 21,
    90–91
Hindu diets, 201
home-meal replacements, 8
hormones, 57, 149
hybrid plant, 150
hydrochloric acid, 78
hydrogenated, 85
hyperglycemia, 74
hypertension, 4, 6, 13, 30, 43
    DASH, 112
    sodium and, 59

I

IFIC (*see* International Food and
    Information Council)
IFT (*see* Institute of Food
    Technologists)
incomplete protein, 79, 95
infused oil, 164
ingredient labeling
    allergens, 55–56
    explanation of, 54
    food additives, 55, 154–156, 159
ingredients
    with food science, 168–169
    modification of, 171, 175
insoluble fiber, 70, 94
Institute of Food Technologists
    (IFT), 11
insulin, 72, 74–75
International Food and Information
    Council (IFIC), 11, 153
Internet
    as food market, 9–10
    nutrition information on, 12
introductory phase, 235
iron, 41, 45, 47, 72, 113, 200
    DVs, 53–54
    enrichment, 156–157, 159
iron-deficiency anemia, 113, 115, 118
Islamic law, 202

J

job aid, 216
jus (juice), 176

K

ketosis, 73
Kids LiveWell program, 42
kilocalorie, 18 (*see also* calories)
kosher, 201, 206

L

labeling
    food, 51–59
    food as healthy, 57
    food as organic, 57, 158

water-soluble vitamins, 21, 100
definition, 118
folate, 111
thiamin, riboflavin, niacin, 110–111
vitamin B$_6$, 111
vitamin C, 111
weaknesses, 131–135 (*see also* SWOT analysis)
weight
adjustments, 30–31
BMI with nutrition and healthy, 29–31, 33
calories balanced to manage, 43–44, 60
carbohydrates and gaining, 73, 94

children and, 31
DRIs for protein for persons of average body, 77
factors influencing, 28
gaining, 6, 73
saturated fatty acids by, 173
wheat
as allergen, 55, 61, 82, 95, 188–189, 204–205
gluten, 189
whole grains, 44, 92
components, 71
as MyPlate Food Group 1, 47, 49
reading label with, 72
why eat, 71

women
alcohol and daily consumption rates for, 43
breakfast skippers, 8
calories needed daily for, 46, 60
with gestational diabetes, 75
MyPlate recommendations for, 49
protein DRIs for, 77
with recommendations for future pregnancies, 45
with recommendations for pregnancy or breastfeeding, 45
water intake per day for, 39, 60

NOTES

NOTES

NOTES

NOTES

NOTES

NOTES

NOTES

NOTES

NOTES

NOTES

NOTES